THE
INVASION
OF
CANADA
BY THE
AMERICANS
1775–1776

THE
INVASION
OF
CANADA
BY THE
AMERICANS
1775–1776

*As Told through Jean-Baptiste Badeaux's Three Rivers Journal
and New York Captain William Goforth's Letters*

Edited by

Mark R. Anderson

Translated by

Teresa L. Meadows

Photo credit: Yale University Art Gallery

Published by State University of New York Press, Albany

© 2016 State University of New York

All rights reserved

Printed in the United States of America

No part of this book may be used or reproduced in any manner whatsoever without written permission. No part of this book may be stored in a retrieval system or transmitted in any form or by any means including electronic, electrostatic, magnetic tape, mechanical, photocopying, recording, or otherwise without the prior permission in writing of the publisher.

For information, contact State University of New York Press, Albany, NY
www.sunypress.edu

Production, Jenn Bennett
Marketing, Fran Keneston

Library of Congress Cataloging-in-Publication Data

The invasion of Canada by the Americans, 1775–1776 : as told through Jean-Baptiste Badeaux's Three Rivers journal and New York Captain William Goforth's letters / edited by Mark R. Anderson ; translated by Teresa L. Meadows.
    pages cm
Includes bibliographical references and index.
ISBN 978-1-4384-6003-1 (hc : alk. paper)—978-1-4384-6004-8 (pb : alk. paper)
ISBN 978-1-4384-6005-5 (e-book)
  1. Canadian Invasion, 1775–1776. 2. Badeaux, J. B. (Jean Baptiste), 1741–1796—Diaries. 3. Goforth, William, 1731–1807—Correspondence. 4. Canadian Invasion, 1775–1776—Sources. I. Anderson, Mark R., 1966– editor. II. Meadows, Teresa L., 1955– translator. III. Title: Jean-Baptiste Badeaux's Three Rivers journal. IV. Title: New York Captain William Goforth's letters. V. Title: Jean-Baptiste Badeaux's Three Rivers journal and New York Captain William Goforth's letters. VI. Title: Invasion du Canada par les américains en 1775.
  E231.I63 2016
  971.02'4—dc23
                                                    2015015564

Contents

List of Illustrations and Maps	vii
Acknowledgments	ix
Abbreviations Used in Footnotes	xi
Introduction	xiii
Historical Prelude	xvii
Chronology	xxv
Jean-Baptiste Badeaux—A Short Biography	xxix
William Goforth—A Short Biography	xxxv
The Stage—Three Rivers, Quebec, 1775–1776	xliii
Translator's Notes	xlvii
Summer 1775	1
September 1775	7
October 1775	21
November 1775	35
December 1775	47
January 1776	55
February 1776	65
March 1776	79
April 1776	109
May 1776	145
June 1776	163
Notes on the Provenance of Badeaux's Journal	167
Appendix 1—The Accounts of the Three Rivers Ursuline Nuns	171
Appendix 2—Officers and Unit Identification	185
Select Bibliography	191
Index	199

Illustrations and Maps

Figure 1.	A General Map of the Northern British Colonies in America	xix
Figure 2.	Operations of the Northern Army	xxiii
Figure 3.	Unidentified Man, 1765–1770	xxix
Figure 4.	New York Soldier, 1775	xxxvii
Figure 5.	*View of Three Rivers at the End of the XVIII Century*	xliii
Figure 6.	*The Town of Three Rivers*	xliv
Figure 7.	Opening Page of the Badeaux Journal	xlviii
Figure 8.	General Sir Guy Carleton	8
Figure 9.	William Goforth Letter to John Jay	13
Figure 10.	Alexander McDougall	15
Figure 11.	Vicar General Pierre Garreau *dit* Saint-Ongé of Three Rivers	22
Figure 12.	Government House Barracks, Three Rivers	65
Figure 13.	*Ste-Anne de la Pérade Church and Other Buildings*	69
Figure 14.	British Winter Uniform	71
Figure 15.	Benjamin Franklin	75
Figure 16.	*The Forges, River St. Maurice*	82
Figure 17.	*Sledge and Habitants in a Snowstorm*	87

Figure 18.	New Jersey Continental Soldier	101
Figure 19.	Ursuline Convent, Three Rivers	110
Figure 20.	Benedict Arnold	117
Figure 21.	John Jay	132
Figure 22.	Ursuline Nun	173
Map 1.	Three Rivers City, 1775–76	xlv
Map 2.	Montreal District and the Lake Champlain Corridor	3
Map 3.	Three Rivers District	10
Map 4.	Quebec District	92

Acknowledgments

This work was made possible only by the help of many associates and institutions. The kind staffs at the Library and Archives Canada, the New-York Historical Society, and Bibliothèque et Archives Nationales de Québec offered tremendous access to their wonderful collections. Those institutions, as well as Columbia University in the City of New York, the American Philosophical Society, and the Public Library of Cincinnati and Hamilton County have also given invaluable assistance in accessing treasured materials from more than a thousand miles away, as we work from our homes in Colorado. The interlibrary loan staff at Pikes Peak Library District provided vital support in obtaining the full range of books and articles necessary to complete this project.

It is a fantastic time to do historical research, as virtual access to primary and secondary sources grows by leaps and bounds each year. We commend the Bibliothèque et Archives Nationales de Québec for their expansive digitization of manuscript collections, providing researchers the ability to remotely view documents deep in some of the most obscure portions of their holdings. The Université de Montréal Research Program in Historical Demography parish records database was another critical tool—a means to readily access vital details of most of the Canadian historical characters' lives and families.

We also must thank our family, friends, and fellow professionals for their contributions: Transcription assistant Kira Anderson, who helped decipher William Goforth's messy and nearly illegible letters; Pam Anderson and Dave Eblen, who willingly proofread drafts at every stage; Professor Michael Gabriel, who has generously continued to encourage and guide this editor/author through the world of academic history and publishing; Associate Professor Fabienne Moore who kindly lent her expertise in eighteenth-century French language and culture to both appropriate translation and reading of difficult script; and colleagues at the University of Colorado Colorado Springs, the University of Oregon, and the University of Rochester who were interested enough to spend time simply discussing the period, the text, and the translation.

Abbreviations Used in Footnotes

AA4 = Force, Peter, ed., *American Archives: Fourth Series*

AA5 = Force, Peter, ed., *American Archives: Fifth Series*

AMP = Alexander McDougall Papers, 1759–1795, NYHS

BAnQ = Bibliothèque et Archives nationales Québec

DCB = *Dictionary of Canadian Biography Online/Dictionnaire biographique du Canada en ligne*

JCC = Ford, Worthington, *Journals of the Continental Congress, 1774–1789*.

LAC = Library and Archives Canada

LoD = Smith, Paul H., ed., *Letters of Delegates to Congress, 1774–1789*

NARA = United States National Archives and Records Administration

NYHS = New-York Historical Society

NYPL = New York Public Library

PGWRWS = Chase, Philander, ed., *The Papers of George Washington: Revolutionary War Series*

PSP = Philip Schuyler Papers, NYPL

SoFR = "State of the Four Regiments," 4 August 1775, NARA, M853, rg93, v5, r15, p152

UMPRDH = Université de Montréal, Programme de recherche en démographique historique

Footnotes that begin with "(date)" are cross-referenced.

Introduction

On its own merits, Canadian notary Jean-Baptiste Badeaux's record, commonly known as the "Journal of the Operations of the American Army during the Invasion of Canada in 1775–76,"[1] warrants a long-overdue translation to the English language. Badeaux's document, written in Three Rivers (Trois-Rivières), Quebec, is one of three principal French Canadian journals of this period, all written by notaries, which have served as invaluable primary sources for the various historical examinations of this American invasion. These three accounts were published in their original French, in an 1873 collection edited by Hospice-Anthelme Verreau.[2] The most prominent of these, the "Eyewitness Account of the Invasion of Canada by the Bostonians during the years 1775 and 1776,"[3] by Simon Sanguinet, is anchored in that author's hometown of Montreal, the political center of the American occupation. Another account, "Extracts from a Memoir by M. A. Berthelot on the Invasion of Canada in 1775,"[4] from Quebec City's Michel-Amable Berthelot Dartigny, provides a French Canadian perspective originating inside the capital—the besieged focal point of the military campaign for six months of the invasion. In a period when approximately 75 percent of French Canadians were functionally illiterate, these journals demonstrate their

---

1. "Journal des Opérations de l'Armée Américaine Lors de L'Invasion du Canada en 1775–76."
2. Hospice-Anthelme Jean-Baptiste Verreau, ed., *Invasion du Canada, Collection de Memoires Recueillis et Annotes* (Montreal: Eusebe Senecal, 1873).
3. "Le témoin oculaire de la guerre des Bastonnois en Canada dans les années 1775 et 1776."
4. "Extraits d'un mémoire de M. A. Berthelot sur l'invasion du Canada en 1775."

authors' remarkable writing skills—the notarial skills they required for documenting local civil and judicial activities were easily transferred to journal keeping during such momentous times. Badeaux's account, however, stands out from the others.

Most importantly, Jean-Baptiste Badeaux provides a uniquely objective view of the invasion. While he repeatedly and explicitly clarified his staunch loyalist stance in his journal, Badeaux, unlike his vehemently partisan counterparts Sanguinet or Berthelot, made a remarkable effort to simply state the facts surrounding events. He avoided the temptation to put all of the invading Continentals' actions in the worst light, and he deliberately weighed the veracity and bias of secondhand reports received from outside his home district. Additionally, Badeaux offers the reader occasional glimpses of his sly wit, and a sprinkling of self-deprecation, giving his journal a warmer, more intimate feel.

One obvious drawback of Badeaux's account is that he was distant from the most momentous events in the campaign, since he largely remained in the Three Rivers District. His relative remoteness from the center of action is an important consideration, however; it gave him opportunity for thoughtful deliberation of the circumstances, and less personal emotional investment in key developments. While his journal is undeniably dependent on others' accounts and rumors of activities in the principal seats of action—the Richelieu River Valley, Montreal, and Quebec City—Badeaux's thoughtful interpretation of those events adds a value of its own. Additionally, readers and historians can gain valuable insight by examining what was happening away from the frontlines: How did the Continentals and Canadians get along in day-to-day interactions? How strong was Canadian support for the royal government . . . or for the Continentals? How did the invasion impact the lives of urban and rural Canadians, of all political persuasions, away from the battle lines? Badeaux's journal is important to understanding all these significant "background" aspects of the American foray into Quebec.

Among the many episodes in Jean-Baptiste Badeaux's journal is a particularly interesting professional relationship that developed during a two-month period of the occupation. The notary observed, on February 8, 1776, that "a detachment under the command of Captain William Goforth . . . arrived to take possession of the city" of Three Rivers. The same Captain Goforth, with substantial extant correspondence from the period, wrote to the colonies from Three Rivers about his "[h]aving been ordered by his Excellency Genl. Wooster on the 3d Feb with a small party to take the command of this place." When Goforth asked for Badeaux's assistance, the Canadian notary recorded his thoughts about cooperating with the enemy, in his journal: "I could not refuse him, especially in the circumstances in which we found ourselves."[5] By Badeaux's account, the two established an effective, cooperative partnership to properly administer Three Rivers and the surrounding district, characterized by mutual respect, in the middle of a divisive, revolutionary invasion.

Yet Captain William Goforth warrants examination for more than just his effective Three Rivers District military governorship described in Badeaux's journal. The captain also serves as an important, representative revolutionary American leader—both in New York politics and through his military activity. William Goforth's thoughtful correspondence offers some particularly interesting elements, and his dedication to rights, his country, and his family shine through in his writing. The intended recipients of the captain's correspondence reflect an importance and reach beyond his second-tier position as a New York City patriot activist, political agent, and industrious artisan. Notable leaders such as Benjamin Franklin, John Jay, and Alexander McDougall received Goforth's letters. And, as a particularly reliable reporter from the Quebec theater, Captain Goforth's observations carried unusual weight with these movers and shakers; and extracts from his letters, reprinted in contemporary newspapers, helped inform home-front New Yorkers of the Canadian campaign's progress and challenges.

Like Badeaux, Goforth was a distant reporter of most action. He missed the initial phases of the invasion's Richelieu Valley campaign overture, and was later forced to rely on secondhand accounts from the decisive Quebec City siege lines. His relative distance from the scene of action, in both time and space, gave him time to reflect—something generally lacking in other military accounts. Additionally, no other American source so thoroughly recorded the unfortunate, occasionally violent, and significant events that directly affected the Americans' ability to attain their Canadian objectives as Continental reinforcements transited the 150-mile span of otherwise quiet and hospitable parishes

---

5. February 18 entry, Badeaux journal.

that sat between Montreal and Quebec City. Another intriguing aspect of Goforth's correspondence is that the captain was clearly thinking at a strategic level, beyond the strict operational bounds of his specific military post. In his missives, he offered diverse solutions for the many challenges that the thirteen colonies faced in their Canadian venture.

Finally, Badeaux's journal and Goforth's correspondence have greater value side by side, as parallel narratives. The Canadian notary's interpretation of events and accounts of the Continental captain's leadership contrast with Goforth's fairly matter-of-fact narration. Badeaux makes frequent reference to "the Commander," Captain Goforth, while the New Yorker is notably silent about his Canadian counterpart. However, in comparing their records, it is clearly evident that the notary played a critical role in shaping the captain's views of the larger Canadian situation. Together, in comparison and contrast, they make an even more significant source for understanding the political, cultural, and behind-the-scenes military factors that affected the American invasion of Canada in 1775–76. Through the personal observations and musings of a lifelong French Canadian official, committed to royal rule, and the writings of an educated New York artisan, serving as a mid-level officer in the "rebellious" Continental Northern Army, the reader receives insight into more than just a military campaign. Badeaux and Goforth offer a valuable cultural vignette of the American Revolution and Canadian-American relationships of the late eighteenth century.

Historical Prelude

Jean-Baptiste Badeaux's journal begins in May 1775, shortly after simmering tensions between Great Britain and her traditional North American colonies boiled over into armed conflict. Prior to this, relations between the metropolis and the thirteen colonies had grown increasingly strained. The protest-destruction of the Boston "Tea Party" brought about London's sharp response in the form of the Coercive Acts, which in turn spawned new levels of collective colonial action, prompting the first Continental Congress, which met in Philadelphia. Among that assembly's several acts, the delegates composed and sent a letter to the inhabitants of the Province of Quebec, asking their northern neighbors to join them in a second congress that would meet in May 1775.[1] Before the second Continental Congress could meet, however, British troops and Massachusetts militia fought at Lexington and Concord in April 1775. Shortly thereafter, as Badeaux records early in his journal, Ethan Allen and Benedict Arnold captured Fort Ticonderoga and Crown Point, securing these key military posts at the southern end of the Lake Champlain corridor on behalf of the colonies. Coincidentally, this occurred on the same day that the new Continental Congress convened. The unexpected capture of the forts was the key moment that transformed Quebec into the Revolutionary War's northern front.

The restive thirteen colonies' relationship with their northern neighbor was fraught with historical tensions, offset by recently expanding economic interaction and newly developing opportunities for political

---

1. 26 October 1774, Worthington C. Ford, ed., *Journals of the Continental Congress* (hereafter cited as *JCC*) (Washington, DC: Government Printing Office, 1904), 1: 104–13.

cooperation among those displeased with Parliament's treatment of the North American colonies. Canada had been a French colony, New France, until it was ceded to the British Empire in 1763, as spoils from the French and Indian War (Seven Years' War). The French colony's inhabitants, fewer than one hundred thousand, were predominantly rural tenant farmers known as *habitants*. Their *seigneur* landlords, a few score men, formed Quebec's elite. Additionally, there was an extremely small bourgeois element of French Canadian merchants and minor government officials. Despite class differences, these Canadians were bound by two common ties that sharply separated them from their counterparts in the rest of the American colonies: their French language and their Catholic faith. For French Canadians, the Church was the only structure with province-wide quotidian influence on their lives, as every substantial community had a parish priest, answering to the Bishop of Quebec and two regional vicars-general.

Quebec's population primarily dwelt along the shores of the St. Lawrence in a near-constant line of farmsteads that abutted the riverbanks, wherever terrain permitted. The only other areas of substantial Canadian settlement were along two Laurentian tributaries—the Richelieu River, near Montreal, and the Chaudière River, near Quebec City. The province's small urban population resided in three cities: the fortified capital Quebec City, the fur trade center of Montreal, and the oversized village of Three Rivers, sitting midway between the others on the north bank of the St. Lawrence.

After the Conquest, New France became the British Province of Quebec, initially ruled by a military regime. A small number of imperial officials and military provisioners followed the conquering British Army, and Anglo-Canadian merchants—English, Scots, Irish, New Englanders, New Yorkers, and others—began to settle in the colony. With their British business connections, these entrepreneurs helped integrate Quebec's economy into the empire, but they also brought their own concerns about British rights and forms of government. For its first decade under British rule, the Province of Quebec was administered by an ill-defined government. The regime was led by a royal governor and a small tier of officials who guided an infrastructure that largely stayed true to New French tradition for local rule, while incorporating imperial practices as able. However, the Canadian elite were unable to participate in provincial government due to British laws that effectively restricted

Catholics from officeholding. In 1770, Quebec's Governor Guy Carleton returned to London in an effort to remedy these considerable shortfalls by developing a government structure that would protect French Canadian interests, relative to the vocal, constitutionally privileged, and economically influential Anglo-Canadian minority. Carleton helped draft the bill to establish a newly defined government. The Quebec Act was signed into law on June 17, 1774, to take effect on May 1, 1775. Word of the act's content began to spread through the colonies in September, just as the first Continental Congress assembled.

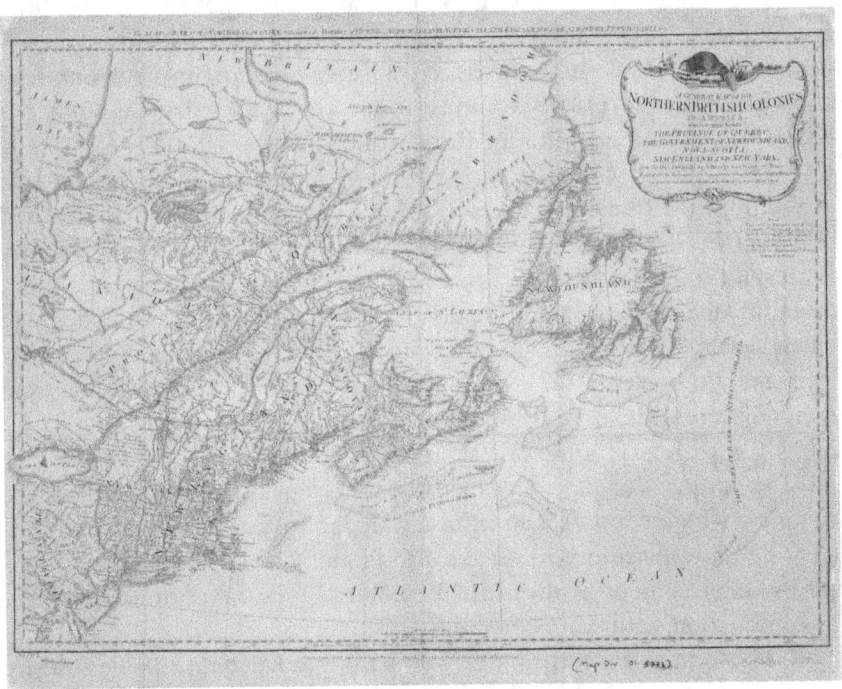

FIGURE 1. A general map of the Northern British Colonies in America. Note that the Royal Proclamation of 1763 imposed the unusual geometric boundaries that closely confined the Province of Quebec to the settled St. Lawrence region and immediate watershed. This 1776 printing failed to reflect the expanded borders introduced by the Quebec Act of 1774, which included the Great Lakes and the northern Ohio River Valley. From the Lionel Pincus & Princess Firyal Map Division, The New York Public Library.

The Quebec Act had a tremendous impact across North America. In Canada, the act established a hybrid British-French law, recognized the Catholic Church, facilitated Catholic Canadian participation in government—including the governor's council, and expanded provincial boundaries to incorporate the entire Great Lakes region and northern Ohio Valley. The status and position of Quebec's very small elite were reconfirmed—the seigneur-landlords, Catholic bishop, and priests were almost unanimously satisfied with this solution. On the other hand, many in the Anglo-Canadian minority were quite distressed by the act. They felt that London had reneged on earlier promises of English-style government and that they were to be indefinitely denied their own provincial legislative assembly. Additionally, the Quebec Act had little appeal for the rural habitants—those with any provincial political awareness saw the resultant buttressing of seigneurial rights and enforced church tithes as a relapse to forms of elite favoritism that they had not previously experienced under British rule.

In the other colonies, the Quebec Act was considered to be part of the punitive Intolerable Acts. Canada's new government was deemed to be an indirect attack by a hostile British ministry. In the zealously Protestant thirteen colonies, the act fed deep-seated concerns about "establishment" of the traditionally threatening Catholic faith. The huge expansion of Quebec's boundaries struck directly at colonial economic interests, both in the fur trade and Ohio Valley land speculation. And more directly, the establishment of a "non-English," executive-dominated, government structure seemed to be a means "to dispose the inhabitants [of Canada] to act with hostility against the free Protestant colonies, whenever a wicked ministry shall chuse so to direct them"[2]—creating an opportunity to "make use of the Canadians as instruments for the enslavement of the British colonies,"[3] by threat or actual force, in conjunction with Ministerial arms.

These concerns contributed to the troubled, defiant colonies' desire to bring Quebec into their Continental Congress—a means both to neutralize the threat and unite the continent in opposition to London's policies. Some of the colonies sought to establish correspondence with like-minded Canadians. Massachusetts even sent an envoy, John Brown,

---

2. Continental Association, 20 October 1774, *JCC*, 1: 76.

3. "Queries Proposed to America," *Pennsylvania Journal* (Philadelphia), 28 September 1774.

to visit Montreal in the spring of 1775. He shared the rebel message and gathered intelligence on political sentiments in Quebec Province.

A small group of Anglo-merchant Canadians had united in opposition to the province's royal government since its earliest days, seeking a Protestant-based legislative assembly and disputing the governors' seeming favoritism for the French-Catholic elite. Early radical Thomas Walker had spearheaded the so-called British Party for its first decade. But the Quebec Act resulted in an immediate change in the group's focus, and a shift in leadership as well. The party's one and only goal became revocation of the Quebec Act. While Walker still played a role as an agitator, the politically savvy Montreal merchant James Price began to rise as the principal opposition leader. Of note, French Canadians failed to provide any substantial support for this cause at this stage—only the French-born François Cazeau took an active role in the pre-invasion period.

James Price and his fellow Anglo-merchant Whig activists began political agitation and proselytization campaigns, particularly in the rural regions around Montreal. With tensions rising in New England, Quebec's Governor Carleton and allies of his administration were particularly worried about the effect these radicalizing elements were having upon the "ignorant" habitant farmers. The seeds planted by the "British Party" radicals in the spring of 1775, however, would take time and the right conditions to produce fruit.

Badeaux's journal effectively commences with the capture of Fort Ticonderoga and subsequent raids on Canada's key border post, Fort St. John's (Fort St. Jean). These incursions into the Province of Quebec occurred on May 18, as Benedict Arnold and an armed party sailed across Lake Champlain and captured a government sloop at St. John's, thereby ensuring that British troops in the north could not immediately recover the rebel-held forts in northern New York. The same day, Ethan Allen's Green Mountain Boys followed in an ill-conceived invasion attempt, but during their first night in Canada, they quickly decided to abandon their mission. These raids were a critical impetus for Governor Guy Carleton's decision to declare martial law in Quebec on June 9, 1775.

Badeaux describes the summer of 1775 as "fairly calm." However, away from the serene isolation of Three Rivers, there was significant unrest. Canadian habitants largely chose to defy government attempts to establish the militia. Sometimes they responded passively, and in a few notable events, they reacted in mass demonstrations. In July, there were at least three parish "rebellions" in which habitants forcibly refused their seigneurs' attempts to mobilize local militia units. Concurrently, the dissenting Anglo-merchant minority continued its propaganda campaign, fostering an increasing degree of Canadian antigovernment sentiment in some areas, particularly the Montreal District.

Meanwhile, the thirteen colonies were entering a new phase in their rebellion. Drawing closer in their common cause, the provinces began to refer to themselves collectively as the United Colonies. Believing that they had no choice but to cooperate in arms to defend their rights, the heretofore loosely confederated Congress established an overarching Continental Army in June 1775. Shortly thereafter, the assembly created the army's Northern Department, initially committed to guarding Ticonderoga and Crown Point. The department commander, Major General Philip Schuyler, was directed to gather additional intelligence on the situation in the north. On June 27, driven by erroneous reports of imminent Indian and British army attacks from Quebec, Congress gave General Schuyler additional discretionary authority to invade Canada and seize Fort St. John's and Montreal. There was a key caveat, however, that he should only move north if such a measure would "not be disagreeable to the Canadians."[4]

Schuyler spent July and August gathering intelligence regarding Canadian sentiments and the scope of the military threat from the north. Two key influences prompted a final decision to launch the Continental invasion of Canada: radical Canadians' requests for support in the Richelieu Valley, and the imminent completion of new British military ships at Fort St. John's. General Schuyler's deputy, Brigadier General Richard Montgomery, assembled the rebel troops and led them north in late August. They landed in Quebec at Ile-aux-Noix, a Richelieu River island twelve miles south of the fort, on September 4.

The invasion began slowly, as Continental forces made a few botched attempts to establish themselves on the mainland in early September. For the first half of the month, the invaders' only real success was in prompting friendly Richelieu Valley Canadians to take up arms against the royal government, under the emerging leadership of Chambly merchant James Livingston. The Continentals finally established footholds near Fort St. John's on September 15 and soon established a blockade, followed by a siege.

---

4. 27 June 1775, *JCC*, 2: 109–10.

Concurrently, General George Washington approved another Quebec invasion. Colonel Benedict Arnold took a select corps of men from the main Continental camp at Cambridge, and led them up the Kennebec River, over the poorly mapped, wild Appalachian highlands, to Canada's Chaudière River. The expedition's objective was to seize Quebec City by surprise or to divert forces away from the Richelieu Valley operation.

FIGURE 2. Operations of the Northern Army. Generals Schuyler and Montgomery led the main Northern Army along the well-established Lake Champlain–Richelieu River route. Benedict Arnold's expedition used the meandering and ill-defined Kennebec-Chaudière path, to the east. This 1806 print was produced for John Marshall's *The Life of George Washington*. Library and Archives Canada, Coverdale Collection, R3908-1-2-E.

At this point both Badeaux and Goforth began to narrate the Canadian invasion in their own words. Their journal and letters offer descriptions of the slowly developing rebel campaign, shifting Canadian sentiments, and the rapid turn of tides following the loyalist surrender of Fort St. John's. Badeaux shared his firsthand experiences during Governor Carleton's flight for shelter in the Quebec City stronghold, as Goforth related the Continental capture of Montreal and General Montgomery's swift movement across the rest of the province. Both Goforth and Badeaux offered different perspectives on General Montgomery's failed siege and New Year's Eve attack on the capital. In the ensuing military stalemate, Goforth and Badeaux were brought together, as rebel leaders attempted to manage an occupation with too few troops, too little money, and indecisive Canadian political support. Badeaux alone was left to conclude the story, as Governor Carleton and his loyalist garrison held out long enough for British relief forces to arrive in May. Within two months the invasion was over and the province firmly returned to the British government's side.

For further detail on the Canadian campaign, see Mark R. Anderson, *The Battle for the Fourteenth Colony: America's War of Liberation in Canada, 1774–1776* (2013), Gustave Lanctôt, *Canada and the American Revolution, 1774–1783* (1967), George F. G. Stanley, *Canada Invaded, 1775–1776* (1977), Justin H. Smith, *Our Struggle for the Fourteenth Colony: Canada and the American Revolution* (1907); or Gavin Watt's loyalist-focused *Poisoned by Lies and Hypocrisy: America's First Attempt to Bring Liberty to Canada, 1775–1776* (2014).

Chronology

8 September 1760—New France surrendered to British Army

10 February 1763—Canada ceded to Great Britain in Treaty of Paris

10 August 1764—Province of Quebec civil government inaugurated under Governor James Murray

1765—Governor Murray disbands the Canadian Militia

12 April 1768—Guy Carleton commissioned governor, replacing Murray

16 December 1773—Destruction of Tea in Boston Harbor

1774

March–June—Parliament passes the Coercive Acts (or "Intolerable Acts"), punishing Boston and reasserting imperial control

22 June—King George III assents to the Quebec Act

5 September–26 October—First Continental Congress meets in Philadelphia

17 September—Governor Carleton returns to Quebec from London

26 October—Continental Congress approves "Address to Inhabitants of the Province of Quebec"

1775

19 April—Battles of Lexington and Concord

28 March—John Brown visits Montreal, representing the Massachusetts Provincial Congress

1 May—Quebec Act enters into effect

10 May—Second Continental Congress convenes in Philadelphia; Fort Ticonderoga captured

18 May—Benedict Arnold and Ethan Allen raids on Fort St. John's, Quebec

9 June—Governor Carleton Proclaims Martial Law in Quebec

June–August—Canadian protests against militia mobilization

27 June—Continental Congress authorizes invasion of Canada

30 August—Continental Northern Army departs Crown Point under General Montgomery

4 September—Continental camp established on Ile-aux-Noix, Quebec

17 September—Continental forces blockade Fort St. John's

25 September—Ethan Allen's Continental–Canadian force defeated at Longue-Pointe; Arnold's Kennebec corps advance guard departs Fort Western (Maine)

18 October—British surrender Fort Chambly

30 October—Continental detachment defeats Carleton's Loyalist relief force at Longueuil; Arnold's advance guard reaches the first Canadian settlements

3 November—British surrender Fort St. John's

13 November—Montgomery enters Montreal; Arnold's corps crosses St. Lawrence and temporarily blockades Quebec City

19 November—Arnold's corps withdraws to Pointe-aux-Trembles; General Prescott surrenders eleven ships on the St. Lawrence, near Sorel

22 November—Carleton proclamation requiring active militia service, or departure from Quebec City

1 December—Montgomery and troops unite with Arnold's corps at Pointe-aux-Trembles

5 December—Continental forces reestablish Quebec City blockade

31 December—Failed Continental assault on Quebec City; Montgomery killed, Arnold wounded

1776

6 January—General David Wooster issues orders restricting Canadian loyalist activity

25 March—Loyalist uprising suppressed at St-Pierre-du-Sud

1 April—General Wooster joins Continental camp outside Quebec City

29 April—Continental Congress committee reaches Montreal

2 May—General John Thomas arrives outside Quebec City to take command of Continental forces

6 May—British relief force reaches Quebec City; Continental forces retreat to Deschambault

18–20 May—Loyalist forces attack Fort Cedars; Continental defenders and relief force surrender

8 June—Battle of Three Rivers

18 June—Continental Council of War decides to evacuate Fort St. John's

1 July—Last retreating Continentals reach Crown Point

Jean-Baptiste Badeaux—A Short Biography

FIGURE 3. Unidentified Man, 1765–1770. Jean-Baptiste Badeaux's actual appearance is unknown, but he presumably would have dressed in a gentlemanly fashion similar to this painting. A German staff officer serving in the Three Rivers District in 1776 specifically observed, "People living in the cities . . . such as notaries, merchants, and the like, dress in the English or French fashion, but without wearing gold or silver jewelry" (Stone, *Letters of Brunswick and Hessian Officers*, 34). Library and Archives Canada, e010936238.

Jean-Baptiste Badeaux is remembered in Canadian history as a minor figure—a dedicated, loyalist provincial official from Three Rivers, Quebec. Born on April 29, 1741, in Quebec City, he was one of Charles and Marie-Catherine Badeaux's two children who survived to adulthood. He came from a long Canadian line: his first ancestors arrived in the colony from La Rochelle in 1647. His father, a tailor, died when Jean-Baptiste was only fifteen years old.[1]

The young Badeaux appears to have been sent to live with an aunt in Three Rivers by age seven, when he began participating in the parish church choir. Within just six years, he became the church's master cantor, being recognized for his "enjoyable and vibrant voice," with "perfect accuracy" in song. During this time, Jean-Baptiste received a substantial education, perhaps at a school run by the Recollet convent.[2]

Local elites recognized some exceptional characteristics in the maturing Badeaux, and he was encouraged to enter official government circles. In 1763 or early 1764, as British administration was being established in newly conquered Quebec's military regime, Jean-Baptiste was hired as clerk to a pair of key officials in Three Rivers: Conrad Gugy, secretary to Governor Frederick Haldimand; and Louis de Mestral who coordinated civil-military affairs as the town major. Governor Haldimand was forced to rely on such French-speaking Protestants as intermediary officials for regional government, since the British Empire's traditional Test Oath for office was not compatible with practicing Catholics' faith. It is noteworthy that the Canadian governors opted to permit minor officials, such as clerks, bailiffs, and notaries, to continue to serve without an oath, easing government transition at the local level. Gugy and Mestral were both of Swiss heritage and had faithfully served the crown in the

---

1. Raymond Douville, "Badeaux, Jean-Baptiste," in *Dictionary of Canadian Biography (hereafter cited as DCB)*, vol. 4 (University of Toronto/Université Laval, 2003), http://www.biographi.ca/en/bio/badeaux_jean_baptiste_4E.html (accessed August 16, 2014);.Université de Montréal Programme de recherche en démographie historique/Research Program in Historical Demography (hereafter cited as UMPRDH), Parish records database, http://www.genealogie.umontreal.ca (accessed September 29, 2014), individual record 161861, indiv. #251841, Charles and Marie-Catherine Badeaux couple record #20587.

2. Benjamin Sulte, *Mélanges historiques, Trois-Rivières d'Autrefois*, vol. 19 (Montréal: Editions Edouard Garand, 1932), 21, 75 (editor's translation); J.-Edmond Roy, *Histoire du Notariat au Canada: Depuis La Fondation De La Colonie Jusqu'à Nos Jours*, vol. 2 (Levis, QC: La Revue du Notariat, 1900), 2: 47; Marcel Trudel, *Le régime militaire dans le gouvernement de Trois-Rivières 1760–1764* (Trois-Rivières, QC: Bien public, 1952), 12.

French and Indian War as foreign-recruited Royal American Regiment officers. Badeaux received a degree of patronage in ongoing professional relationships with Gugy, whose influence grew as he became a Canadian seigneur-landlord, justice of the peace, and, eventually, a provincial legislative councilor.³

In October 1764, Jean-Baptiste Badeaux married Marie Marguerite Bolvin, daughter of noted ornamental woodcarver and successful merchant Gilles Bolvin. Badeaux was elected by the citizens of Three Rivers to serve as a sub-bailiff in June 1766—another distinct honor for this young, ascendant gentleman. In this position, he played a direct role in local administration and justice, helping to serve "both civil and criminal process and also acting as police," and in maintaining public roads and bridges. Jean-Baptiste also studied for a profession, under the tutelage of one of the city's two active notaries, Louis Pillard or Paul Dielle.⁴

As soon as he met the minimum age requirements, Badeaux entered his lifelong career. On March 20, 1767, he received his first provincial government commission as a notary for Three Rivers. Jean-Baptiste Badeaux had to seek this appointment directly from Lieutenant Governor Guy Carleton, and his request would have been accompanied by certificates of good conduct and recommendations from prominent locals—priests, judges, or some other influential individuals—Conrad Gugy was a likely candidate to have given him such support. As a notary, Jean-Baptiste entered a world where he was in daily

---

3. Jean-Baptiste Badeaux to Frederick Haldimand, 23 February 1781, Roy, *Histoire du Notariat*, 2: 131; Raymond Douville, "Gugy, Conrad," in *DCB* 4, http://www.biographi.ca/en/bio/gugy_conrad_4E.html (accessed November 17, 2013); Francis-J. Audet, "Louis de Mestral," *Bulletin des Recherches Historiques* 33 (1927): 695–96; Alexander Campbell, *The Royal American Regiment: An Atlantic Microcosm, 1755–1772* (Norman: University of Oklahoma, 2010), 204; Trudel, *Régime militaire*, 204.

4. "Badeaux, Jean-Baptiste," DCB, 4; UMPRDH indiv. #167878; Michel Cauchon and André Juneau, "Bolvin, Gilles," in *DCB* 3, http://www.biographi.ca/en/bio/bolvin_gilles_3E.html (accessed August 16, 2014); Trudel, *Régime militaire*, 174; Donald Fyson, "Judicial Auxiliaries Across Legal Regimes: From New France to Lower Canada," A paper presented to the colloquium *Les auxiliaires de la justice: intermédiaires entre la justice et les populations, de la fin du Moyen Âge à l'époque contemporaine*, Québec, September 2004, p. 10, http://www.hst.ulaval.ca/profs/Dfyson/Auxiliaries.pdf (accessed January 17, 2010); Ordinance Establishing Civil Courts, 1764, in *Documents of the Canadian Constitution, 1759–1915*, ed. W. P. M. Kennedy (Oxford, Toronto: 1918): 39–40; André Vachon, *Histoire du Notariat canadien, 1621–1960* (Quebec: Les Presses de L'Université Laval, 1962), 64; Roy, *Histoire du Notariat*, 2: 11, 14.

contact with the local notables—government and church officials, landlords, and merchants of all sorts.[5]

In this new professional role, Badeaux recorded legal and commercial actions in official documents. At this point, he had become firmly ensconced in Canada's very small bureaucratic middle class. Jean-Baptiste adapted well within the British regime and developed an exquisite mastery of the English language. Badeaux's three decades of precise notarial documents serve as a detailed record of Three Rivers civic life spanning his generation. In 1769, in recognition of his contributions to the community, Jean-Baptiste and his heirs were given the privilege of a reserved pew in the parish church, free from the usual fees. This was an honor normally reserved for seigneurial landlords and bailiffs or militia captains. By 1772, Jean-Baptiste also began serving as an attorney for the Three Rivers Ursuline nuns. He managed external business for the convent and for that order's seigneurial landholdings.[6]

Domestically, Jean-Baptiste and Marguerite had their first child, daughter Marie-Louise, in December 1765. They would have another eleven children over the next seventeen years; but only three would survive to adulthood. In the period of Jean-Baptiste's 1775–76 journal, there were five young children in the Badeaux household. The notary, however, kept his family life out of that chronicle—even the birth of son Jean-Baptiste on May 8, 1776, and the death of their nineteen-month-old daughter at the end of that same month were not mentioned in the journal.[7]

Jean-Baptiste Badeaux's comfortable bourgeois village lifestyle was rudely interrupted by the Canadian unrest that began in 1775,

---

5. "Badeaux, Jean-Baptiste," DCB, 4; Roy, *Histoire du Notariat*, 2: 42; Vachon, *Notariat canadien*, 63; Michel Guénette, "Les notaires de Laprairie, 1760–1850: étude socio-économique" (MA, Université de Montréal, 1992), 35.

6. "Badeaux, Jean-Baptiste," DCB, 4; Francis-J. Audet, *Les Députés des Trois-Rivières (1808–1838)* (Trois-Rivières, QC: Bien Public, 1934), 5; Bishop Jean-Olivier Briand Circular Letter, October 15, 1768, in Henri Têtu and C.O. Gagnon, *Mandements, Lettres Pastorales et Circulaires des Évêques de Québec*, vol. 2 (Quebec: Imprimerie Générale, 1888), 214; Olivier Hubert, "Ritual Performance and Parish Stability: French-Canadian Catholic Families at Mass from the Seventeenth to the Nineteenth Century," in *Households of Faith: Family, Gender, and Community in Canada, 1760–1969*, ed. Nancy Christie (McGill-Queens University Press: Montreal, 2002), 40–41.

7. UMPRDH couple #41876. Six of Jean-Baptiste's seven younger siblings had also died before the age of two; Charles Badeaux and Marie-Catherine Loisy Desrochers UMPRDH couple #20587.

and the subsequent American invasion. However, these tumultuous developments inspired him to keep a journal of political and military events—covering both local Three Rivers affairs and province-wide happenings. This record would prove to be his most durable historical legacy. Throughout the period, Jean-Baptiste remained a "convinced royalist," and despite his cooperation with Continental Army occupation leaders in semiofficial capacities, regional elites offered him high praise in the invasion's aftermath. Now a Quebec legislative councilor, Conrad Gugy referred to Badeaux as "a man very fond of government," and the most prominent district seigneur, Militia Colonel Louis-Joseph Godefroy de Tonnancour, praised the notary as "a very perfectly honest man."[8]

With his loyalist *bona fides* reinforced, Jean-Baptiste reaped additional offices and duties. His fellow parishioners elected him as a churchwarden in 1776. Despite Badeaux's earlier reluctance to take up arms with the militia, as related in his October 13, 1775, journal entry, the governor recognized his civic leadership by giving him a militia captain's commission. Upon the passing of the district's master notary Paul Dielle, in December 1778, Governor Haldimand also entrusted Badeaux with primary responsibility for all Three Rivers District notarial records. Three years later, the governor expanded Jean-Baptiste's notarial jurisdiction to encompass the entire Province of Quebec. In 1790, he was appointed a district justice of the peace. With the official end of the Revolutionary War, Badeaux had also been asked to present claims to the new United States government, outside of his official duties: prominent merchant Aaron Hart desired compensation for supplies and services provided to the invading army in 1775–76; and the Ursuline nuns still sought payment for medical services they had provided for sick Continental Army soldiers in Three Rivers.[9]

During this period, Badeaux lost his first wife in November 1789. In the immediate aftermath of this unfortunate event, his fellow church members provided another enduring measure of their respect for Jean-Baptiste and for his many services for the community—the

---

8. Conrad Gugy to Frederick Haldimand, November 2, 1778, and Louis-Joseph Godefroy de Tonnancour to Frederick Haldimand, October 28, 1778, in Roy, *Histoire du Notariat*, 2: 64, 65.

9. Audet, *Députés des Trois-Rivières*, 5; Conrad Gugy to Frederick Haldimand, November 2, 1778; Roy, *Histoire du Notariat*, 2: 64. See Appendix 1 for details of the Ursuline Sisters' claims.

parish covered all funeral expenses. A year later, he married Marguerite Pratte, eight years his junior. Approaching his final half-dozen years, the ever-dutiful and respected Jean-Baptiste was charged with one last significant responsibility, "preparing the land roll for the properties being claimed by the Abenakis of Saint-François"—the "settled" Odanak Indians living south of Lake St. Pierre, about twenty-five miles up the St. Lawrence from Three Rivers.[10]

On March 12, 1796, Jean-Baptiste passed away at age fifty-five after "a long and severe illness." The *Quebec Gazette* reported his death with a short eulogy, "His active and able conduct in the execution of his duty as a magistrate and a notary, always received the merited approbation of all those who knew him, and the regret expressed by all ranks of persons on this melancholy occasion, sufficiently evinces, that the public have cause to lament the loss of a useful and respectable citizen, and his family that of a most tender and kind protector." His sons would continue in their father's footsteps: Antoine-Isidore, the older son, served as a notary until his early death at age twenty-six; Joseph Badeaux served as a notary, justice of the peace, chief cantor, militia officer, and in numerous other official appointments. Most conspicuously, Joseph was elected as a Lower Canadian House of Assembly member, representing the city of Three Rivers, Buckingham County, and Yamaska County during different sessions.[11]

Journal author Jean-Baptiste Badeaux rose from his urban artisan-class youth through the ranks of local officialdom in Quebec Province's third and smallest city. By demonstrating exceptional administrative skills, a good touch of political acumen, and a deep well of simple human kindness, he earned a broad portfolio of responsibilities and a solid position on the periphery of Canada's ruling elite. In the process, he also left future generations with an invaluable account of Canada's experiences as a scene of conflict in the American Revolution.

---

10. Roy, *Histoire du Notariat*, 2: 47; UMPRDH indivs. #3823234 and #224764.
11. "Three-Rivers, March 14, 1796," *Quebec Gazette*, 17 March 1796; Renald Lessard and Jean Prince, "Badeaux, Joseph," in *DCB* 6, http://www.biographi.ca/en/bio/badeaux_joseph_6E.html (accessed August 16, 2014).

William Goforth—A Short Biography

William Goforth played some very important roles in New York, Pennsylvania, and Ohio in the age of the American Revolution and the Early Republic. Yet even though he corresponded with, or directly cooperated with several very famous counterparts—the likes of Alexander McDougall, Benjamin Franklin, John Jay, Alexander Hamilton, and Thomas Jefferson—Goforth has remained in history's shadows. Only in the records of his short Canadian military duty do modern researchers find an enduring, direct account of his strong character, inquisitive mind, sagacity, and effective leadership—a sampling of attributes he demonstrated throughout his life.

William Goforth's youth is scantly documented. There is a twenty-nine-year lacuna spanning from his Philadelphia birth on April 1, 1731, until 1760, when he was first recorded as a "labourer" in New York City's rolls of freemen. That same year, he was married to Catherine Meeks, thirteen years his younger, by Reverend John Gano in New York City's First Baptist Church. Goforth made his living as a cordwainer (leather shoemaker) and small-scale merchant.[1]

Goforth's earliest political activity seems to have been prompted by his Baptist affiliation. In 1769, he was a founding member of New York City's Society of Dissenters, a group of eighteen men who cooperated "for the preservation of their common and respective civil and religious Rights and Privileges," which they felt were impinged upon by the colony's established Anglican Church. Society efforts brought Goforth

---

1. Goforth Family Bible (1728), Public Library of Cincinnati and Hamilton County; New-York Historical Society (hereafter cited as NYHS), "The Burghers of New Amsterdam and the Freemen of New York, 1675–1866," in *Collections of the New-York Historical Society for the Year 1885* (New York, New-York Historical Society, 1886), 194.

into close contact with rising revolutionaries Alexander McDougall and John Morin Scott. In the early 1770s, he focused on his business and supported Catherine in raising their three young children—William, Mary, and Tabitha—born from 1766 to 1774.[2]

The momentous revolutionary events of 1774 called Goforth to new political action. As a representative of New York City's "mechanics," or artisan class, he rose to new levels of responsibility. Goforth was elected to both the Committee of Sixty and the Committee of One Hundred, the major political bodies established to channel the city's growing Continental spirit. The character of his civic duties soon changed, though.[3]

In June 1775, Goforth's friend Alexander McDougall was given command of the newly formed First New York Regiment. The forty-four-year-old Goforth soon heeded the call to arms. As characterized in the conclusion of a poem he composed in his personal daybook, playing upon his own name, he asked "What! not Goforth? when Awl's at Stake." He was appointed as the captain of McDougall's fourth company and had notable recruiting success. The new captain eventually led ninety-three men and two lieutenants when they marched from New York City. Goforth's relatively low social position, however, was reflected in an appeal that he and three fellow officers made to the provincial congress. The officers sought assistance in acquiring uniforms and weapons, as they had did not have the personal wealth of those traditionally called to serve in such ranks. Goforth led his men north to Fort Ticonderoga en route to Canada in September 1775.[4]

Just seven months later, Goforth's military obligations in Quebec were complete. On May 16, 1776, the captain returned to Ticonderoga

---

2. "The Society of Dissenters Founded at New York in 1769," *The American Historical Review* 6, no. 3 (April 1901): 498–502; Goforth Family Bible.

3. "New Committee of Sixty Elected," 22 November 1774; "New General Committee for the City and County of New-York Elected," 1 May 1775; Peter Force ed., *American Archives, Fourth Series* (hereafter cited as *AA4*) (Washington, DC: 1837–1853), 1: 330, 2:459.

4. "Captains Appointed by the New-York Provincial Congress," July 6, 1775, *AA4*, 2: 1592; William Goforth Day Book, John Armstrong Papers, Indiana Historical Society; "State of the Four Regiments raised in the colony of New-York," August 4, 1775 (hereafter cited as "SoFR"), U.S. National Archives and Records Administration (hereafter cited as NARA), M853, Numbered Record Books . . . , rg93, v5, r15, p152; "Muster Roll of Captn Goforth's Compy," September 19, 1775, NARA, M246, Revolutionary War Rolls, 1775–1783, rg 93, r65, f1, p33; "To the Honourable Provincial Congress," July 26, 1775, *AA4*, 2: 1729.

FIGURE 4. New York Soldier, 1775. Goforth's men would have been uniformed in this manner as they entered Canada. The First New York regimental colors were a blue jacket with red facings. Charles MacKubin Lefferts, Uniforms of the American Revolution: 3rd N.Y. Regiment; Object #1920.147, New-York Historical Society.

and delivered official messages from Canada to General Philip Schuyler. Goforth then continued back home and arrived in New York City five days later. Completing his latest task, he presented Schuyler's correspondence to General Israel Putnam, temporarily in command as General Washington was in Philadelphia. After spending a few days with Catherine and his children, including five-month-old son Aaron, Goforth went back to Ticonderoga on another courier mission, bearing messages from George Washington to Schuyler.[5]

In June, it seemed as if Goforth might progress up the officer ranks, having been given the rank of major in a newly formed New York regiment. Goforth, however, saw this appointment as a slight, rather than an honor. During his time in the army, Goforth shared a very common "republican" attitude as a stickler for the principle of seniority as the primary basis for military promotion; and the new regiment's commander and lieutenant colonel had both been junior in rank to him.[6] As a result, Major Goforth wrote to the New York Provincial Congress on July 5 and declined further service. He expressed that he considered an appointment "under two junior officers" was "no more than taking the most genteel way of discharging" him from "the publick service as an officer." New York's assembly accepted the resignation with apparent good will, recognizing him as "a brave and good officer." When New York made subsequent attempts to call on him for officer duty in the following year, he declined further service.[7]

Back in New York City in the summer of 1776, Goforth turned to other less martial venues in his support of the Continental cause. Shortly after resigning his commission, he joined more than one hundred

---

5. Philip Schuyler to George Washington, May 16 1776; George Washington to Philip Schuyler, June 15, 1776, Philander D. Chase, ed., *The Papers of George Washington, Revolutionary War Series* (hereafter cited as *PGWRWS*) (Charlottesville: University of Virginia, 1983–1991), 4: 316–19, 531–39.

6. See Goforth's January 19 letter for his thoughts on the importance of seniority for military promotion and posting. Lewis Dubois was appointed commander of this new regiment, and although he had been junior to Goforth when they marched north in 1775, Dubois had been field-promoted to major at the Quebec City siege camp. Jacobus Bruyn was the new regiment's lieutenant colonel, and by all accounts he was junior in rank to Goforth. However, Bruyn had also seen combat duty around Quebec City. Notably, on the day before the officer appointments were made, Continental Congress delegate George Clinton wrote a letter to New York Provincial Congress secretary John McKesson, mentioning Bruyn as an officer whose merits warranted an appropriate posting—perhaps characterizing the exact sort of partisan political influence that Goforth despised. Transcript of General Schuyler, "A List of officers . . . as they Rank 28 Feby 1776," NARA, M247, Papers of the Continental Congress, rg93, r178, f181, p230; George Clinton to John McKesson, June 25, 1776, *AA4*, 6: 1064.

7. William Goforth to New York Provincial Congress, July 5, 1776, Peter Force ed., *American Archives, Fifth Series* (hereafter cited as *AA5*) (Washington, DC: 1837–1853), 1: 203–204; New York Convention to the President of Congress, July 11, 1776, *AA5*, 1: 202; Rudolphus Ritzema to New York Convention, August 1, 1776, *AA5*, 1: 1467; Henry Beekman Livingston to George Washington, February 15, 1777, *PGWRWS*, 8: 342–43.

memorialists who made a direct appeal General Washington. They were deeply concerned about the region's internal loyalist threat, and asked "that orders may be given for the removal of dangerous persons from this city." Washington subsequently honored Goforth as one of just six civilians authorized to grant travel passes in the New York City region, home to many loyalists, and occupied by the main Continental Army at the time. In a concurrent business endeavor, Goforth joined four fellow veterans by responding to a New York City appeal for establishment of a salt-works; however that enterprise proved to be short-lived. When the conquering British army arrived in the city in September, the Goforth family departed their home, rather than suffer under tyrannical occupation.[8]

It is possible that William, Catherine, and their four children stayed in the New York countryside for a short while. Family tradition related that Goforth served as a spy in the region as late as 1780. This story might be embellished to some degree—Catherine was in Philadelphia for the birth of daughter Jemima on May 9, 1778; and William was confirmed to be in Pennsylvania by October 1779, when he purchased loyalist Gilbert Hicks's "Four Lanes" estate in Bucks County. Other cherished family stories from later generations said that the Goforth family hosted Washington and Lafayette at their new home for "secret meetings" during the Valley Forge winter of 1778.[9]

The Goforths remained in Bucks County for the rest of the war, where Catherine bore their last two children. In 1781, William served for a short time as a Pennsylvania state auditor, handling army pay depreciation claims. Apparently in financial distress, he made unproductive attempts to sell "Four Lanes" as early as December 1782. Still short of cash, Goforth subdivided the estate into smaller parcels in early 1783 to encourage sales and to form a planned settlement with designated plots for churches and schools. This enlightened hamlet, dubbed "Washington Village," was to have streets named after Goforth's notable associates

---

8. Memorial of Sundry Inhabitants of the City of New York to George Washington, July 14, 1776, *AA5*, 1:335; William Goforth and John Houston to New York Provincial Congress, August 3, 1776 and New York Convention, August 5 and 6, 1776, *AA5*, 1: 1475–76; General Orders, *PGWRWS*, 5: 672–75; William H. Chatfield, *Two Revolutionary War Patriots: Major William Goforth and Captain John Armstrong; Epic Struggles Against British Suppression and Indian Warfare* (Cincinnati: Pendleton House, 2011), 16.

9. Chatfield, *Two Revolutionary War Patriots*, 16, 18–19, 29; Supreme Executive Council of Pennsylvania, October 4, 1779, *Minutes of the Supreme Executive Council of Pennsylvania* (Harrisburg: Theo. Fenn, 1853), 12: 156; Goforth Family Bible.

from military service, including Montgomery, McDougall, Willett, and Lamb; but the effort never came to fruition.[10]

With the British army's November 1783 departure upon the war's end, the Goforths returned to New York City. William promptly distinguished himself as "an earnest advocate of popular rights and popular education." In January 1785, he co-founded the New York Manumission Society. Later members such as Alexander Hamilton and John Jay have received more historical recognition for their prominent participation; Goforth, however, was one of the society's leading workhorses. In 1786, he participated in a committee seeking funds for a "negro childrens' school," and in 1787, served as the society's vice president.[11]

Concurrent with his society duties, in 1784, Goforth was elected to the New York State Assembly with the endorsement of the "Sons of Liberty." He was one of just two "mechanics" elected in the first postoccupation legislature. Serving two consecutive terms, he built upon his Manumission Society activities by promoting a law to free children born to slave women after 1785.[12]

Yet while William Goforth was making a social and political impact, his financial situation continued to decline. As an associate recorded, "the war injured him & he has met with Losses in Trade, he has failed . . ." By 1787, he owed the tremendous sum of £5,100 sterling. William and Catherine made the difficult decision to join their grown children's families that had already decided to head west, staking their future on the Ohio frontier. Goforth settled accounts as best he could, but was forced to leave his real estate property in the hands of creditors, who eventually sold it at public auction. On September 26, 1789, fifty-eight-year-old William left New York City for the last time and headed to the Northwest Territory.[13]

---

10. Supreme Executive Council of Pennsylvania, March 3 and June 6, 1781, *Minutes*, 12: 646, 747; Goforth Family Bible; W. W. H. Davis, *The History of Bucks County, Pennsylvania, From the Discovery of the Delaware to the Present Time* (Doylestown: Democrat Book and Job Office, 1876), 172; intent to sell, *Freeman's Journal* (Philadelphia), 5 February 1783; Washington Village plan, *Independent Gazetteer* (Philadelphia), 29 November 1783.

11. New-York Manumission Society Records, 1785–1849, 5: 27, 122, 126, NYHS; *New York Packet* (New York City), 17 November 1786.

12. *Independent Journal* (New York), 21 April 1784; Edwin G. Burrows and Mike Wallace, *Gotham: A History of New York City to 1898* (New York: Oxford University Press, 1999), 280; Stephen C. Hutchins, *Civil List and Constitutional History of the Colony and State of New York* (Albany: Weed, Parsons, 1880), 282–83; Chatfield, *Two Revolutionary War Patriots*, 14, 30.

13. David Jones to George Washington, January 13, 1790, *Papers of George Washington, Presidential Series*, ed. Dorothy Twohig (Charlottesville: University Press of Virginia, 1993),

Goforth reached what would become his new home on January 18, 1790, a small Ohio River settlement called Miami, later becoming Columbia, Ohio. Two days after his arrival, he joined in establishing the community's Baptist church, and in less than two years, was spearheading plans for a local "educational academy." In 1790, Territorial Governor Arthur St. Clair recognized Goforth's prominence when he appointed William as a judge for the newly established Hamilton County court of common pleas. In this service, he was recognized for his "integrity and independence," controversially arresting federal soldiers and shutting down local liquor peddlers. In 1801, Secretary of State James Madison appointed Goforth as a federal commissioner to settle disputed territorial land claims. Meanwhile, William and his extended family constantly improved their settled property. They also accumulated hundreds of additional acres in the region, although some of it was of questionable value.[14]

Goforth's next major task was advocacy for Ohio statehood. Despite Federalist Governor St. Clair's opposition, in 1797 Goforth helped generate a circular letter seeking other counties' support in the cause. In January 1802, he boldly wrote to President Thomas Jefferson. Goforth conveyed his fellow Ohio republicans' issues with "the Government of the Northwestern territory," and enclosed a statehood petition. His letter complained that Ohioans had suffered "deprivation of those privileges injoyed by our fellow citizens in the States in the Union," and appealed to the president "to restore us to the precious privilege of a free Elective Republican Government." Hearkening back to the great revolution, which was almost thirty years in the past, he complained that "our ordinance Government it is a true transcript of our old English Colonial Governments, our Governor is cloathed with all the power of a British Nabob, he has power to convene, prorogue and dissolve our legislature at pleasure, he is unlimitted as to the creation of offices, and I beleive his general rule is to fill all the important leading offices with

---

4: 568–69; Chatfield, *Two Revolutionary War Patriots*, 30–33; "Extracts from memorandums made by Judge William Goforth, in his day book," in *The Cincinnati Miscellany, or Antiquities of the West*, ed. Charles Cist (Cincinnati: 1845), 1: 172.

14. "Extracts from memorandums made by Judge William Goforth, in his day book," Cist, *Cincinnati Miscellany*, 1: 173–74; John C. Hover et al., eds., *Memoirs of the Miami Valley*, vol. 2 (Chicago: Robert O. Law, 1919), 618; Roderick Burnham, *Genealogical Records of Henry and Ulalia Burt . . . from 1640 to 1891* (Hartford: Case, Lockwood and Brainard, 1892), 71–72; note from Albert Gallatin to Thomas Jefferson, October 6, 1801, *The Papers of Thomas Jefferson*, ed. Barbara B. Oberg (Princeton: Princeton University Press, 2008), 35: 391–92; Chatfield, *Two Revolutionary War Patriots*, 40, 42.

men of his own political Sentiments." Goforth recorded several specific cases of Governor St. Clair's manipulative misrule and provided specific population estimates to support the statehood appeal. In April 1802, Congress authorized the inhabitants to meet that November to form a state constitution. William Goforth attended that convention, serving as president *pro tem*. His mission was complete when the State of Ohio officially joined the union the following year.[15]

Goforth accepted one final political role in 1804, leading Ohio's Republican Electoral ticket and casting votes for Thomas Jefferson and George Clinton. Thereafter, Goforth effectively disappeared from the historical record until his November 2, 1807, death at age seventy-six, in Columbia, Ohio. His wife Catherine survived him for another twenty years. His son Dr. William Goforth was renowned as the first prominent medical doctor west of the Appalachians, and for his role in excavating mastodon bones at Big Bone Lick, Kentucky—drawing President Jefferson's attention and a visit from Meriwether Lewis. In the extended Goforth family, two of the elder William Goforth's sons-in-law achieved regional prominence as well: John Stites Gano, husband of eldest daughter Mary, became a major general in the Ohio Militia; daughter Tabitha's husband John Armstrong was also an officer and served as a county and territorial official.[16]

Biographer William H. Chatfield reflected on the sum of William Goforth's life, "Few colonial gentlemen could match Goforth's varied and unique accomplishments. His values, ethics, manners, and civic accolades set a high standard for ensuing generations." An obituary penned by one of his associates noted that Goforth distinguished himself in every one of his roles: "As a soldier he had patriotism, courage, and honor; as a legislator he had wisdom & Republicanism; as a judge he had integrity and independence . . . in the humble & domestic relations of husband, father and neighbour he shone with a steady and native lustre. . . . He loved us, his <u>country</u> & the world: he practiced the strictest justice, purest morality & most disinterested benevolence."[17]

---

15. Julia Perkins Cutler, *Life and Times of Ephraim Cutler* (Cincinnati: Robert Clarke, 1890), 319; William Goforth to Thomas Jefferson, January 5, 1802, *The Papers of Thomas Jefferson*, 36: 297–303; "Chillicothe, NWT, Nov. 6," *Mercantile Advertiser* (New York City), 7 December 1802.

16. *Scioto Gazette* (Chillicothe, OH), 29 October and 10 December 1804; Goforth Family Bible.

17. Chatfield, *Two Revolutionary War Patriots*, 59; Daniel and Benjamin Drake Papers, 1787–1853, Draper Manuscripts, State Historical Society of Wisconsin, 2O, v2, 197.

The Stage—Three Rivers, Quebec, 1775–1776

FIGURE 5. *View of Three Rivers at the end of the XVIII Century*, by James Peachey, ca. 1784. This view is from the banks of the St. Lawrence, south of the town. The Parish Church is leftmost of the spires; the Recollet Church and Ursuline Convents are to the right. The Government House barracks is the large multistory building in the center. Library and Archives Canada, Acc. No. 1983-33-1609.

The following contemporary descriptions provide four diverse views of Three Rivers (Trois-Rivières), Quebec, the principal scene for Jean-Baptiste Badeaux's journal and William Goforth's letters:

> Tis a beautiful town, about as large as Plymouth, situated on the river. (Continental Chaplain Ammi R. Robbins, 5 May 1776)[1]

---

1. Ammi R. Robbins, *Journal of the Rev. Ammi R. Robbins, A Chaplain in the American Army in the Northern Campaign of 1776* (New Haven: B. L. Hamlen, 1850), 16.

Three Rivers, although the oldest French colonial town in Canada, is small and straggling. It contains scarcely three hundred houses, most of which are of wood and but one story high. Still, many merchants occupy them as residences. . . . The Convent of the Recollets has been abolished; the former Government-House turned into a barrack for 300 men; and the Ursuline Convent converted into a hospital for our troops. The chief resident *Curé* [parish priest] bears the title of Grand Vicar. Many pretty and lively girls are met with in this town who dress themselves very neatly. Quite a number of Seigneurs have here their winter residences. . . . An extremely important magazine is also located here; and occasionally you will meet with exceedingly nice houses furnished very respectably. (Brunswick Officer's Journal, 3 November 1776)[2]

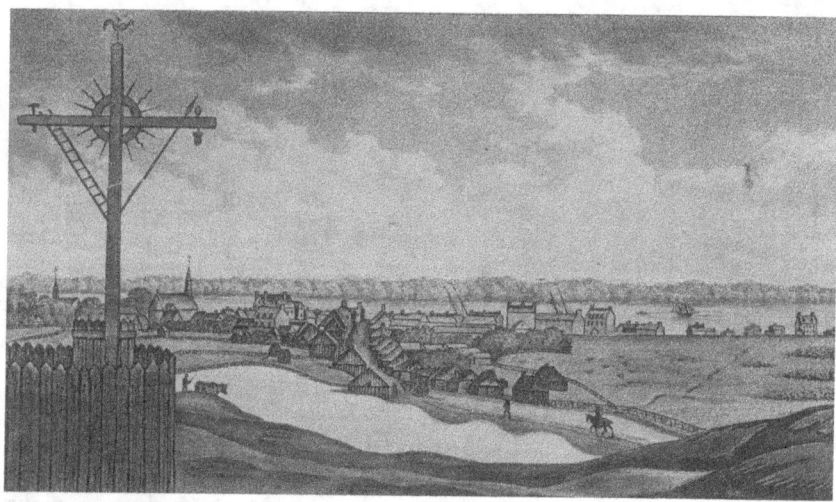

FIGURE 6. *The Town of Three Rivers*, by John Lambert, 1810. This perspective is just north of the Rue des Forges, west of the town. A roadside shrine is in the foreground. The larger multistory riverfront merchants' warehouses were built after the Revolution. Library and Archives Canada, C-001458.

---

2. William Stone, trans., *Letters of Brunswick and Hessian Officers During the American Revolution* (Albany: Munsell's, 1891), 45–46.

Their houses are built of wood, except the churches and convents, which are of stone, and very magnificent; yet, upon the whole, the village of Trois Rivieres has all the appearance of an infant settlement, situated in a barren part of the country; . . . the land there is well cultivated, seemingly fertile, and abounding in every thing. (Captain John Knox, August 1760)[3]

The Town of Trois Rivieres . . . is built upon the North Shore of the River St Lawrence, and Consists of about One Hundred Houses a Parochial church, a Convent of Ursuline Nuns, & Another of Recollet Priests. (Col Ralph Burton's Report on the State of Government at Three Rivers, April 1762)[4]

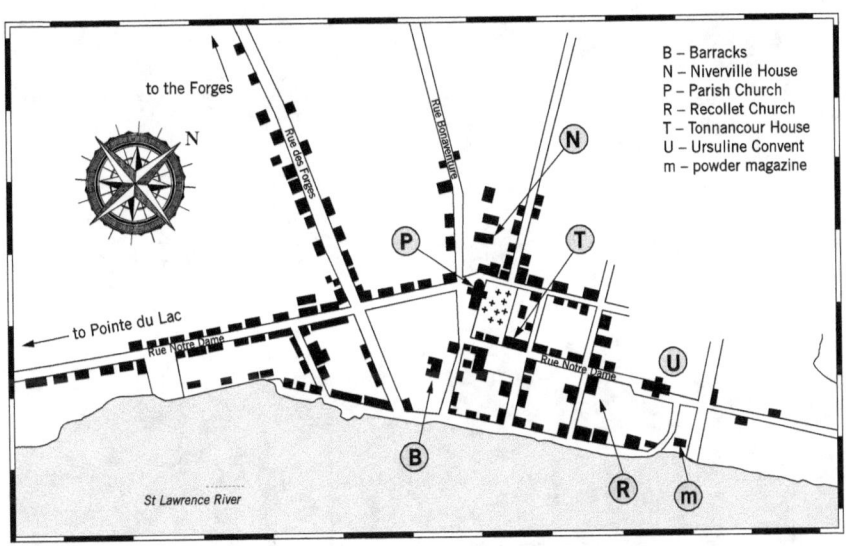

MAP 1. Three Rivers City, 1775–76. This is an interpretation of the city's layout in the late eighteenth century, compiled from historical maps and illustrations, and local heritage studies.

---

3. Captain John Knox, *An Historical Journal of the Campaigns in North America, 1757, 1758, 1759, 1760* (London: W. Johnston, 1769), 361.
4. Adam Shortt and Arthur Doughty, eds., *Canadian Archives: Documents Relating to the Constitutional History of Canada, 1759–1791* (Ottawa: S. E. Dawson, 1907), 1: 62.

Translator's Notes

The translation does not attempt to reproduce the irregular spellings and punctuation issues from Badeaux's journal, and keeps only proper names in their misspelled and widely varying forms. If words in the original journal or marginalia are difficult to discern, they are noted with [?]. Where the manuscript copies are illegible, those portions are noted [Ms. illegible]. Editorial insertions are indicated in brackets. The notation [*sic*] has been limited to situations where a word or content would be otherwise unclear.

The translation maintains contemporary usage of most words. Note that the notion of a "notaire" (Badeaux's profession), both in the eighteenth century and modern usage is closer to that of a contract attorney than to that of a notary in today's world. As the reader can see from the text, Badeaux is responsible for a wide range of legal duties, from real estate transactions to bill collection.

Also note that the term *sauvages*, referring to the Native Americans fighting both with and against the loyalist forces, has been translated as "Indians." This is common usage and does not reproduce the immediately negative connation of "savages." The translator notes, however, that the original term and its more direct translation reflect a widely held view of native peoples as "savages" in comparison to the "civilized" Europeans. This usage was common in eighteenth-century English as well as French.

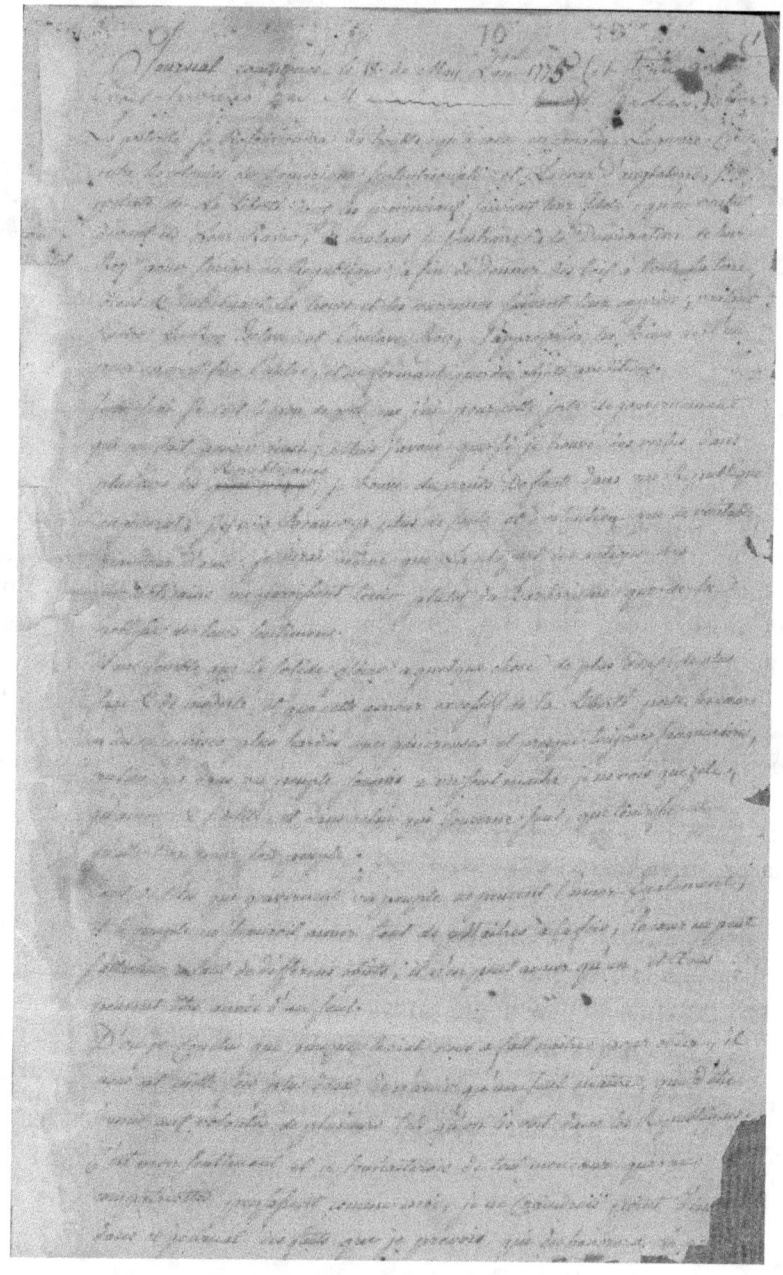

FIGURE 7. Opening page of the Badeaux Journal. The notary's smooth, professional penmanship is evident in this manuscript. Library and Archives Canada, Collection Amable Berthelot, MG23-B35.

Summer 1775

Jean-Baptiste Badeaux's Journal Begun on the 18th of May in the Year 1775[1]

Posterity will remember the trouble caused in Canada by the civil war between the Colonies of North America and the Court of England upon pretext of liberty, which the provincials made their idol and which they claimed was being taken from them; but they rather wished to remove themselves from their King's domination in order to set themselves up as a republic, so as to give laws to the entire world, taking and distributing thrones and crowns according to their whim, wishing to make the king a slave and the slave a king, appropriating the goods of the one to gratify the other and forming nothing but ambitious goals.

    I do not know if it is the little taste I have for this form of government that makes me think this way, but I admit that if I find virtues in many republicans,[2] I find great defects in a republic in general; I see therein a great deal more splendor and ostentation than true greatness of soul; I will even say that the majority of the republicans' actions

---

1. Historian and collector François-Xavier Garneau added "(and kept at Three Rivers by M. ——— (M. Badeaux) notary" to the manuscript title. Alfred Garneau to Douglas Rymney, June 1, 1876, Library and Archives Canada (hereafter cited as LAC), MG23-B35. See Notes on the Provenance of Badeaux's Journal, following the journal and correspondence.

PRESENTATION NOTES:
Section headings come from marginal notes added to the manuscript by Amable Berthelot (see Notes on the Provenance of Badeaux's Journal). Otherwise added material is noted or bracketed. Words without specific, direct translations, or with additional French connotations, are appropriately footnoted.

2. The term *Republicans* replaces the original, crossed-out *provincials* in the manuscript.

seem to me to have more to do with barbarism than with the nobility of their sentiments.

It seems to me that real glory has something softer, wiser & more modest to it, and that this excessive love of liberty moves hearts to undertakings more hardy than generous, and nearly always bloody. On the contrary, in a people subject to a sole master, I see only zeal, love & faithfulness, and in he who governs alone—nothing but tenderness and care for his people.

So many heads governing a people cannot love it equally, and the people cannot know how to love so many masters at one time; the heart cannot attach itself to so many different objects; it can only love one and all can be loved by one alone.

Letter from Congress[3]

From whence I conclude that since the Heavens made us born to obey, it is a thousand times sweeter to have only one master, than to be subject to the wishes of several such as we see in republics. This is my feeling, and I would hope with all my heart that my compatriots think as I do; I have no fear of inserting events that I foresee will dishonor the Canadian[4] nation into this journal. For I perceive that at present the Canadians have changed their feelings based on the letter they received from Congress, dated the 26th October, of the year 1774,[5] which each interprets according to his own fancy. May the Heavens grant that I be wrong and that the Canadians may preserve their honor and faithfulness.

---

3. The section headings are translations of Amable Berthelot's margin notes on the original manuscript. (see Notes on the Provenance of Badeaux's Journal).

4. In usage common for his time, when Badeaux used the term *Canadians* (*Canadiens*), he was specifically referring to French Canadians. Anglo-Canadians were simply "English."

5. On October 26, 1774, the First Continental Congress approved a letter "To the Inhabitants of Quebec," inviting them to participate in the next congress. It also "educated" Canadians about the benefits of English government, and identified key reasons why the United Colonies felt oppressed by the British government; *JCC*, 1: 105–13. Copies began to reach Canada in late 1774 and early 1775.

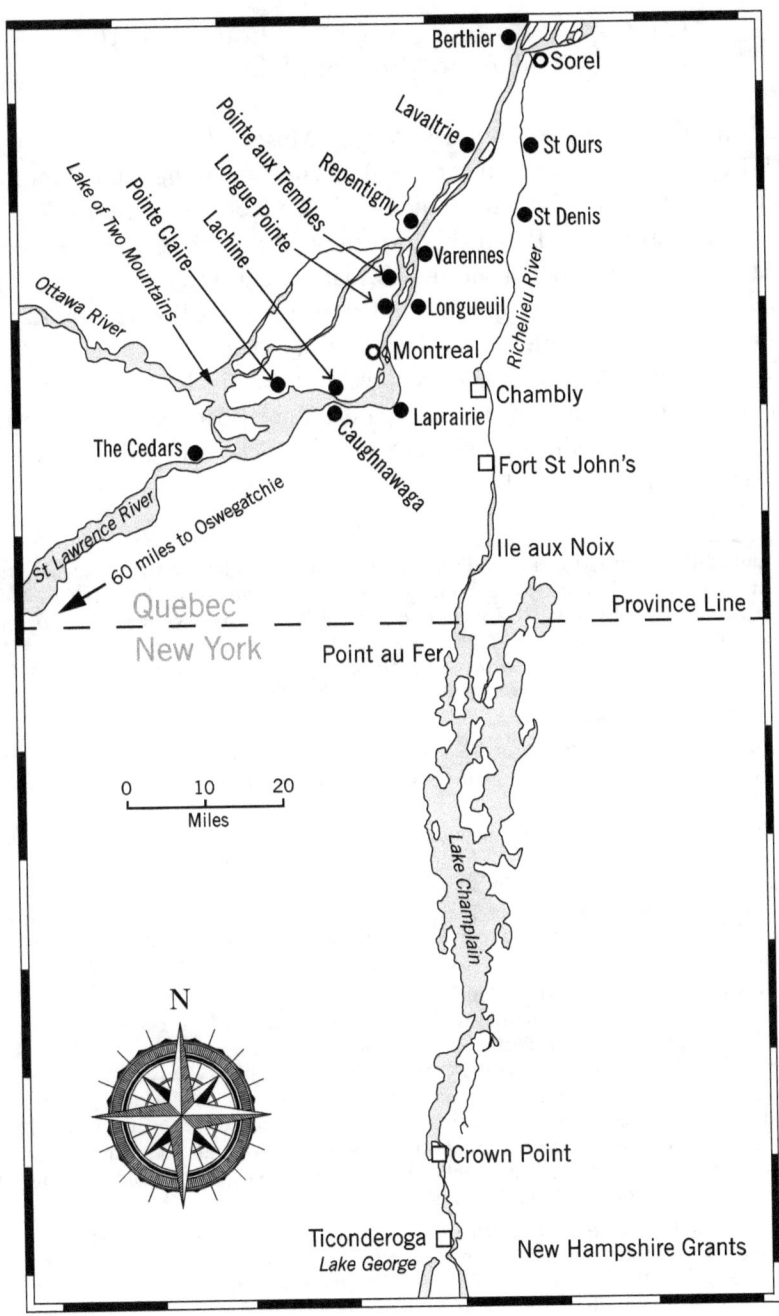

Map 2. Montreal District and the Lake Champlain Corridor.

Capture of Carillon, of Crown Point, and the Pillage of Fort St. John's

Towards the end of May 1775, Mister Moses Hazen,[6] officer of the 44th Regiment, while passing through this city coming from Montreal, told us that a party of "Bostonians"[7] had taken the forts of Carillon [Ticonderoga] and la Pointe [Crown Point];[8] that they had even come as far as St. John's,[9] taken the troops that were at the fort as well as the King's provisions and munitions, and retreated to la Pointe, where they built boats to penetrate deeper into this province.

As soon as Mr. Carleton[10] was warned of this, he had troops from Quebec [City][11] come to defend against the "Bostonians'" entry into this province. Captain Strong's company,[12] which was garrisoned in this city, left on the 20th of May.

---

6. (End of May entry) Moses Hazen was a half-pay (inactive) British Captain, who settled in Canada after the Conquest and eventually became a seigneur on the upper Richelieu River. See Allan S. Everest, "Hazen, Moses," in *DCB* 5, http://www.biographi.ca/en/bio/hazen_moses_5E.html (accessed November 11, 2013); Allan S. Everest, *Moses Hazen and the Canadian Refugees in the American Revolution* (Syracuse: Syracuse University, 1976); Philippe Demers, *Le Général Hazen, seigneur de Bleury-Sud: essai de monographie régionale* (Montreal, Librairie Beauchemin, 1927).

7. The Canadians used the term *Bostonians* (*Bostonnois* or *Bastonnais*) for colonists from any of the traditional thirteen British North American provinces: New Englanders, Yorkers, Pennsylvanians et al.

8. These were the British Army–manned forts at Ticonderoga [*Carillon*] and Crown Point [*Pointe à la Chevelure*], seized by rebel parties on May 10 and 11, 1775. The raids were conducted by the Green Mountain Boys, from the disputed New Hampshire Grants region (Vermont), and men from western Massachusetts. Both Connecticut and Massachusetts had, coincidentally, authorized missions on the forts, with Ethan Allen and Benedict Arnold being appointed leaders of the respective detachments.

9. On May 18, Benedict Arnold led a party of soldiers down Lake Champlain to Fort St. John's [*St. Jean*], the southernmost Canadian settlement, which consisted of a small barracks, ruined French fortifications and a minor shipyard. Arnold's objective was to seize a nearly completed sloop being built for British military service, which would contest the rebels' newly obtained control of the lake. Shortly after Arnold and his men withdrew with the captured vessel, Ethan Allen landed a second, completely separate detachment of Green Mountain Boys, occupying the fort overnight. This force withdrew in the face of an advancing British regular army party from Montréal on the following morning, which recovered Fort St. John's for the Crown.

10. Governor Guy Carleton, a British army general appointed as Quebec's lieutenant-governor, in 1766, and governor in 1768. See G. P. Browne, "Carleton, Guy, 1st Baron Dorchester," in *DCB* 5, http://www.biographi.ca/en/bio/carleton_guy_5E.html (accessed November 11, 2013); and Paul David Nelson, *General Sir Guy Carleton, Lord Dorchester: Soldier-Statesmen of Early British Canada* (Cranbury, NJ: Associated University Presses, 2000).

11. (May 1775) When Badeaux or Goforth refers to "Quebec," they mean Quebec City. They generally refer to the province or region as "Canada."

The troops from Quebec passed through on the 26th of May and Captain Baillie[13] lodged in my home. Nothing happened from this time until the ninth of June, on which day the General published a Proclamation establishing the militias;[14] this proclamation was addressed to Chevalier De Tonnancour[15] who charged me with reading it on the 13th of June, the Feast of St. Anthony,[16] which I did after mass at the Recollets'.[17]

The 23rd of June, Mister de Montesson, Chevalier of Saint Louis,[18] received a packet of blank commissions from the General, who noted in

---

12. Captain John Strong was from the Twenty-Sixth Regiment, one of the two remaining regular British army units that garrisoned Canada at the start of the Revolutionary War. He would serve at Fort St. John's and became a prisoner of war with that fort's surrender on November 3, 1775. "Minutes of a Court of Enquiry, St. Johns, 5 October 1775," in "Appendix B: Papers Relating to the Surrender of St. Johns and Chambly," in *Report on the Works of the Public Archives for the Years 1914 and 1915*, ed. Arthur Doughty (Ottawa: L. Taché, 1916), 10; "List of Prisoners taken at Chambly and St. Johns," *AA4*, 3: 1427.

13. Captain James William Baillie, Seventh (Royal Fusiliers) Regiment; he also served at Fort St. John's, and became a prisoner of war with its surrender. "Minutes of a Court of Enquiry, St. Johns, 5 October 1775," in Doughty, "Papers Relating to the Surrender," 10; "List of Prisoners," *AA4* 3: 1427.

14. Governor Carleton declared martial law on June 9, 1775, as a result of the Arnold and Allen raids on Fort St. John's, and subsequent rebel scouting missions and informal "rebel" envoys crossing into the Province of Quebec. Governor Carleton's June 9 Proclamation, *Quebec Gazette*, 15 June 1775.

15. Nineteen-year-old Charles Antoine Godefroy de Tonnancour, the third surviving son of prominent regional seigneur Louis Joseph de Tonnancour (see note to 6 September entry). Charles-Antoine inherited the French title *Chevalier* associated with the *Croix de St. Louis*. See Normand Paquette, "Godefroy de Tonnancour, Charles-Antoine (1755–98)," in *DCB* 4, http://www.biographi.ca/en/bio/godefroy_de_tonnancour_charles_antoine_1755_98 (accessed November 11, 2013); Pierre-Georges Roy, *La Famille Godefroy de Tonnancour* (Quebec: Laflamme, 1904), 61.

16. Traditionally, militia captains read government proclamations to the people, but the captain's office had been eliminated when British authorities disbanded the militia in 1765. Local bailiffs (judicial auxiliaries) assumed many of the militia captains' responsibilities. It appears that as a notary, Badeaux was called to "publish" government orders as well. This was the Feast of St. Anthony of Padua.

17. The Recollets were a reformed branch of the Franciscan brothers, serving as missionaries in Canada since 1615. After the Conquest, the British government forbade the order from accepting new initiates, so only a few brothers remained. The Recollet church was still one of the few public buildings in Three Rivers, and was shared with the city's small Anglican congregation.

18. Joseph-Michel de Montesson was a regional seigneur and veteran colonial officer. The fifty-nine-year-old had earned the *Croix de St. Louis* for his service in the French and Indian War, earning him the title *Chevalier de St. Louis*. He subsequently served as a volunteer at Fort St. John's, and was taken prisoner upon its surrender, dying during loose captivity in Pennsylvania. See Malcolm MacLeod, "Legardeur de Croisille et de Montesson, Joseph-Michel," in *DCB* 4, http://www.biographi.ca/en/bio/legardeur_de_croisille_et_de_montesson_joseph_mich. (accessed November 11, 2013).

his letter that he should take me with him to make the rounds of the district, setting up elections for militia officers,[19] but, whether I wished [to go] or not, Mr. Baucin,[20] in town from Rivière du Loup,[21] spared me this trouble and went with Mr. Montesson. Upon their return they held the election for this city's officers.

Everything was fairly calm during the months of July and August. The general had assembled his council[22] in Quebec to work on establishing regulations for the province, but he was obliged to abandon his council to rush to the defense of Fort St. John's, which was threatened by the "Bostonians."[23]

---

19. Along with the implementation of martial law, Governor Carleton restored the militia in the summer of 1775. Traditionally, each parish nominated their own militia captain, who was then confirmed and commissioned by the governor. It appears Carleton was employing this system in Three Rivers District. In some regions, he simply appointed the new militia officers—often the same men who had been parish captains when the militia was disbanded in 1765.

20. (June 23) Michel Beaucin, a French-born loyalist merchant and Rivière-du-Loup militia captain. Henri Têtu, *Histoire des Familles Têtu, Bonenfant, Dionne et Perrault* (Quebec: Dussault et Proulx, 1898), 588; UMPRDH indiv. #98351.

21. Rivière-du-Loup (modern Louiseville, see Map 3—Three Rivers District) was a Three Rivers District parish roughly twenty miles south (upstream) of the city of Three Rivers, on the center north shore of Lake St. Pierre, a twenty-five-mile-long widening of the St. Lawrence River. It is not to be confused with modern Rivière-du-Loup, north (downstream) of Quebec City.

22. Governor Carleton called one session of his new Quebec Act legislative council, starting August 17. This assembly was notable as the first time Catholic Canadians could serve in this high appointed office. Eight of Carleton's twenty appointees were French Canadian. None of the council members came from Three Rivers city, although Councilor Conrad Gugy was a seigneur from Yamachiche in Three Rivers District. See Simon Sanguinet, "Témoin Oculaire de L'Invasion du Canada par les Bastonnois," in Verreau, *Invasion du Canada*, 46; Hilda Neatby, *The Administration of Justice under the Quebec Act* (Minneapolis: University of Minnesota, 1937), 25.

23. Fort St. John's had been overhauled during the summer and consisted of two earthen redoubts that surrounded preexisting buildings. There were also two small warships, which were nearly complete. Carleton concentrated about 450 regular troops and Canadian volunteers at the post, augmented by Indian parties, to bar rebel access to the province on the Lake Champlain–Richelieu River corridor. Late on September 4, a Continental force under Major General Philip Schuyler and Brigadier General Richard Montgomery landed at Ile aux Noix, twelve miles south of the fort. The Continentals launched their first mission on the Canadian mainland on September 6, encountering a British-led Indian party that night. After a short firefight, the Continentals withdrew to Ile-aux-Noix the following morning. "Intelligence received by the Congress from General Schuyler," September 18, 1775; *AA4*, 3: 727.

September 1775

The 6th of September, the general arrived from Quebec and was lodged in the home of Mr. de Tonnancour,[1] who provided him with a Canadian guard. This sentry was Charles l'Etournau, a blacksmith. The General, seeing this man going back and forth in front of his windows, and not knowing what was going on, asked Mr. de Tonnancour what this armed man was doing outside the door? Mr. de Tonnancour told him, "He is guarding your Excellency." So, he went out the door, called the guard to him and told him, "This is the first Canadian I have had the honor to see armed;"[2] he took two guineas[3] from his pocket and gave the man one for himself and the other for his companions on the watch. If all sentries had been paid in this manner, they would have mounted watch with more courage than they did.

---

1. (September 6) Louis Joseph Godefroy de Tonnancour, the most prominent regional seigneur and merchant in Three Rivers. Governor Carleton appointed Tonnancour as militia colonel for the Three Rivers District when the militia was reinstated in 1775. See Frances Caissie, "Godefroy de Tonnancour, Louis-Joseph," in *DCB* 4, http://www.biographi.ca/en/bio/godefroy_de_tonnancour_louis_joseph_4E.html (accessed November 11, 2013); Roy, *Famille Godefroy de Tonnancour*, 51-57. See also journal entry from Batiscamp, November 3, 1776, in Stone, *Letters of Brunswick and Hessian Officers*, 45-46, for an interesting perspective of Tonnancour's character.

2. As noted in the Historical Prelude, Canadians had generally ignored the governor's attempts to mobilize the militia in 1775. In the Montreal District, there were actually three minor habitant rebellions sparked by seigneurs attempting to force mobilization. Francis Maseres, *Additional Papers concerning the province of Quebec* (London: W. White, 1776), 69-80.

3. A guinea coin was worth slightly more than a Canadian *livre*, which was less than one day's pay for a Continental private. While seemingly a trifle, habitants were traditionally uncompensated for militia duty. Currency exchange table in Fernand Ouellet, *Economic and Social History of Quebec, 1760–1850: Structures and Conjunctures* (Ottawa: Carleton University, 1980), 60; Michael P. Gabriel, ed. *Quebec during the American Invasion: The Journal of François Baby, Gabriel Taschereau, and Jenkin Williams*, trans. S. Pascale Vergereau-Dewey (East Lansing: Michigan State University Press, 2005), 126 (note 5).

FIGURE 8. General Sir Guy Carleton. Library and Archives Canada, Acc. No. 1997-8-1.

Poor Disposition of Montreal District

The 7th of September, the General left for Montreal and had the discomfort of seeing that the more he advanced upriver, the more he found the habitants[4] opposed to his designs.

The 8th. A command was issued in the city as well as in the rural communities [*côtes*],[5] to go to Fort St. John's, but the Chamblies parishes,[6] having sided with the "Bostonians" had sown the idea in all the other parishes to not take up arms against the "Bostonians"; that those people

---

4. The habitants were tenant farmers in Canada's traditional seigneurial land system. They are sometimes referred to as peasants.

5. "During the French regime *côte* meant a line of settlement along the St. Lawrence, a tributary, or a road. As used here the word is given a sharper focus to mean a line of

had come to draw us out of oppression. The Canadian people, credulous when one ought not be, went along with the Chambly parishes' belief and nearly all of the Three Rivers District refused to march, with the exception of a few volunteers from the parishes of Rivière du Loup, Machiche & Masquinongé.[7] The parishes of Nicolet, Bécancour, Gentilly and St. Pierre-l'ebequet[8] refused to furnish a single man in spite of the reproaches made to them; all was useless.

September 10th. Today Mr. de Tonnancour, Jr.,[9] and Mr. Bellefeuille,[10] militia ensign, with a dozen men from the city and Pointe du Lac,[11] left for St. John's, where several Montreal gentleman volunteers had already

---

settlement which was short and isolated enough so that its inhabitants thought of the settlement as a distinct community"; it was not a village or rural center, "simply a loose grouping of farmers each living close to" his neighbors, driven by the pattern of land grants given to habitants in long strips perpendicular to rivers. Richard C. Harris, *The Seigneurial System in Early Canada: A Geographical Study, with a New Preface* (Montreal: McGill-Queen's Press, 1984), 176, 186.

6. The "Chamblies" parishes were those along the Richelieu (or Chambly) River—roughly a forty-mile strip of settlement stretched on the river banks between the village of Chambly and the town of Sorel on the St. Lawrence River. A cell of "patriot" Canadian partisans formed in the Chambly region, gathering hundreds of Richelieu Valley habitants to actively support the Continental invaders by providing supplies and taking up arms to cut government communications with Fort St. John's.

7. Maskinongé, Rivière-du-Loup and Yamachiche parishes sat along the north shore of Lake St Pierre (see Map 3).

8. Nicolet, Bécancour, Gentilly, and St-Pierre-les-Becquets were south shore parishes, stretching thirty-five miles from Lake St Pierre, downstream to the Quebec District boundary (see Map 3). Details of habitant passivity and resistance to mobilization in the latter three parishes are documented in Gabriel, *Quebec during the American Invasion*, 43–50.

9. Joseph-Marie de Tonnancour, son of Louis-Joseph. The young noble had just returned from university studies in Paris and Oxford, passing through restive New York on his trip home. He would serve as a volunteer at Fort St. John's and became a prisoner of war upon its surrender. See Martin Rochefort, "Godefroy de Tonnancour, Joseph-Marie," in *DCB* 6, http://www.biographi.ca/en/bio/godefroy_de_tonnancour_joseph_marie_6E.html (accessed November 11, 2013).

10. Antoine Lefebvre Bellefeuille, the twenty-year-old son of prominent regional seigneur François Lefebvre Bellefeuille. Antoine was another of the young French Canadian elite who served as a volunteer at Fort St. John's and became a prisoner of war after its surrender. See A. C. Léry de Macdonald, "La famille Le Fébure de Bellefeuille," *Revue Canadienne* 20 (1884): 241–42; "List of Prisoners," *AA4* 3: 1428. Antoine's seigneur father, François, would be one of just sixteen Trifluviens (residents of Three Rivers) identified as ardent loyalists by a local patriot in 1776; see Badeaux's 30 April entry.

11. Pointe-du-Lac was a north shore parish (see Map 3), sitting at the point where Lake St. Pierre narrows back into the St. Lawrence, only nine miles upstream from Three Rivers; also the Tonnancour family's principal seigneury.

gone. This same day, Mr. Champlain,[12] who had refused to mobilize, sang high mass and vespers in the guardroom, because it was Sunday.

12th. We learned from the Montreal courier that a detachment of volunteers under the command of Mr. de Longueil[13] had been surprised by the enemy while scouting;[14] a certain Perthuis,[15] Indian interpreter, lost his life and the Chevalier La Bruyère[16] had both arms broken.

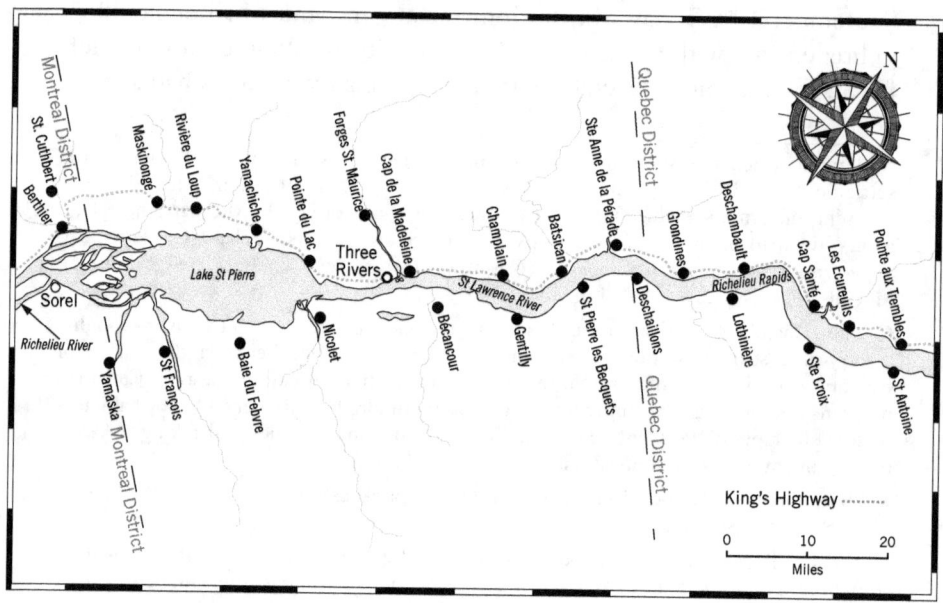

MAP 3. The Three Rivers District

---

12. Mr. Champlain is unidentified.

13. Joseph-Dominique-Emmanuel le Moyne de Longueuil, seigneur and French and Indian War veteran. He led a detachment of approximately one hundred French Canadian volunteers from Montreal to Fort St. John's on September 7. He too became a prisoner with the fort's surrender. See Gérald Pelletier, "Le Moyne de Longueuil, Joseph-Dominique-Emmanuel," in *DCB* 5, http://www.biographi.ca/en/bio/le_moyne_de_longueuil_joseph_dominique_emmanuel_5E.html (accessed November 11, 2013).

14. This engagement occurred late in the evening of September 10, when the Continentals made a second landing near Fort St. John's. Once again, they withdrew to Ile aux Noix the following morning.

15. Interpreter Louis Perthuis, who coordinated Indian auxiliary activities around Fort St. John's; Paul L. Stevens, "His Majesty's 'Savage' Allies: British Policy and the Northern Indians during the Revolutionary War, The Carleton Years, 1774–1778," (doctoral dissertation, State University of New York-Buffalo, 1984), 84, 383, 428.

Beaubien

22ⁿᵈ. We learn from Montreal that the "Bostonians" and the Chambly habitants have blockaded Fort St. John's and have taken several carts filled with provisions, herds of animals, and munitions; that the garrison of the fort having been informed of this, made a sortie against the "Bostonians," repelling them vigorously and taking several prisoners, among whom was Mr. Moses Hazen of the 44ᵗʰ Regt. with his servant.[17] We lost Mr. Beaubien[18] of Quebec in this action, and a certain Tessier from Pointe du Lac was wounded.[19]

The Affair of Longue Pointe

The 26th of this month the "Bostonians" & Chambly Canadians, numbering 200, went to Longue Pointe,[20] about a league from Montreal city, in an attempt to surprise the city and pillage it, but the nobility and bourgeoisie, warned of their undertaking, came out with unparalleled

---

16. Although the Chevalier de la Bruyère's identity is not specifically clear, he was presumably from the seigneurial Boucher de la Bruere family. In his 'Témoin Oculaire," Simon Sanguinet called him "Sieur de la Bruire;" Verreau, *Invasion du Canada*, 44.

17. (September 22) Major John Brown led a corps of Continentals and Canadian partisans to establish pickets north of Fort St John's, and ambushed a supply convoy on the night of September 17. This detachment had detained Moses Hazen and his servant prior to the ambush, being uncertain where that seigneur's loyalties stood. After the British and Canadian loyalist force recaptured Hazen, garrison commander Major Charles Preston was similarly doubtful of Hazen's allegiance and had him covertly escorted through Continental lines to Montreal, where Governor Carleton decided to imprison him. Claude de Lorimier, *At War with the Americans*, trans. and ed. Peter Aichinger (Victoria, BC: Press Porcépic, 1987), 32–35.

18. Sources do not specifically identify who this might have been. In his journal, Fort St. John's defender Feu Foucher records the casualty as "Mr. Baubien des Ruisseaux," otherwise known as "Desaunier;" Feu Foucher, "Journal Tenu Pendant Le Siege du Fort Saint-Jean, en 1775," *Le Bulletin des Recherches Historiques* 40, no. 3 (1934): 139; in his "Témoin Oculaire," Sanguinet refers to him as "Le Sr Beaubien Desauniers;" Verreau, *Invasion du Canada*, 69.

19. It seems this Tessier was one of Joachim Tessier's four sons, but the documentary record does not offer any clarifying details. In the published version, Verreau added a footnote reference here to Sanguinet's "Témoin Oculaire," Verreau, *Invasion du Canada*, 68–69, which offers another description of the event.

20. Longue-Pointe was on the Island of Montreal, a small St. Lawrence parish opposite the south shore ferry point of Longueuil (see Map 2). Continental troops had reached this region's southeast river banks within the past week.

boldness, went after the enemy and repelled him most vigorously,[21] took 30 prisoners, among whom were Colonel Ethan Allen[22] and 20 or 25 Chambly Canadians, who were led to Montreal and then put on the ships, shackled hand and foot. The Royalists lost in this action: Captain Carden,[23] previously of the 8th Regiment, Mr. Paterson[24] fatally wounded; Mr. Beaubassin[25] was slightly wounded. The "Bostonians" dispersed into the woods; otherwise they would all have been taken prisoner.[26]

The 27th. I volunteered for guard duty and the sergeant did me the honor of making me acting corporal; I leave it to the imagination whether

---

21. The combined Canadian-Continental force was to be supported by another Continental force under Major John Brown, crossing from La Prairie (south of Montreal), and a Canadian habitant force from L'Assomption (see Map 2), formed under the direction of notorious Montreal merchant-rebel Thomas Walker.

22. (September 26) Ethan Allen was the principal leader of the Green Mountain Boys, from the disputed New Hampshire Grants region (future State of Vermont). Although Allen had led the Green Mountain Boys to seize Ticonderoga and in the Fort St. John's raid in May 1775, he was not given command when a Continental Green Mountain Boys Regiment was formed in the summer. He joined the Canadian expedition as a volunteer, and General Richard Montgomery primarily employed him as a liaison with the Chambly Canadians and regional Indians. David Bennett, *A Few Lawless Vagabonds: Ethan Allen, the Republic of Vermont, and the American Revolution* (Havertown, PA: Casemate, 2014).

23. John Carden was referred to as a major, and "a brave Man and gallant Officer," in the *Quebec Gazette*'s accounts of the Battle of Longue-Pointe. He was apparently a half-pay, inactive, or retired British army officer settled in Canada; "Quebec, September 21, 1775," and "Extract of an authentick Letter from Montreal, dated September 28," *Quebec Gazette*, 5 October 1775; [Nauticus] "To the Printer of the Quebec Gazette, *Quebec Gazette*, 19 October.

24. Montreal merchant Alexander Paterson was "shot through the body." In 1774, he had been a very active participant in Canada's anti-Carleton and anti–Quebec Act "British Party," but aligned himself with the Crown as tensions flared in 1775; "Extract of an authentick Letter from Montreal, dated September 28," *Quebec Gazette*, 5 October 1775; [Nauticus] "To the Printer of the Quebec Gazette," *Quebec Gazette*, 19 October; "Montreal, January 10, 1774. Petition from the Free-holders, etc. of Quebec," and "Extract of a Letter from a Gentleman in Montreal . . . , dated October 9, 1774," and "Petition from the Province of Quebec . . . to the King," November 12, 1774, in *AA4*, 1: 1844, 853–54, 1849.

25. Seigneur and veteran Indian officer Pierre Hertel-de-Beaubassin, who had helped coordinate Indian scout parties at Fort St. John's in the summer of 1775. In early 1776, Continental authorities would arrest Beaubassin because of his disruptive influence in the occupation, and then detained him in the rebel colonies. Stevens, "His Majesty's 'Savage' Allies," 378, 382–83, 508; "Letter from General [David] Wooster to General [Philip] Schuyler, March 13, 1776, in *AA4*, 5: 417.

26. Verreau offered a footnote reference to Sanguinet's "Témoin Oculaire," 49–51, for another description of the battle at Longue Pointe.

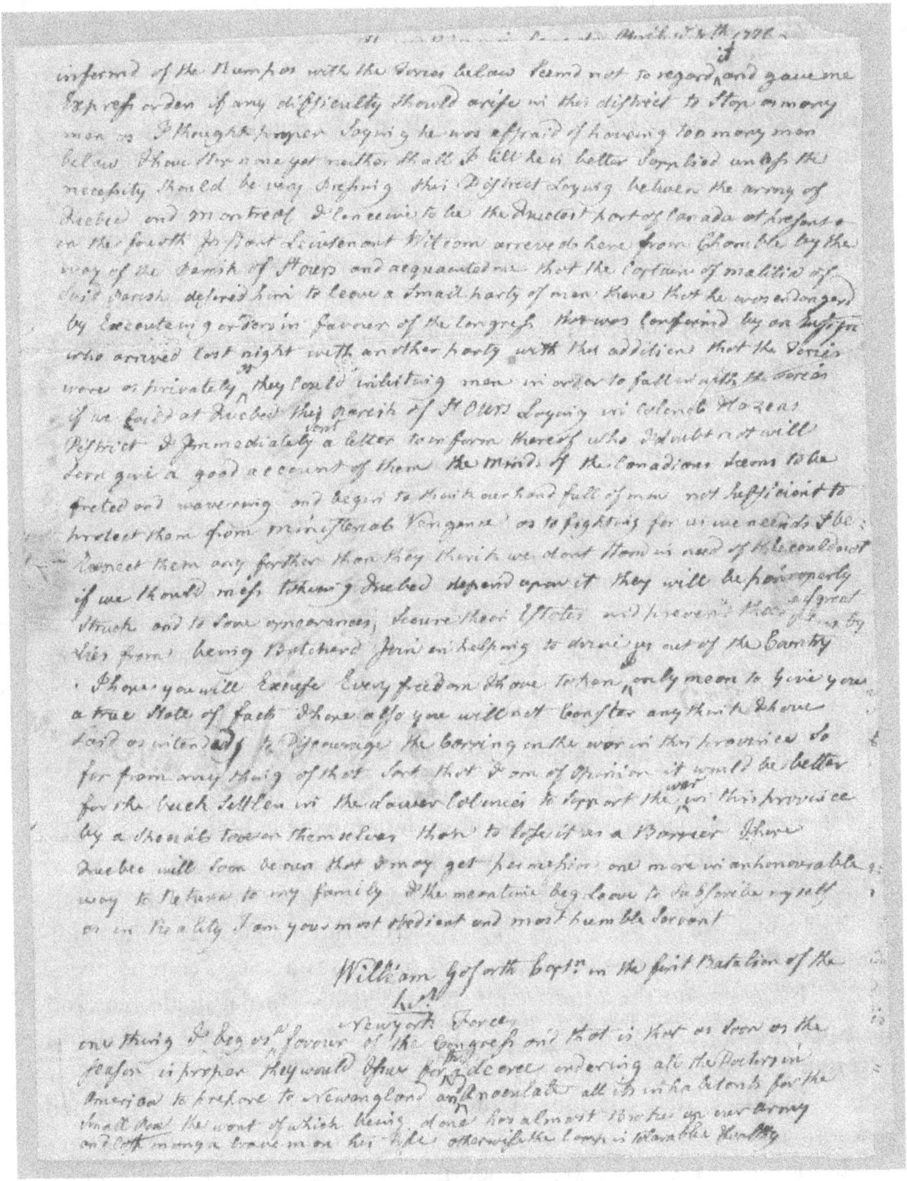

FIGURE 9. William Goforth Letter to John Jay, 8 April 1776. It is clear that the captain took extra care in writing to Jay and Franklin, as their letters are his most legible. John Jay Papers, Rare Book & Manuscript Library, Columbia University in the City of New York.

or not I was pleased to be given this duty, having never been more than a simple soldier.

As we were required to patrol hourly, when I returned around eleven o'clock, another detachment left to do a tour of the city. Noticing that they were late returning and that it was time to change the guard, Mr. Leproust,[27] officer of the watch, & I went to see where they were. Passing by Macbean's[28] [Inn] we heard talking and we listened in at the shutters by opening them a crack, and we saw that our lads were "patrolling" full cups, with no fear of the enemy whatsoever; they returned a minute after us, each, by their own admission, with a bottle of wine in their belly: what a night.

William Goforth Letters—September and 1 October

Editor's Notes on William Goforth's Correspondence

With erratic spelling, grammar, and punctuation, William Goforth's letters seem to present a stark contrast to Jean-Baptiste Badeaux's well-ordered journal. However, the reader should keep in mind several considerations before making assumptions about Goforth. First, that irregular spelling was common through the late eighteenth century; and that the many irregular spellings and punctuation issues with Badeaux's journal have been lost in the translation process, since as pointed out in the Translator's Notes, only proper names were kept in their misspelled form in this work. Captain Goforth was a reasonably well-educated artisan—but comparing his writing to that of a career government administrator is also unfair. Finally, many of Goforth's early letters were written in austere field conditions or poorly equipped quarters, and paper was a scarce commodity—

Badeaux, on the other hand, produced his journal in the comfort of his notary's office or home, and the available manuscript was almost certainly transcribed from an earlier draft, as well.

In these transcriptions, Goforth's spelling has been maintained wherever it is likely that a general reader could discern the author's intended word choice; but modern punctuation has been inserted throughout. The captain's occasional use of "ye" has been rendered

---

27. (September 27) Louis-Joseph Leproust, son of Antoine-Claude Leproust; *Les Ursulines de Trois Rivières Depuis Leur Établissement Jusqu'à nos Jours.* (Trois Rivières, QC: Pierre Ayotte, 1892) 1: 500 note; UMPRDH indiv. #142967.

28. Joseph Jean McBean, a Scots-Canadian, married to a French Canadian wife; UMPRDH indiv. #218071; *Ursulines de Trois Rivières,* 1: 503.

as "the" throughout the correspondence. Editorial insertions are indicated in brackets. Transcription use of [?] and [Ms. illegible] follow the description in the Translator's Notes. The notation [*sic*] has been limited to situations where a word or content would otherwise be unclear, or where words were unintentionally repeated in the manuscript.

Transcription assistance was provided by Kira Anderson.

Prelude: *NEW-YORK JOURNAL*, 7 September 1775

"Since our last Capt. Goforth and his Company, and Capt. John Lamb's Company of Artillery embarked for Albany, to join our Army under General Schuyler, at Ticonderoga."[29]

FIGURE 10. Alexander McDougall, by Max Rosenthal. Print Collection, Miriam and Ira D. Wallach Division of Art, Prints and Photographs, The New York Public Library, Astor, Lenox, and Tilden Foundations.

---

29. Goforth is next observed on September 18, at the Northern Army's Canadian base camp on Ile-aux-Noix. "Mate of a Vessel on Lake Champlain to the New-York Convention," September 18, 1775, *AA5*, 2: 386.

Letter: William Goforth to Alexander McDougall[30]

from the Camp before St. Johns, October 1 [1775][31]

Dear Sir,

on the 25th Sept' we arrived at the Camp on which a new Scene opened. the Enemies have their Bombs but have done very little Damage by them, one more only being Killd by them. he belongd to the artillery. one more lost by their Grape Shot.[32] we have but one Small mortar[33] that we Can use. On the[34] 28th I had the honour with one hundred men to [take] my turn to Command the Bomb Battery[35] in the Evening. Capt" Lamb[36] came down to give them some shells which were duly noticed by the Tories. their shells were well directed but overreached us only one falling within our works. Different Bodies are sent in the Country under Command of Colonel Biddle,[37] Collonel allen and Major

---

30. Colonel Alexander McDougall, commander of the First New York Regiment, was a prominent figure in the New York Sons of Liberty, and had risen to be a preeminent patriot political leader by 1775. See Roger Champagne, *Alexander McDougall and the American Revolution in New York* (Schenectady: Union College Press, 1975).

31. From the Alexander McDougall Papers (hereafter cited as AMP), 1756–1795, NYHS.

32. Grapeshot was a clustered round consisting of many smaller balls, having an effect on "soft" targets much like a giant shotgun.

33. Mortars are artillery pieces designed to loft rounds on a high, indirect, arcing trajectory; useful for firing over walls.

34. Goforth uses the fairly common early Modern English "ye," (as used in the King James Bible) in which the "y" actually represented a character known as thorn, pronounced "th"; "ye" has been transcribed as "the" throughout Goforth's correspondence.

35. The first Continental bomb battery (heavy artillery) was established about four hundred yards south of Fort Saint John's; "Narrative of the Siege of St Johns Canada," September 17, 1775, in Doughty, "Papers Relating to the Surrender," 20.

36. Captain John Lamb, commander of New York's Artillery Company and one of New York City's early Sons of Liberty radicals; see Isaac Leake, *Memoir of the Life and times of General John Lamb* (Albany: Joel Munsell, 1850).

37. Veteran frontier warrior Colonel Timothy Bedel led three companies of New Hampshire Rangers, and another New Hampshire volunteer company, to join the Canadian campaign in September 1775, and commanded a detachment posted north of Fort St. John's, isolating the fort in collaboration with local partisans; Edgar Aldrich, "The Affair of the Cedars and the Service of Colonel Timothy Bedel in the War of the Revolution," *The Proceedings of the New Hampshire Historical Society, Volume 3, June, 1895 to June, 1899* (Concord: New Hampshire Historical Society, 1902): 194–205.

Brown.[38] Collonel allen is taken By being too Ventersom and attempting to take Montreal when supported by only about 30 other people and a few Canadians.[39] I heard major Brown say (who came last night into Camp) that the accounts from the Country were as favourable as could be Expected. Yesterday our Chaplain[40] arrived and to day we should have had Divine Service had it not Raind. Your son[41] is well and is now on Command on the Bomb Battery where Captn Quaqenbos[42] Commands to day with an other Lieutenant and one hundred men. I am with the Greatest Respect your most oblidged and most Humble Servant—William Goforth

[P.S.]

Octob 5th

When your Son was on G[u]ard at the Bomb Battery they had very bad Wet Weather when he Returned he was taken with a high fever and with bloody flux, by my advice and his Brother[']s Impetuosity he went on board the Vessel which your son John[43] has the Command of and Just now 5th octobr Came ashore much better—

---

38. General Montgomery used Ethan Allen and John Brown as liaisons with the local Richelieu Valley Canadians and nearby Indian villages. See notes to Badeaux's September 26 entry. Major John Brown had played an important role in establishing Canadian relations before the invasion, making an important, semi-covert trip to Montreal on behalf of Massachusetts in the spring of 1775. During that summer, he made several covert scouting trips into Canada to gather intelligence and coordinate with Richelieu Valley partisans. At this time, Brown was second in command in James Easton's western Massachusetts regiment.

39. See Badeaux's September 26 entry and notes regarding Allen's defeat at the Battle of Longue Pointe.

40. Israel Evans, the First New York Regiment's chaplain; "SoFR," also in *AA4*, 2: 1334.

41. Colonel Alexander McDougall had two sons participating in this campaign as officers in his regiment. Goforth is referring to his own second lieutenant, the younger Ranald Stephen McDougall. First Lieutenant John McDougall served in Captain Frederick Weisenfels's First Company.

42. Captain John Quackenbos, commander of the Eighth Company, First New York Regiment; "SoFR."

43. Lieutenant John McDougall was given command of one of the ten bateaux stationed upriver from Fort St John's, as part of the naval blockading force. The bateaux were double-ended, flat-bottomed utility boats, about forty feet long, capable of carrying forty men. The rest of the Continental flotilla consisted of the sloop *Enterprise* (46 ft., 6x6

Yesterday being the 4th St John [*sic*] LaCorn[44] sent in a Belt of Wampum asking a Conference with General Montgomery to be held at Chamblee on Saturday next. Last night Lieutenant Collonel Wynkoop[45] arrived with a Reinforcement of about 200 fresh men which Seem'd to give fresh Vigor to our Fateagued troops. with them Came up what they Call the old Sow, which in plain English is a 13 Inch Mortar,[46] about which we are very Busy today in order to get it fix'd, and by tomorrow Morning will begin to play from our Bomb Battery which Lays within about 250 or 300 Yards of the Enemies Fort. We are now Cut[t]ing a New Road in order to Raise more Cannon on, or against, the Northern Part of the Fort. a New Battery is opening on the East Side of the River. we shall I hope in a Small time have three Batteries besides our Bomb Battery playing on them. Our Camp Lays within Gun shot of the Enemie. they throw their Bombs when they please 50 Rod beyond us. the Ground on which we are is very Wet. many of our people Sick, but Considering our Situation, I am Surprized we are not more so. We have nothing more than a Lieutenant Colonel among us that is of the

---

pounder guns), the schooner *Liberty* (41 ft., 4x4 pounder guns), and simple gondolas (also called row galleys) *Schuyler* and *Hancock* (60 ft., 1x12 pounder each); James L. Nelson, *Benedict Arnold's Navy* (Camden, ME: International Marine, 2006), 91; Douglas Cubbison, *The American Northern Theater Army in 1776: The Ruin and Reconstruction of the Continental Force* (Jefferson, NC: MacFarland, 2010), 84–85, 181–82.

44. Goforth is referring to Luc de La Corne, commonly called La Corne Saint Luc; Pierre Tousignant and Madeleine Dionne-Tousignant, "La Corne, Luc de, Chaptes de La Corne, La Corne Saint-Luc," in *DCB* 4, http://www.biographi.ca/en/bio/la_corne_luc_de_4E.html (accessed October 10, 2014). La Corne and several prominent Montréal merchants offered to initiate separate peace talks with General Montgomery, through the Caughnawaga Indians, but got cold feet after Allen's defeat at Longue-Pointe and La Corne terminated the treasonous communication by handing Montgomery's response to Governor Carleton, who destroyed the letter without opening it.

45. Lieutenant Colonel Cornelius Wynkoop, Third New York Regiment; "SoFR."

46. The "Old Sow" was one of the heaviest artillery pieces captured at Ticonderoga and Crown Point; Benedict Arnold to Massachusetts Committee of Safety, May 19, 1775; *AA4*, 2: 645; "Narrative of the siege of St Johns Canada," September 17, 1775, in Doughty, "Papers Relating to the Surrender," 19. Montgomery "principally depended" upon his mortars, of which the Old Sow was the largest, "for distressing the garrison" in Fort St John's; Richard Montgomery to Philip Schuyler, 28 September 1775, *AA4*, 3: 954.

York Force.⁴⁷ I am very Sorry you are not on the Ground. I hope you will excuse me when I tell you I have heard it Complained of that the York head Collonels are not on the Spot.

47. Because of his tremendous political influence, Colonel McDougall was encouraged to stay in New York to help the patriot cause there, rather than joining his regiment in Canada. Lieutenant Colonel Rudolphus Ritzema was the senior regimental officer in the field. James Duane to Alexander McDougall, November 15, 1775, in Paul H. Smith, ed., *Letters of Delegates to Congress* (hereafter cited as *LoD*), *1774–1789* (Washington, DC: Library of Congress, 1976), 2: 350–51; see also Roger Champagne, "New York's Radicals and the Coming of Independence," *The Journal of American History* 51, no. 1 (June 1964): 33–34. Regarding the commanders of the other New York regiments, while some companies from those units joined the Canadian campaign, the Second New York Regiment commander, Colonel Goose Van Schaick, was detained in Albany, under circumstances similar to McDougall's in New York City; while the Fourth New York's Colonel James Holmes got no farther north than Ticonderoga. Only Colonel James Clinton, Third New York Regiment, actually entered Quebec Province, reaching Montreal by November 23; James Clinton et al. to Richard Montgomery, November 23, 1775, *AA4*, 3: 1695, and Goforth's January 5 letter to Alexander McDougall, below.

October 1775

October 2nd. At the beginning of this month several of us went to Vicar General St. Ongé's,[1] to beg him to grant us some public prayers, which he did most willingly. He even ordered the Relics of St. Clement and St. Modeste,[2] housed in our church, to be brought down, since we had on many occasions received obvious proofs of the credibility these great saints have with the Lord. So they were brought down and there was a procession in which they were carried by the vicar general & the Reverend Father Isidor,[3] parish priest of this city. We left the parish [church] singing the hymn, *Sanctorum meritis*.[4] We went to the Recollet Fathers', then to the Ursuline Ladies',[5] where, after the nuns had sung

---

1. Vicar General Pierre Garreau *dit* St-Ongé of Three Rivers. Along with Montréal's Vicar General Etienne Montgolfier, St. Ongé was one of Bishop Jean-Olivier Briand's two regional subordinates in the Catholic Church hierarchy. It was common for French Canadians to go by family nicknames, indicated by the French *dit* (called). See Raymond Douville, "Garreau, Saint-Onge, Pierre," in *DC* 4, http://www.biographi.ca/en/bio/garreau_pierre_4E.html (accessed November 11, 2013).
2. The relic bones of ancient martyrs St. Clement and St. Modeste were brought to Quebec in 1689. In 1712, they were taken to Three Rivers, and when the "new" Recollet Church was built in 1754, they were placed in reliquaries on its main altar; John R. Porter and Léopold Désy, "L'ancienne chapelle des Récollets de Trois-Rivières," *Le Bulletin et le Bulletin annuel du Musée des beaux-arts du Canada* 18 (1971): 5.
3. Popular Recollet Father Superior Charles-Antoine Isidore Lemire *dit* Marsolet. The Recollets served as parish priests for Three Rivers from 1693 to 1776. Cyprien Tanguay, *Répertoire Général du Clergé Canadien* (Montreal: Eusèbe Senecal et fils, 1893), 119; Porter, "L'ancienne chapelle," 5.
4. "The Merits of the Saints," an ancient hymn, used in the liturgy for first vespers and matins in the "Common of Many Martyrs"; John Julian, ed., *A Dictionary of Hymnology, Setting Forth the Origin and History of Christian Hymns of All Ages and Nations* (New York: Charles Scribner's Sons, 1892), 998.
5. The Recollet and Ursuline convents were east of town center on the main Rue Notre Dame (see Map 1).

a few motets,[6] the vicar-general began singing the *Te Deum*,[7] which we sang while returning to the parish [church]. When we arrived, we received the blessing of the most Holy Sacrament and we were told that there would be a novena,[8] for which this procession was to be the overture. During the entire novena, everyone was very diligent at both Mass and prayers. There were some very good Christians to be found among them, but how many others were there? I myself heard several people leaving the church, saying that they went but only to pray to God that the "Bostonians" would win. This is the point to which irreligion has been pushed, and so, should we be surprised if God has weighed his heavy hand on this miserable province? After the end of the novena, we went to thank the vicar general, who received us most favorably.

FIGURE 11. Vicar General Pierre Garreau *dit* Saint-Ongé of Three Rivers. Bibliothèque et Archives nationales du Québec, E6 Fonds ministère de la Culture et des Communications, S8, SS1.

---

6. A motet is a short piece of music set to Latin words; *The Catholic Encyclopedia* (New York: Encyclopedia Press, 1911) 10: 600.

7. (October 2) *Te Deum*—A hymn in rhythmical prose, beginning *Te deum laudamus*, commonly used for praise or thanksgiving; *Catholic Encyclopedia*, 14: 468.

8. (October 2) novena—Nine days of devotion to obtain special graces; *Catholic Encyclopedia*, 11: 141.

The 8th. The General sent orders to all the parishes, ordering the mobilization of fifteen men of every hundred.[9] Nearly all refused, especially in the parish of Nicolet. The captain came to report to Colonel de Tonnancour.[10] He called for me and I went. He asked if I wanted to go with his son the Chevalier, to get the Nicolet habitants to understand the import of the General's order. I said that I would gladly go. A canoe was quickly prepared for us and we left. Since the wind was extremely strong from the southwest, we disembarked a little above Sainte Thérèze,[11] and we went on to Nicolet on foot, not without a great deal of trouble, as we had to cross very deep swamps. We crossed on trees, sometimes with one foot on the tree, sometimes in the water. None of that mattered, as long as we were able to accomplish our mission. Once we had arrived in Nicolet, we went straight to the parsonage, believing we would find the parish priest there, but he was in St. François[12] and didn't return until around 4 o'clock. Nonetheless, the house girl made us dinner and we ate while the sergeants assembled the inhabitants. Many told them to go to the devil; others showed no desire to come, so we had very few attendees at our sermon. Nonetheless, we began our harangue by telling them that we had no intention of giving them orders; that we had no power to do so; that it was only out of friendship for them that we had come to make them see the error in disobeying the order of such a good master, & that their religion commanded them to be loyal to the King; that they had taken the oath and that it was their duty to fulfill it; that the general's order declared anyone refusing said order to be rebels, and that they would be punished as such, and

---

9. Militia was typically mobilized by calling a quota of men per parish or company (for those parishes with more than one company). Individuals would then be chosen at the parish level to fill the quota. Ernest Chambers, *The Canadian Militia: A History of the Origin and Development of the Force* (Montreal: L. M. Fresco, 1907), 10, 14.

10. Governor Carleton appointed Three Rivers' leading seigneur-citizen Louis Joseph Godefroy de Tonnancour as the senior militia officer in the Three Rivers District, one of three militia colonels in the entire province. The Chevalier was Tonnancour's son Charles Antoine. See note to September 6 entry.

11. This unidentified point is presumably a point on the sparsely populated, low-lying south bank of the St. Lawrence, northeast of the Nicolet River, or on the lower stretches of that river. This would perhaps be a two or three mile overland journey to the Nicolet parish church.

12. (October 8) St-François-du-Lac was the next parish southwest of Nicolet, approximately fifteen miles away. It was well known for its nearby Jesuit mission village of settled Catholic Abenaki Indians, also known as Odanak. There were several strong supporters of the rebel cause in this village.

that the punishment for rebellion was the gallows: that we would be sad to see any of them be subjected to this punishment; that this was the only thing we were determined to tell them. Finally, after many debates back and forth, there were ten who decided to come with us. We took advantage of their good will and asked for priest Monsignor Brassard's[13] large canoe, which he was happy to lend us, but not before we had supped. We sat down to the table and ate rather quickly, afraid that our people would change their minds. After supper, we thanked the priest and when we were at the river's edge ready to leave, our young people threw themselves at the feet of their priest and asked his blessing, which he gave them. We pushed off with many cries of joy, although there was someone who was crying. At first, when we were on the great river we recited the litanies of the Holy Virgin, and after the prayer *Gratiam tuam*,[14] our warriors sang all the way to the city, where we arrived at 10 o'clock in the evening. The joyous cries of our young men brought everyone out of their houses and down to the riverbank. After our arrival, I went with Chevalier De Tonnancour to report on our management of things; and then I went to bed.

The 10th. The Three Rivers District detachment of sixty-seven men, commanded by Mr. de Lanaudière Jr. and Mr. Godefroi de Tonnancour Jr.,[15] left from this city to go to Montreal.

This same day, a ship passed through on its way from Montreal, carrying the "Bostonians" & Canadian prisoners taken in the action of the 26th of last month near the city of Montreal.[16]

---

13. Louis Marie Brassard, had been Nicolet's parish priest for almost a quarter-century. He also served two small neighboring parishes. See Claude Lessard, "Brassard, Louis-Marie," in *DCB* 4, http://www.biographi.ca/en/bio/brassard_louis_marie_4E.html (accessed November 11, 2013); Tanguay, *Clergé canadien*, 125.

14. (October 8) *Angelus* refers to a short Catholic devotion "repeated three times each day, morning, noon, and evening, at the sound of the [church] bell," It concludes with a prayer beginning *Gratiam tuam quæsumus, Domine, mentibus nostris infunde* (Pour forth, we beseech thee, O Lord, Thy grace into our hearts); *Catholic Encyclopedia*, 1: 486.

15. Charles-Louis Tarieu de Lanaudière, was a French and Indian War veteran, owned several seigneuries, and had been Governor Carleton's aide-de-camp since 1770. See Yves Beauregard, "Tarieu de Lanaudiere, Charles-Louis," in *DCB* 5, http://www.biographi.ca/en/bio/tarieu_de_lanaudiere_charles_louis_5E.html (accessed November 11, 2013). "Mr. Godefroi de Tonnancour, Jr." referred to Pierre André Godefroy de Tonnancour.

16. H.M.S. *Gaspé* carried these prisoners to Quebec City. Ethan Allen and thirty-four other Battle of Longue-Pointe prisoners were promptly shipped to England. Ethan Allen, *A Narrative of Col. Ethan Allen's Captivity* (Burlington, VT: Chauncey Goodrich, 1846).

The 12th. This morning at 6 o'clock, Mr. Leproust, a militia officer, and Joseph Bolvin,[17] a militiaman, arrived from the detachment that had left the day before yesterday, informing us that the Chicot Parish[18] habitants, under the orders of a certain Merlet,[19] captain of that parish, had stopped them in the woods between Berthier and Chicot,[20] where they had been awaiting them for three days. After stopping them, they disarmed Mr. Lanaudière and Mr. Godefroy de Tonnancour and took them prisoner, then took them to the home of Buron,[21] captain of St Cuthbert, where the parish priest, Mr. Pouget,[22] happened to be. He appealed so strongly to Captain Merlet that he finally obtained their release. What must certainly have been mortifying for our gentlemen is that after they were made prisoner, all the women they passed on the road mockingly called out to their husbands: "You certainly had a good hunt today." Mr. Leproust said that while having a glass of wine at Buron's, Captain Merlet asked him, "Who are you?" He replied, "I am an officer of the King." "Well then," responded Merlet, "get the hell out of here," and without giving him the time to have a second glass of wine, he took him by the arm and put him out the door. He sorely missed that glass of wine, since he was very thirsty, but he was

---

17. See notes on September 27 entry for Leproust. Joseph Bolvin was Badeaux's brother-in-law; UMPRDH indiv. #125229 (Joseph), #167878 (Marie Marguerite Badeaux) and #80497.

18. This parish sat on the Chicot River, a few miles off the St. Lawrence. It had actually been renamed St-Cuthbert Parish in 1766, by its new Scots-Canadian seigneur, half-pay Captain James Cuthbert. "Berthier," in Joseph Bouchette, *A Topographical Dictionary of the Province of Lower Canada* (London: Longman, Rees, Orme, Brown, Green, and Longman, 1832), n.p.

19. French-born Ardouin (also spelled Hardoin) Merlet Delaboulais; UMPRDH indiv. #156152.

20. The region around Berthier-en-Haut (modern Berthierville) had also been the site of one of the most notable militia mobilization resistance episodes in the summer of 1775. Armed habitants peacefully, but sternly, resisted seigneur James Cuthbert's attempt to call them to arms, and took oaths to resist any future mobilization attempts. "A Narrative of the tumultuous conduct of the freeholders of divers[e] seigniories in the province of Quebeck in the summer of the year 1775," in Maseres, *Additional Papers*, 75–76.

21. Jean Baptiste Buron was a merchant by trade, UMPRDH indiv. #78592.

22. Priest Jean Baptiste Pouget had just been given responsibility for restive St-Cuthbert Parish two years earlier, replacing a financially troubled priest who had also enraged seigneur James Cuthbert by refusing to say customary prayers for the king. See Pierre Dufour, "Pouget, Jean-Baptiste-Noël," in *DCB* 5, http://www.biographi.ca/en/bio/pouget_jean_baptiste_noel_5E.html (accessed November 11, 2013).

most satisfied to be away and to be out of Mr. Merlet's hands. I don't know if it is fear or fatigue that had so changed our arriving men, but I can say that they were very pale when I met them at the water's edge.

The 13th. Mr. Godefroy de Tonnancour arrived in this city from Chicot. This same day the Quebec courier arrived, announcing the arrival of a 64-gun frigate with many hands.[23] At the same time, Mr. Dainse,[24] an officer in the Royal Emigrants[25] arrived, informing us that Colonel Maclean[26] is in Champlain[27] with his troops. On the 14th, Colonel Maclean arrived in this city with his force to establish a new command, and I accompanied Mr. Godefroy de Tonnancour in carrying the orders to the captain of Cap La Magdeleine,[28] so they might be passed

---

23. There is no historical record indicating a Royal Navy ship arrived in Quebec City at this time. The next British warships did not reach the capital until two vessels (sloop *Hunter* and frigate *Lizard*) came on November 4. "Quebec News," *Quebec Gazette*, 9 November 1775.

24. Ensign George Daine, formerly of the Eighth Regiment; "Officers of the 1st Battalion of the Royal Highland Emigrants (H.M. 84th Regiment), 1775–1778," in *Blockade of Quebec in 1775–1776 by the American Revolutionists (Les Bastonnais)*, ed. Frederick Wurtele (Quebec: Literary and Historical Society of Quebec, 1905), 267.

25. In early 1775, Colonel Allan Maclean was authorized to recruit a new provincial regiment, the "Royal Highland Emigrants," from the numerous Scots Highlander settlers in North America. The first battalion was recruited from northern colonies, including Quebec, New York, and the Maritime Provinces, the second from the Carolinas. In return for service "during the present Troubles in America only," recruits were promised two hundred acres of land in the North American province of their choice. Although the regiment was not fully manned, it proved critical in Canada's defense in 1775–76. "Quebec News" and recruiting announcement, *Quebec Gazette*, 20 and 27 July, and 10 August 1775; Mary Beacock Fryer, *Allan Maclean, Jacobite General: The Life of an Eighteenth Century Career Soldier* (Toronto: Dundurn Press, 1987), 121–29.

26. (October 13) The resolutely loyal Maclean was a fifty-year-old veteran of the French and Indian War, who had personally presented his plan for the new regiment in London. He returned to North America and met with General Thomas Gage in Boston. After covertly recruiting in New York, he headed north in midsummer to reach safer Canadian territory. See G. F. G. Stanley, "Maclean, Allan," in *DCB* 4, http://www.biographi.ca/en/bio/maclean_allan_4E.html (accessed November 11, 2013).

27. North shore Champlain Parish sat about a dozen miles downstream (northeast) of Three Rivers. While a few residents supported either side, most parishioners remained indifferent to both loyalist and rebel efforts during the invasion; Gabriel, *Quebec during the American Invasion*, 40–41.

28. Cap-de-la-Madeleine Parish sat across the St. Maurice River from Three Rivers, only two miles to the northeast (see Map 3). The parish remained passively neutral in 1775–76; Gabriel, *Quebec during the American Invasion*, 42–43.

on as far as Ste. Anne.[29] Since many among those receiving the orders in that village refused to mobilize, Colonel Maclean issued a general order and Sergeant Major Pratte[30] made it so broad that he only omitted those persons exempted by reason of their public duties; such that he came at 8 o'clock in the evening to order me to appear the next day on the parade grounds with my arms. I responded that I would not be of great help to them, as the only weapon I had was a pen-knife with a broken point. Nevertheless, he ordered me to be there, but since Colonel Maclean had me depart for Quebec in the night, I was exempt from that appearance, which I would not have made even had I stayed.

Col. Maclean Wants to Force Nicolet to Take Arms

The 15th. Colonel Maclean's party, and the Three Rivers men under Mr. Godefroy de Tonnancour's command, left this city for Sorel,[31] and

---

29. Ste-Anne-de-la-Pérade Parish (see Map 3) and Figure 13. Its militia captain, Louis Gouin, zealously supported mobilization orders, despite opposition by many habitants. Gouin led twenty-two militiamen to support Governor Carleton in Montreal. Maclean apparently levied a fine against those who did not heed the call to arms; Gabriel, *Quebec during the American Invasion*, 34–36. Around this time, some of the more rebellious parishioners allegedly "threatened to fire on the people of the parish next to them if they dared to march" in support of the loyalists; Hugh Finlay to Anthony Todd, November 1, 1775, in K.G. Davies, ed. *Documents of the American Revolution, 1770–1783* (Dublin: Irish University, 1975), 11: 171.

30. Charles Dupras Pratte, who may have been the senior Three Rivers militia sergeant Pratte (b.1712 or 1740; see below), helped recruit the Three Rivers company formed for British Pontiac's War service in 1764; Trudel, *Régime militaire*, 190; UMPRDH indiv. #78096 (born 1712), or son (born 1740) with same name, indiv. #105292. Notably, after the death of his first wife, Jean-Baptiste Badeaux would marry the elder Pratte's daughter Marie-Marguerite in November 1790 (UMPRDH indiv. #224764).

31. Sorel Parish sat at a strategic point on the southeast bank of the Richelieu River, where it flowed into the St Lawrence. This is about fifty miles downstream (northeast) from Montreal and forty miles upstream (southeast) of Three Rivers (See Map 2). Colonel Maclean had orders to lead his Emigrants to Sorel, gather and arm militiamen, and prepare to march up the Richelieu River. Governor Carleton planned to cross the St. Lawrence from Montreal with a militia-heavy force, advance toward Fort St John's, unite with Maclean's force and relieve the fort's beleaguered garrison. Lorimier, *At War*, 38.

the colonel, along with Chevalier De Tonnancour and some Emigrants, went to Nicolet to bring to heel the inhabitants of that parish who refused to take arms. Upon arrival, he was informed that a certain Rouillard[32] strongly opposed any mobilization of the habitants. He went [there] with Mr. de Lanaudière, Chevalier de Tonnancour and a few soldiers. When he was at the house, he found no one there but the wife (the men having carefully hidden themselves). He asked where her husband and son were. She said that she had no idea. "Well then," said the colonel, "if you do not tell me where your husband and son are, I will put fire to your house." She answered him, "Well, go ahead; for an old [one] you will give me a new." So the colonel ordered the fire lit. When she saw the fire at the gable of her house, she came out and ran toward the woods screaming, "St. Eustache,[33] save me from the fire. St. Eustache, save me from the fire. This band of brigands wants to burn me up." The colonel, seeing that he would gain nothing from burning the house, ordered it [the fire] to be put out, which was quickly done. He returned to the parsonage, where he was informed that the habitants (upon hearing that they [their properties] were to be burnt) had all assembled on an island[34] with their weapons. He immediately left to go there with Mister de Lanaudière and the Chevalier de Tonnancour with a few Emigrant soldiers. When they arrived across from the island where the habitants were, they found nothing with which to cross except for a little wood canoe, in which Colonel Mclean embarked with Mr. de Lanaudière. The Chevalier de Tonnancour forded across and, following his example, the rest of the

---

32. Fifty-year-old Joseph Rouillard Larivière; UMPRDH indiv. #141704; J. E. Bellemere, *Histoire de Nicolet, 1669–1924* (Quebec: Athabaska, 1924), 152 note.

33. Saint Eustace, considered "one of the Holy Helpers . . . invoked in difficult situations," who was martyred by burning in the second century—coincidentally also a patron saint of hunting; "Eustachius and Companions," in *Catholic Encyclopedia*, 5: 627.

34. There were a few relatively small Nicolet River islands in the heart of this parish, each less than one hundred yards in length; Joseph F. W. Desbarres and Samuel Holland, *River of St. Lawrence, from Chaudière to Lake St. Francis, &c. surveyed in pursuance of instructions and orders from the Right Honourable Lords of Trade to Samuel Holland Esqr. &c*, 1781, Bibliothèque et Archives Nationales de Québec (hereafter BAnQ), http://services.banq.qc.ca/sdx/cep/document.xsp?id=0002663083 (accessed November 4, 2012).

party did the same. When the habitants saw that the colonel and his party were crossing, they gave proof of their bravery, since, without giving our men time to cross, they began fleeing into the woods as if the devil had promised them five *sols*:[35] there is every reason to presume that they are still running, since none of them have been seen in this city since this ever so glorious action in Nicolet parish. As it was late, the colonel judged it not worth pursuing them; he returned to the parsonage, from there he continued on his way to Sorel with the rest of his party.

18th. Today, two boats filled with muskets and ammunition for Sorel arrived from Quebec. This same day, Sir Chabot[36] also passed through, in command of an armed ship, on his way to Sorel.

20th. We have learned that the Chamblis [*sic*] parishes offered their services to Colonel Maclean: God grant this to be true.

Desertion of Colonel Maclean's Troops and Betrayal of the Chambly Inhabitants

24th. The reports of this day are very different from those of the 20th since it is said that several Canadians from the Chambly parishes were in Colonel Maclean's camp on the pretext of lending him a hand, but that after being armed by Colonel Maclean, they deserted to the "Bostonian" camp. What is sadder yet is that we are assured that even men from Colonel Maclean's party desert daily. If this is so, we have every reason to fear for our poor province.

---

35. The source of this expression is unknown; a *sol* was a small coin, one twentieth of a Canadian *livre*.

36. (October 18) Other than this appearance in Badeaux's account, and a very similar reference in Berthelot's journal, this Captain Chabot's background is unclear; Michel Amable Berthelot, "Extraits du Mémoire du M. A. Berthelot," in Verreau, *Invasion du Canada* 230; "Le Capitaine Chabot," *Bulletin des Recherches Historiques* 7, no. 1 (1901): 280-281. The French *sieur* has been translated as Sir.

Carleton's Defeat at Longeuil

28th.[37] We learn that General Carleton, Colonel Prescot[38] and the Montrealers, wishing to descend upon Longueil,[39] were repulsed by the "Bostonians":[40] and that Mr. Jean Bte. Despins[41] and a certain LaCoste,[42] a wigmaker from Montreal, were made prisoners.

29th. Today, men from Colonel Maclean's party arrived saying that the colonel, desiring to pass through St Denis[43] to go to St. John's, had found all the bridges dismantled, obliging him to withdraw to Sorel.

---

37. This entry and the next must have been erroneously dated after the fact, as the battle and retreat mentioned here occurred on and after October 30.

38. (October 28) Colonel Richard Prescott was a veteran of the Seven Years' War, and had been assigned to Canadian duty in 1773. Posted temporarily in Boston with General Thomas Gage, Prescott was ordered back to Quebec in June 1775, to serve as Carleton's principal military deputy, with the local rank of brigadier general. He established his headquarters in Montreal; note to "Journal of Col. Guy Johnson from May to November, 1775," in *Documents Relative to the Colonial History of the State of New York* . . . , ed. E. B. O'Callaghan (Albany: Weed, Parsons, 1857) 8: 659; Thomas Gage to Dartmouth, June 12, 1775, in *Concerning Canadian Archives for the Year 1904* (Ottawa: S. K. Dawson, 1905), 358; "Quebec News," *Quebec Gazette*, 13 and 20 July 1775; James Grant Wilson and John Fiske, eds., *Appleton's Cyclopaedia of American Biography*, vol. 5 (New York: D. Appleton, 1900), 109.

39. Longueuil village sat across the St. Lawrence from Montreal, the northernmost of two main ferry points from the south bank to the Island of Montreal (see Map 2). The Continentals had established a post there in late September, commanded by the Green Mountain Boys Regiment's Lieutenant Colonel Seth Warner.

40. Governor Carleton led 600 militiamen, 130 British regulars, and 80 Indians in this mission to cross the St. Lawrence and relieve Fort St. John's. For several hours, Seth Warner maneuvered his 350 Continentals up and down the river banks to drive off every landing attempt, leading the governor to abort the mission, much to the dismay of many of his loyalist supporters; John Fassett Jr., "Diary of Lt John Fassett Jr . . . ," in *The Follet-Dewey Fassett-Safford Ancestry of Captain Martin Dewey Follett*, ed. Harry P. Ward (Columbus, OH: Champlin, 1896), 223–28; Lorimier, *At War*, 38–39.

41. Twenty-four-year-old Jean-Baptiste was the first son of prosperous Montreal merchant Jacques-Joseph Lemoine Despins. See José E. Igartua, "Lemoine Despins, Jacques-Joseph," in *DCB* 4, http://www.biographi.ca/en/bio/lemoine_despins_jacques_joseph_4E.html (accessed November 11, 2013); UMPRDH indiv. #15429.

42. Although La Coste's only stated, distinguishing identification was that he was a wigmaker (*perruquier*), parish records indicate that this may have been Jacques Courraud Lacoste, age twenty-four; UMPRDH indiv. #48128.

43. St-Denis Parish sat on the Richelieu River, seventeen miles from the St. Lawrence, and almost equidistant to Chambly (see Map 2). Its "village" served as an important granary and merchant center in the valley's wheat trade; Allan Greer, *Peasant, Lord, and*

William Goforth Letters—October

Letter: William Goforth to Alexander McDougall

[Note: this letter is barely legible due to ink bleeding and poor handwriting in field conditions]

Camp before St Johns, Sunday 22d Octob[r] 1775[44]

Dear Sir,

I hope you will not think me troublesom[e] by my frequent scribbling. two reasons opperate with me, the one is I think it my duty Considering my Relation to you in the Army to attempt to acquaint you of our success in my fortunes in the martial way, the other arises from the friendly Confidence with with [sic] which you placed your Son under my Care. In my last I acquainted you of an intention to Erect a Battery on the East Side of the Lake, which has had the happy Effect to [Ms. illegible] to their side[?] or [Ms. illegible] for 14 Guns and Disabled the whole of their Navigabels[45] [Ms. illegible] this Grand Object. The said Battery has in my opinion anoyd them in the Fort more in a few days than the other Battery had done[?] in three[?] weeks. Chamblee[46] has surrendered to the American Arms, by taking which we have made the Grand

---

Merchant: Rural Society in Three Quebec Parishes, 1740–1840 (Toronto: University of Toronto, 1985), 163, 195–96.

44. From AMP, NYHS.

45. The final impetus for the Canadian invasion came with late-August intelligence reports that two British ships were nearing completion at Fort St. John's, as these vessels would threaten rebel naval superiority on Lake Champlain, and pose an immediate danger to Fort Ticonderoga and other northern posts. The largest ship, the schooner, was sunk by fire from the east battery on October 16. Richard Montgomery to Philip Schuyler, August 29, 1775, Philip Schuyler Papers (hereafter cited as PSP), microfilm reel 12, New York Public Library (hereafter cited as NYPL); Doughty, "Papers Relating to the Surrender," 23.

46. Fort Chambly was a stonework fort, midway along the Richelieu River. At the time, it was the only post, other than Fort St. John's, still held by British forces in the area southeast of Montreal. Canadian partisan leader Jeremiah Duggan and Continental Major John Brown led a combined attack on the fort, resulting in a quick surrender and the capture of its large supply of military stores.

Acquisition of 6 Ton of powder, 300 hundred [*sic*] Shots, Some Mortars, Howitzers, &c. and thirty odd thousand Musket Cartridges ready filld. I have Enclosed you the Articles of Capitulation. In the 22nd Instant,[47] in the Morning I took the Command of the Bomb Battery. in the meantime some of the officers prisoners had prevaild on Major Brown to Ask a Parley with the Commanding officer of St. Johns in order to procure the Ease and Conveniency of transporting the Bagage, women & Children by water to our Camp.[48] Soon after the G[u]ards were relieved and I had placed my out Centries, the parley was beat Immediately. Sent Mr Platt[49] to Collonel Ritzema,[50] who waited on the General and was desired by him to come down with the drum Major and answer the parley, which he did. the truce took place. 8[?] officers,[51] 75 privates with the women, Children and Bagage Came in Boats under the Guns of St Johns, and are now Among us and treated with all the tenderness and and [*sic*] Politeness our Officers have in their Power to Confer And go down to Ty[conderoga] with them. Your Son John[52] mounted G[u]ard with me as Chief Lieut. the 20th Instant. the night was Long and dark and Raind Excessive hard. he seems Calculated for fateague and hardship, Braves Every thing and is Lookd Upon to be a brave Soldier. Your Son Stephen[53] Recover'd from his Illness I acquainted you of before, and

---

47. "Instant," referring to the current month.

48. Fort Chambly not only held its own garrison's family members, but those of some of Fort St. John's regular soldiers, as well. In order to get the prisoners, families, and baggage to the siege camp, Ticonderoga, and elsewhere in the colonies, they had to pass Fort St. John's, which still controlled the Richelieu River.

49. Second Lieutenant Richard Platt, of Captain Weisenfels's First Company, First New York Regiment, "SoFR."

50. Lieutenant Colonel Rudolphus Ritzema, the acting commander of the First New York Regiment, as Colonel McDougall remained in New York City. General Montgomery relied upon Ritzema, a European-trained veteran, as a key deputy in the Fort St. John's campaign. William Hall, "Colonel Rudolphus Ritzema," *Magazine of American History* 2 (March 1878): 162–67.

51. Although this number is difficult to discern in Goforth's manuscript letter, other accounts indicate there were eight officers taken prisoner; "List of Officers Taken at Chambly," *AA4* 3: 1133.

52. First Lieutenant John McDougall, First Company. He soon succumbed to "a bilious fever" and was buried near Laprairie, across the St. Lawrence from Montreal, on November 12; Rudolphus Ritzema to Alexander McDougall, November 19, 1775, AMP, NYHS; Fassett, "Diary," 234.

53. Ranald Stephen McDougall, Goforth's second lieutenant, and the youngest son of First New York Regiment commander Colonel Alexander McDougall, went by his middle name.

has since been quite hearty, but yesterday haveing the quarter G[u]ard and being very wet, he this morning finds himself very poorly. but don't be Uneasy, a little Rest and Dry weather I hope will Cure him. The Ground on which we Encamp is Excessive bad, over shoes in Mud. Our little Army haveing suffered Several Divisions, our men are much fateagued [and have] Grown Sickly in camping. Our Success seems to linger by the day, bear with me when I beg you to press on the forces. Late as it may be in the Season I think they will be wanted. I doubt not but we shall penetrate into the Heart of Canady, and I trust in God [will] Subject our Foes to the Noble Priviledge of being Freemen. Capt Mot[54] Gives his Compliments to you and will write if time permits. Last Sunday we had fine weather and Mr. Evens[55] opend Divine Service on the Banks of Lake Champlain [—] is Generally Approved of and Gains great Respect. With my best Respects to you, I conclude asking your Kindness to acquaint my Family I am well, and tell my dear wife I shall Embrace the first opportunity to Return which may be consistent with my obligations to that avowed Cause of Liberty. Tell Mr Vanwagenen[56] his son is well and much Respected.

William Goforth

[In margins of first page]

You will see a disagreement between the account of Stores taken at Chamblee as given in my letter and the copy I have sent you. I spoke by information, but as I have procured you a Coppy to which you must trust, I hope you will not Even Suspect that I meant to misinform, farewell—

---

54. Captain Gershom Mott, commander of the Seventh Company, First New York Regiment. He was a friend of Goforth and a well-known member of New York City's Sons of Liberty, dating back to the Stamp Act crisis; "SoFR;" Leake, *Memoir*, 112; Joseph Tiedeman, *Reluctant Revolutionaries: New York City and the Road to Independence, 1763–1776* (Ithaca: Cornell University Press, 2008), 94.

55. Chaplain Israel Evans, First New York; see note to Goforth's October 1 letter.

56. Mr. Huybert Van Wagenen was owner of a New York City hardware store; Gerrit Hubert Van Wagenen, *Genealogy of the Van Wagenen Family from 1650 to 1884, Part First* (Private printing, 1884), 22–24. His son was Second Lieutenant Gerrit Van Wagenen, Eighth Company (Quackenbos), First New York Regiment; "SoFR;" Van Wagenen, *Genealogy*, 28.

November 1775

Colonel Maclean Abandons Sorel

November 2nd. The Three Rivers men, the last remaining with Colonel Maclean, just arrived in this city. They say that the colonel, seeing his force's desertion, had been compelled to raise camp. He had all the cannons loaded onto the ships, and had all the gun carriages and other tools of war broken.

5th. We learn today of Fort St. John's surrender to the "Bostonians."[1]

Col. Maclean Stops in 3-Rs[2]

8th. Today Colonel Maclean came down river with the rest of his troop, in Etienne Papillon's ship.[3] Before disembarking from the ship, he sent a bateau to see if there were "Bostonians" in this city. Having been informed that there were none, he disembarked with some of his officers

---

1. Fort St John's surrendered on the morning of November 3. Two days earlier, General Richard Montgomery had sent prisoner of war Lacoste—captured at the Battle of Longueuil—to the fort under a flag of truce, demonstrating that Governor Carleton was not coming to relieve the siege. Provisions were running low, and with the little remaining shelter having been riddled by the ongoing bombardment, Major Preston agreed to terms on November 2. "Narrative of the Siege of St. John's Canada," in Doughty, "Papers Relating to the Surrender," 24–25.
2. "3-Rs" is common shorthand for Three Rivers/Trois Rivières.
3. Etienne Papillon of Pointe aux Trembles (Neuville), a St. Lawrence pilot-navigator.

and soldiers. He had all the King's provisions and the barracks stores[4] loaded on board, and even went so far as to take the merchants' powder.

The Trifluviens[5] Decide to Surrender to the Americans

9th. Seeing that there was no more hope, nor recourse for us, we assembled in the house of the Reverend Recollet Fathers, to deliberate on the most advantageous course of action for saving our goods. It was decided, that having no force of arms or munitions, and unable to hope for a surrender, we would delegate two men to go to Mr. Montgomery,[6] who would be bearers of a request conceived in the following terms:

Humble Address to his Excellency General Montgomery, &tc, &tc. "The Citizens of the City of 3-Rivers very humbly beg; That it please you to allow them to tell Your Excellency, that for the past few days, they have been awaiting the arrival in their city of a detachment of the troops honored to be under your orders and that, given the uncertainty in which they find themselves, as to whether or not Your Excellency would be in charge, they dare beg you to please order that they be

---

4. (November 8) The government maintained stores in the unoccupied Three Rivers barracks and powder at a separate magazine. The barracks was an imposing two-floor stone building on the *Platon* town center. The structure had previously served as a governor's residence and administrative building under both French and British regimes, most recently functioning as barracks for the small British army garrison from 1765 until the detachment's 1775 departure (see May 20, 1775 entry). One of the city's few large stone structures, it had been constructed in 1723, and was known variously as the *maison du roi*, Castle (*château*), Government House, or barracks (*caserne*). Daniel Robert and Norman Séguin, "Trois-Rivières, 1634–2009, Chronologie essentielle du patrimoine bâti," *Patrimoine Trifluvien* 19 (2009): 7; Trudel, *Régime militaire*, 11. The powder magazine, rebuilt by the British around 1770, appears to have been kept northeast of the Ursuline convent, between that building and the river; Sulte, *Mélanges historiques*, 18: 46–47.

5. A "Trifluvien" is a person from Three Rivers, also used as an adjective.

6. General Richard Montgomery was an Irish-born former British army officer who served with distinction in the French and Indian War. In 1772, he resigned his captain's commission and returned to America. He settled in New York, married into the powerful Livingston family, and quickly became involved in patriot politics. In June 1775, the Continental Congress selected him as the Continental Army's second brigadier general. Montgomery served as second-in-command of the Northern Army, under Major General Philip Schuyler, but became the senior officer in Canada when illness forced Schuyler's return to Ticonderoga in mid-September. Michael Gabriel, *Major General Richard Montgomery* (Madison, NJ: Fairleigh Dickinson, 2002); and Hal Shelton, *General Richard Montgomery and the American Revolution* (New York: New York University Press, 1994).

treated as favorably as those who have fallen into your hands in the course of your various conquests.

This is why the petitioners hope that Your Excellency will wish to order the commanding officer taking possession of this place to conscientiously ensure that his soldiers do no insult nor trouble in the ownership of their goods and the peaceful enjoyment of their particular interests, as well as to their personal safety. Knowing the sentiments of honor and humanity to be inseparable from your person, the petitioners have every reason to hope for the grace they ask of you. With all respect, they have the honor of calling themselves most sincerely Your Excellency's very humble servants";—21 signatures.[7]

Delegation from Three Rivers to General Montgomery

After this request had been signed, I was named to be one of the delegates. I thanked the assembly for the confidence that the people composing it had in me, but remonstrated that it was impossible for me to undertake this voyage at a time when my affairs did not allow it, that I was obliged to leave as soon as the next day to go to Rivière du Loup to collect rents for the Ursuline ladies and that if this had happened at another time, I would have accepted with all my heart. Finally, we nominated Mr. Pierre Baby[8] and Mr. William Morriss,[9] whom the assembly enjoined to leave immediately, and to that effect, we made a passport conceived in the following terms.

"We the Undersigned certify that Mr. William Morriss and Mr. Pierre Baby, of the City of Three Rivers, have been named by a committee of the principal citizens of this city, as delegates designated to go to His Excellency, General Montgomery or other commanders of the American forces. We beg the officers of the forward posts to permit the said delegates to pass and to find them the shortest routes to the place where His Excellency Montgomery or other commanders of

---

7. Badeaux does not provide the names of those who signed this letter, only the number of signatures.

8. (November 9) Fifty-four-year-old Pierre Baby was not directly related to the well-known fur-trading Baby brothers who operated from Quebec City, Montreal, and in the upcountry; UMPRDH indiv. #78126.

9. William Morris is otherwise unidentified.

said forces will be; Said Delegates being charged as representatives of the aforementioned committee. Written in Three Rivers, November 9, 1775." (15 signatures.)[10]

The gentlemen delegates were to leave that very evening, but being unable to procure horses, they put it off until the following morning. However, Mr. Baby changed his mind and did not wish to go unless there were to be a sum of money for his travel, so the affair remained in this state until the 18th of the month, on which day I left for Montreal, as I will tell in the following.

There being nothing of interest from the 9th to the 17th, I say nothing about any of these days.

Gen. Carleton's Return

Today, November 17th, General Carleton, accompanied by the Chevalier de Niverville[11] and Mr. Lanaudière Jr., arrived in the city around noon. They came on ships piloted by Captain La Tourtre ["Wild Pigeon"].[12] Once he had disembarked at the port, General Carleton asked Sir

---

10. Again, Badeaux does not provide the names of those who signed this letter, only the number of signatures.

11. (November 17) Chevalier Joseph Boucher de Niverville, a substantial Three Rivers seigneur and a veteran officer of campaigns across the breadth of French North America; Pierre Dufour, "Boucher de Niverville, Joseph," in *DCB* 5, http://www.biographi.ca/en/bio/boucher_de_niverville_joseph_5E.html (accessed November 11, 2013).

12. (November 17) French-born Canadian mariner, Captain Jean-Baptiste Bouchette. He was known as La Tourtre (*Tourterelle*), or Wild Pigeon, for the speed of his travels; W. A. B. Douglas, "Bouchette, Jean-Baptiste," in *DCB* 5, http://www.biographi.ca/en/bio/bouchette_jean_baptiste_5E.html (accessed November 11, 2013); Mémoire sur les actions du capitaine Bouchette lors de l'invasion de Québec en 1775, Collection Centre d'archives de Québec, P1000,S3,D254, BAnQ; Benjamin Sulte, *Histoire de la Milice Canadienne-Française, 1760–1897* (Montreal: Desbarats, 1897), 43. Governor Carleton and many loyalists had attempted to flee from Montreal to Quebec City, aboard eleven ships. However, they were stalled by weather and a threat of Continental batteries and gunboats near Sorel. See November 17 and 19 entries and notes below. Following a council of war, Carleton decided to attempt to escape in the middle of the night with Niverville and the governor's aide-de-camp Lanaudière. Bouchette skillfully piloted a small boat to evade the rebels. On Lake St. Pierre, they met a navy ship, and continued toward the capital, resulting in this encounter in Three Rivers. See also William Goforth to Alexander McDougall, November 22 letter, end of first paragraph.

Malcolm Fraser,[13] whose acquaintance he had made, if the Yankees had come this far? He answered no, but that we had learned that they were in Pointe aux Tremble, near Quebec.[14] The general didn't want to believe it, but when he got to Mr. de Tonnancour's house, this news was confirmed for him by the Chevalier de Tonnancour who had just arrived from Quebec. Mr. Maillet,[15] who was visiting him, announced that there were 600 in Machiche,[16] just waiting for the right time to come on. The general dined and left around three o'clock, hoping to travel all night and get to Quebec without danger. . . . May God make it so!

In 3-Rs, The English Wish to Capitulate Separately

The 18th. On my way to the upper city, I saw that the English citizens were plotting something amongst themselves. I did my best to find out what it was. After many steps and much effort, I learned that they had prepared a request to be sent and presented to General Montgomery in their names. So, fearing that if this request were to be presented without a [French] Canadian request appearing with it, this division could cause trouble in the city, I went immediately to Mr. Morriss and asked him

---

13. (November 17) Malcolm Fraser, Three Rivers merchant, not to be confused with the seigneur and Royal Highland Emigrants captain of the same name; *Ursulines de Trois Rivières*, 2: 548; Sulte, *Mélanges historiques*, 21: 32–34.

14. Benedict Arnold's corps of only 680 men moved to quarters in Quebec District's Pointe-aux-Trembles (modern Neuville), approximately twenty miles from Quebec City on November 19. This force had made a harrowing and deadly two-month voyage up the Kennebec River from Fort Western (modern Augusta, Maine), through the mountains, to Quebec's Chaudière Valley. After reaching the St. Lawrence, Arnold led his men across the river and attempted to coax and intimidate the capital into surrender. They started a short, untenable blockade of Quebec City, and subsequently decided to withdraw to Pointe aux Trembles. They waited there to be joined by General Montgomery's forces from Montreal. See Thomas Desjardin, *Through a Howling Wilderness: Benedict Arnold's March to Quebec, 1775* (New York: St. Martin's Press, 2006); and Arthur S. Lefkowitz, *Benedict Arnold's Army: The 1775 American Invasion of Canada during the Revolutionary War* (New York: Savas Beatie, 2008).

15. (November 17) Presumably Louis Maillet, another Three Rivers notary; Roy, *Histoire du Notariat*, 2: 43.

16. The troops in Yamachiche were Montgomery's advance guard, led my Major John Brown of Easton's Massachusetts Regiment (see November 19 entry and note below).

why our request had not yet been sent. He told me that Mr. Baby had not wanted to go without being paid. "Well then," I told him, "if that is the reason, I am prepared to go with you, and I hope the public will not be opposed to reimbursing our expenses upon our return." He agreed and we left the city at noon. At the first river we met a courier from Quebec who was on his way to Montreal on behalf of the "Bostonians" and we traveled with him both ways.[17] When we arrived in Machiche, we met a "Bostonian" courier who was traveling by horse and who had a carbine slung across his shoulder. He stopped and asked us if there was any news in Quebec (thinking that we were coming from there). We told him no. We asked him for news from upriver. He told us that the city of Montreal had surrendered and that they hoped to soon have the ships at General Carleton's location. We left him thinking this way, without telling him that the general had already gone by. We were most satisfied to see that they were mistaken. We slept in Masquinongé, in spite of the poor roads.

The next day, the 19th, we continued our route as far as Berthier, where we were stopped by brave Canadians who led us to two houses further upriver where Captain Merlette was to be found. They had us get out of our carriages in order to pay our respects to the commanding officer (who was Merlet). We went into the house to receive his orders, but apparently he had been up late, since we found him in bed sleeping. One of his guards went to wake him. He came out rubbing his eyes and asked what was new? We were introduced as people going to Montreal with dispatches for General Montgomery. So he let us pass, but before leaving, he gave us each a cup of rum and we had the honor of drinking with him.

The Americans' Bad Faith

We left Berthier then so as to arrive in Montreal in the same day; but when we got to La Valterie,[18] we were again stopped to take orders

---

17. This was probably a courier from Arnold's camp at Pointe-aux-Trembles, rather than Quebec City itself.

18. The north shore parish of Lavaltrie sat roughly midway between Berthier-en-Haut and the Lachenaie parish ferry point to the northeast end of the Island of Montreal.

from Colonel Eston.[19] We went and were very well received by the colonel and the other officers. He begged us to excuse him for having stopped us, but, as he had sent Major Brown[20] on an embassy to the ships, he asked us to please await his return, so we could take news to General Montgomery. So we stayed about two hours. During this time, we talked about what was happening. The officers asked the courier from Quebec, "What do the lower[21] Canadians say?" He told them that they were quiet and had no desire to meddle in the quarrel. The officers replied, "So much the better; if the Canadians don't get involved, we're in good shape; we'll cajole [*enjolerons*] them a while." They didn't know that I was Canadian, or I think they would have withheld the term "cajole."[22]

Finally, Major Brown arrived from the ships, bringing news that Colonel Prescot[23] was ready to surrender on the condition that he be taken to Quebec with his troops. Colonel Eston rejected the proposal, saying that he sought only what belonged to the King; and so, if the ships did not surrender within four hours, they would be boarded. After the council was ended we were given leave and were able to go on to Arpentigni,[24] were we slept.

---

19. Colonel James Easton commanded a western Massachusetts regiment, originally recruited by Benedict Arnold. Easton had participated in the capture of Fort Ticonderoga. See William L. Root, "The Capture of Fort Ticonderoga," in *Collections of the Berkshire Historical and Scientific Society* (Pittsfield, MA: For the Society, 1894), 379.

20. (November 19) Major John Brown of Easton's Regiment, had served as a key scout in Canada since March 1775, and worked as a liaison with the rebel Richelieu Valley Canadians after the invasion. He commanded the Continental forces that helped capture Fort Chambly in conjunction with the Canadians. See Goforth's October 1 letter and notes. See also Archibald M. Howe, *Colonel John Brown of Pittsfield, Massachusetts, the Brave Accuser of Benedict Arnold* (Boston: W. B. Clarke, 1908), 5.

21. The term *lower Canadians* meant those from the lower part of the province, to the northeast (Quebec District).

22. In this entry's final form, Badeaux chose the word *enjolerons*, to coax, wheedle, or cajole. He had originally used another word, but in his journal it is struck through and completely illegible.

23. See note to October 28 entry for more on Prescott. When Carleton escaped downriver with Bouchette (see November 17 entry and note), General Prescott was left with the ships, troops and stores, their passage still blocked by the rebel batteries at Sorel.

24. Repentigny parish about four miles from the ferry point from the north shore to the north end of the Island of Montreal (see Map 2).

On the 20th, we left Arpentigny on our way to Pointe aux Trembles,[25] where we stopped for about half an hour for lunch. We were taken for "Bostonians" and were given many compliments and thanks for the fact that we had come there (so they said) to give them liberty. When we had finished lunching, I took out a piaster[26] and told the hostess, "Pay yourself for what we have eaten." She took this piaster. Holding it between two fingers she showed it to everyone in the house saying, "You see how these 'Bostonian' gentlemen have no money! They wanted us to believe that they only had paper money, and here is the proof, see, if they talk of paper, they pay with good silver."[27] We left them believing that we were "Bostonians" and that we had lots of money.

The Canadians Are More Feared than the Americans

We arrived in Montreal as the *Angelus* was ringing.[28] We went straight to Mr. Montgomery, to whom we were introduced. We greeted him and handed over the request with which we were charged. He read it, after which he said that he was mortified that we had come from so far; that we were not to fear that his troops would do us any harm. We replied that our fear was not at all of his troops, but rather of the Canadians who would come down with them.[29] He told us, "If I have any Canadians when I arrive, I will know what orders to give them, but for the peace of the citizens of your city, I will give you a written response." Here are the terms translated from English:

---

25. Pointe-aux-Trembles (Montreal District) was the northernmost parish on the Island of Montreal (see Map 1). It is not to be confused with the Quebec District parish of the same name, where Arnold's corps was resting at this time.

26. A silver coin.

27. General Montgomery was carefully rationing his army's limited supply of hard cash, using Continental bills and receipts to pay for everything but the most essential provisions. Loyalist Canadians had also prophetically published frequent warnings that the Continental colonies were bankrupt and would flood Quebec with worthless paper money if their armies entered the province. For examples, see "Reponse d'un Canadien à un Étranger," and "An English Farmer to the People of Canada," *Quebec Gazette*, 27 July and 17 August 1775.

28. *Angelus*, ringing of church bells, see note to October 8 entry.

29. (November 20) The Trifluviens were referring to the Richelieu Valley Canadians under James Livingston who had actively taken up arms to cooperate with the Continental invaders.

Sirs,

"I am mortified that you would be under any apprehension whatsoever regarding your property. I am convinced that the Continental troops will never be tarnished by any charge of oppression. We have come to save and not to destroy. If Providence continues to favor our works, this province will soon be a happy free government. I have the honor to be, Sirs, your very humble servant. Richd. Montgomery, Brigad^r Genl. in Montreal,"

20 November 1775

Walker

Upon receiving this response, we took our leave of His Excellency and departed Montreal immediately, intending to sleep in Pointe aux Trembles. Arriving there around 8:00 in the evening, we met Colonel Eston, who was very friendly towards us and even told us about the surrender of the ships.[30] We also found Mr. Walker[31] who had come from the ships where he had been held prisoner, with irons on his hands and feet. We were made very welcome in the house we were in because, since we spoke English, they thought that we were "Bostonians"; nothing was too good for us.

Finally on the 21st we were back in Three Rivers. We had communicated Montgomery's response; the public as a whole was satisfied,

---

30. Governor Carleton and General Prescott had faced adverse winds, fog, rebel batteries, and gunboats as they attempted to navigate their flotilla past Sorel. After the governor's escape, with his ships full of civilians, and in one case, gunpowder, Preston chose to surrender to Colonel Easton rather than force a fight.

31. (November 20) Thomas Walker was the most radical antigovernment Anglo-Canadian in British Quebec. Arriving in Canada shortly after the Conquest, he took an early opposition stance against the provincial leaders and military, and had been "maimd" by having his ear cut off by unidentified attackers in a dispute over billeting British Troops. Governor Carleton, who had long tolerated Walker's intransigence and openly rebellious stance, finally had him arrested when given evidence that Walker had been gathering Canadians to join Ethan Allen before the Battle of Longue-Pointe. Lewis H. Thomas, "Walker, Thomas (d. 1788)," in *DCB* 4, http://www.biographi.ca/en/bio/walker_thomas_1788_4E.html (accessed November 13, 2013).

but I was a long way from being so myself, since there seemed to be no hurry to reimburse me for the money I had spent on this trip. Nonetheless, I am not really worried because I will find a way to get reimbursed.

William Goforth Letters—November

Letter: William Goforth to Alexander McDougall

Montreal, Nove^m 22^d 1775[32]

Dear Sir,

I received yours dated the 13th October and take as the highest kindness your goodness in Sending and informing me of the State of my Family. as to the Contents of your letter Respecting the Stoppage of Money from the men, I would inform you that all the Capt^ns will try to stop the Moneys paid to the Wives of the Men or their attornies as far as they can be informed,[33] but as to stopping the money from their Cloaths it will not be done.[34] in a word, we are not disposed to do it, and if we were disposed to Conform we dare not, because we all agree in this that it is not only Unjust but Extremely Impolitic. I am well informed that the General declares it never shall be stopt, and by

---

32. From AMP, NYHS.

33. At least six of Goforth's soldiers' wives, or their attorneys, arranged to have a portion of their husbands' pay diverted directly to them. There is a record of payment dated November 4 in AMP, NYHS. See first paragraph of William Goforth's January 19, 1776, letter, and associated note, for more details.

34. By November 1775, the northern Continental Army not only needed additional winter clothes, but replacement uniforms as their old outfits had been worn out in the dirty, wet siege of Fort St John's. After Montreal's capitulation, General Montgomery gave replacement clothing to any Continentals who reenlisted—many of the new uniforms came from captured British stores. Almost immediately, there were rumors that soldiers would be charged for this clothing, and within the next month, the Continental Congress actually considered whether the soldiers should be charged for the uniforms, but decided that the clothing should be considered "as a bounty" due to the severity of the campaign and climate. "Report of the Committee directed to repair to Ticonderoga and Confer with General Schuyler," December 23, 1775, *JCC*, 2: 447–48.

what follows you will not doubt that to be the opinion of the General, for he has orderd the Men a new of [*sic*] warm Suit of Cloaths at the Expence of the Congress. dear Sir you are something Mistaken in your American Soldiers. I hope they will do the Service of their Country and we intend to make you pay them. As to the poor officers, I expect they will all become Bankrupts. our pay would not, till we reacht this [place], Support daily Expences. our Cloaths are wore out and so dirty in our Miserable Encampment that they are not Scarce fit for a servant, and we can b[u]y no more, without we Cheat our men or the Congress will Raise our Pay. You have heard before this of the taking a Chamble, St Johns And Montreal. I have now the pleasure to inform you that we have taken Eleven sails of Vessels with Major Prescott, St Luke Lacorn, and a number of other prisoners. Carleton has Escaped in a small Sciff.[35]

Collonel Arnold is before Quebec with 800 men.[36] we Expect in a few days, perhaps tomorrow, to move towards that place. the Regulars have fired at two flags of truce that have been sent towards the town [Quebec City] by Arnold. I hope we shall soon be their [*sic*] with Cannon and Mortars of which we have now plenty of the best on the Globe, and then we shall offer them arguments of more weight.[37]

As I view you not only as my Colonel but also in the Character of an old Friend, I shall therefore make free to Communicate my Sentiments Concerning this Country, and first I am of Opinion that if the Congress mean to Continue the war and support the Liberties of America, this Colony [is] of the highest Consequence to them, and it Must by no Means be left naked. nothing less than ten thousand Men will be sufficient to Encourage the Canadians and make them hearty in case of an attack, which I doubt not will be made with great Violence in

---

35. See Badeaux's November 17 and 18 entries regarding General Prescott's surrender of the ships and Governor Carleton's escape.

36. General Montgomery had only opened direct communications with Colonel Benedict Arnold on November 8. Until that point, the two corps did not have any operational coordination. Benedict Arnold to Richard Montgomery, November 8, 1775, in Benedict Arnold, "Letters, September 27-December 5, 1775," *Collections of Maine Historical Society* 1 (1861): 480–81.

37. He is referring to the diverse multitude of artillery captured in May 1775, primarily at Crown Point; Benedict Arnold to Massachusetts Committee of Safety, May 19, 1775; *AA4*, 2: 645. However, the largest of these weapons, 24 pounder cannon and 13 inch mortars, were not siege guns, and could do little meaningful damage to fortified Quebec City.

the Spring. I would press from Every Consideration the Raising at least five hundred Artillery Men.[38] All the forces for the defence of Canada should be here Early in April.[39] I Expect my next will be dated from Quebec. Please to Remember me to my family. your Son Stephen is very hearty. I am Sir, with the utmost Respect yours to Serve,

William Goforth[40]

---

38. At this point, only Captain John Lamb's New York Artillery Company had trained artillerists serving in Canada, and they were only one hundred men, at fully authorized strength. As a result, many "regular" infantry soldiers were employed ad hoc throughout the campaign to man guns captured in Canada, as well as those sent north from Ticonderoga and Crown Point. New York Committee of Safety, July 16, 1775, and New York Congress to Philip Schuyler, August 8, 1775, *AA4*, 2: 1791, 3: 525.

39. Quebec Province was effectively isolated from Atlantic communications from early November through late April, as the frozen St. Lawrence was unnavigable. A British relief army was generally expected to arrive at the beginning of May.

40. The army had technically been reorganized into new units from those soldiers who elected to reenlist in Montreal; Proclamation to Troops, November 15, 1775, *AA4*, 3: 1683. Overall, the New York troops generally appear to have remained in their original companies, even though their 1775 regiments officially ceased to exist at the end of the year. The 1776 composite "New York Regiment" that was supposed to be formed from these troops in Canada was not even organized on paper until late in the campaign. The New York troops effectively functioned as independent companies under command of the senior local Continental officer. Most likely, Goforth's "new" company consisted largely of his original recruits, but his junior officers were shuffled about as needed, at General Wooster's direction. At least a few soldiers seem to have returned home before the New Year.

December 1775

Ever since our return, we have expected any day the passage of the "Bostonians" who were supposed to go downriver to lay siege to Quebec. Even though many people thought that it was too late in the season for such an undertaking, the "Bostonians" arrived in the ships that they had taken on the 20th of November, and passed through at the beginning of December.[1] Mr. Price, a merchant from Montreal and a current member of Congress,[2] disembarked to buy rum, blankets, hats and other articles necessary to the troops. Mr. Montgomery went straight through by ship.

Loiseau

A few days after the ships' passage, some sixty Canadians, commanded by Captain Loiseau,[3] arrived here in a row galley and some oth-

---

1. General Montgomery used the ships surrendered by Prescott to transport most of his remaining troops downriver, joining Arnold's force at Pointe-aux-Trembles (Quebec District); Rudolphus Ritzema, "Journal of Col. Rudolphus Ritzema, of the First New York Regiment, August 8, 1775 to March 30, 1776," *Magazine of American History* 1 (1877): 103–104.

2. (Beginning of December) James Price was a wealthy American-born Montreal merchant, who rose to prominence in Canada's anti-administration "British Party" since mid-1774. In the summer of 1775, he visited Congress as an informal ambassador from the Montreal "British Party" committee, but he was not a member of Congress. Price repeatedly lent massive sums of money to support the invading army, and would become its deputy commissary general in Canada.

3. Captain Augustin Loiseau led a company of James Livingston's new Canadian Continental Regiment, authorized by General Montgomery. Loiseau, a former Chambly-area

ers came by land. The day after they arrived, Mr. Loiseau entered nearly every house (that was known to belong to Royalists) to seize their arms. When he went to Mr. de Tonnancour's, he found only a hunting knife and an old pistol barrel, which he took. From there he went to Mr. de Niverville's, took from him two or three muskets; at Mr Cressé's,[4] a sword with a silver handle; at Mr. Leproust's,[5] two muskets. I was warned of the search; I put my musket,[6] my horn and my shot pouch in safety, but it was unnecessary; they didn't come to my home. That evening, Mr. Loiseau went to speak with some persons of this city (who I will not name to save them the shame of such a black betrayal). They told him that they were sure that Mr. de Tonnancour had other arms and that he even had hidden powder. "Well then," said Loiseau, "I will go back there tomorrow and if I do not find the rifles and powder, I will have his house raided." In saying this, he made these individuals so extremely happy, that they didn't make any other requests, but, Providence be thanked, things did not go as far as they hoped.[7]

---

blacksmith, had been a key Canadian partisan leader in the Richelieu Valley campaign, opposing Maclean's advance up the Richelieu, and helping interdict Prescott's ships with Easton at Sorel. Augustin Loizeau Petition to John Jay, n.d., M247, r158 i147 v3 p409–11.

4. Claude Poulin Courval-de-Cressé, seventy-five-year-old seigneur of Nicolet, resident in Three Rivers, serving as the district's militia lieutenant-colonel by Governor Carleton's appointment; "Recensement des Habitants de La Ville et Gouvernement des Trois-Rivieres, 1760–1762," in *Rapport de L'Archiviste de la Province de Quebec pour 1946–1947* (Quebec: Redempti Paradis, 1947), 6; UMPRDH indiv. #60026.

5. (November 21) This would presumably be Antoine-Claude Leproust, sixty-three-year-old father of militia officer Louis-Joseph Leproust, mentioned in September 27 and subsequent entries; UMPRDH indiv. #78084.

6. Of note, when ordered to mobilize on October 14, Badeaux told Sergeant Major Pratte that the only weapon he had was a penknife. Badeaux must either have been provided a weapon in the intervening weeks, or he was dissembling back in October.

7. Perhaps Loiseau was restrained by guidance that Montgomery presumably provided in response to the Three Rivers capitulation, delivered by Badeaux and Morriss (see November 20 journal entry and note). However, there is no extant record or reference to such orders.

La Rose

The 4th of December I learned that Mr. Gugy[8] had been caught up in the intrigues of Sir La Rose,[9] from la Rivière du Loup. The next day, as I was going to the upper city, I met Mr. Gugy. I asked if it was true that he had been arrested. He told me yes. He begged me to go with him to Mr. Hart's;[10] Mr. La Rose was supposed to be there to prove the charges that he had made against him. I went, along with Mr. Baucin.[11] A moment after we went in, Mr. LaRose arrived. Mr. Levingston,[12] a

---

8. (December 4) Conrad Gugy was a British French and Indian War veteran, early Quebec provincial official and seigneur of various properties in the Yamachiche/Rivière du Loup region. Badeaux had served as a clerk for Gugy back in 1764, and continued to work with Gugy in official notarial business in the intervening years; see discussion and notes in Badeaux biography above, and BAnQ, P98, Fonds Famille Gugy, S2 Fief Grand Pré and S8 Rivière du Loup. In 1775, Gugy was one of Governor Carleton's Quebec Act government legislative councilors. "Gugy, Conrad," in *DCB* 4.

9. François Guillot *dit* La Rose was a French-born businessman residing in Canada since the 1740s. He settled in the Rivière-du-Loup region in 1767 and became a bailiff. He was appointed or elected as a militia captain in 1775. He would eventually be commissioned as a Continental captain, and fled to New York when the Province of Quebec was recovered by British forces. See Raymond Douville, "Guillot, Larose, François," in *DCB* 4, http://www.biographi.ca/en/bio/guillot_francois_4E.html (accessed November 17, 2013).

10. (December 4) Aaron Hart was a successful Jewish merchant who came to Three Rivers as a British army purveyor in the French and Indian War. He quickly established himself as a prominent merchant, landowner, and financier. Of note, although Hart had business ties to loyalists such as the Nivervilles, Cressés, and Tonnancours, he also provided supplies and mended weapons for Colonel James Livingston's Canadian Continental troops, in addition to accepting the highly controversial Continental bills. His house could be considered as reasonably neutral ground for resolving this episode. See Denis Vaugeois, "Hart, Aaron," in *DCB* 4, http://www.biographi.ca/en/bio/hart_aaron_4E.html (accessed November 17, 2013); Aaron Hart to James Livingston, 27 December 1775, *Publications of the American Jewish Historical Society* 26 (1918): 257–58.

11. Michel Beaucin, see June 23 entry and note.

12. James Livingston's New York family settled in Montreal after the Conquest. He established himself as a Richelieu Valley wheat trader in the 1770s, and took an early role in the Chambly partisan cell in the summer of 1775. Even though he was the only Anglo-Canadian listed among the original Chambly cell leaders, Livingston quickly rose to principal leadership with the Continental invasion. When General Montgomery established the Canadian Continental regiment on November 19, 1775, he appointed Livingston as colonel in command. See Emma Ten Broek Runk, *The Ten Broeck Genealogy: Being the Records and Annals of Dirck Wessele Ten Broeck of Albany and His Descendants* (New York: De Vinne Press, 1897), 87–88; Memorial of James Livingston, March 7, 1782, NARA, M247, r50 i41v5 p246.

Canadian colonel, asked Sir La Rose what grievances he had against Mr. Gugy. He began by laying out a packet of papers filled with the most atrocious stupidity, saying that Mr Gugy had forced the Canadians to march against the "Bostonians"; that he had threatened to have them whipped if they didn't want to go; that he had said that the "Bostonians" were a band of rogues; that Dugand[13] was a rascal and Levingston a bankrupt who had sided with the "Bostonians" to get out of paying his debts. Mr. Gugy responded that he had said that Dugand was a wig-maker[14] and that he would say it again, since it was well known; that as for Mr. Levingston, that he didn't know him well enough to have said the things he was supposed to have said.

Mr. Levingston told Sir La Rose that he could do very well without inserting anything personal into his writings, that he saw that to be beneath him and that, for the rest, he saw no legitimate cause for arresting M. Gugy. He told Mr. LaRose to calm down, that he had no need of his services and that he should absolutely not behave in this way and he gave Mr. Gugy a document to be published on the church door, making Sir La Rose's character known to the public. In this way, Mr. Gugy was cleared of the false charges made against him.

[Colonel Livingston's declaration on Gugy's behalf (not in Badeaux's journal) read:

> I, the undersigned, commanding Colonel of a Canadian regiment in the service of the honorable Congress, certify to whomever it may concern, that Sir Conrad Gugy of Machiche was brought as a prisoner before me in Three Rivers, under the imposition of the forenamed François Guillot d^{it} Larose. After having heard the forenamed Guillot and the forenamed Sir Gugy, we find that Larose maliciously had Sir Gugy arrested with the intention of vexing him. We are

---

13. Jeremiah Duggan was an Irish Canadian Richelieu Valley wheat trader. Speaking fluent French and with many local acquaintances, he rapidly rose to become James Livingston's chief deputy in organizing Canadian resistance to loyalist forces after the Continental invasion. He participated in Allen's defeat at Longue-Pointe and led Canadian forces in the capture of Fort Chambly. Duggan became Livingston's boldest company commander in the Canadian Continental regiment, and later earned his own commands. See Foucher, "Journal," 151.

14. Duggan had been a Quebec City barber before becoming a Chambly merchant. The French term *perruquier*, literally meant a barber or wigmaker, but also had pejorative, disreputable connotations.

convinced of this, having heard the report of his character and conduct. Consequently, we have given the aforementioned Sir Gugy his freedom to go wherever it pleased him, to look after his affairs. We forbid whomever it may be to bother him in whatever manner whatsoever, be they Canadians or other employees of the honorable Congress, in the name of which we have given the present [declaration] in Three Rivers, the 5th of December, 1775.

Signed, Colon[l] Jas. Livingston;

[margin] Notary Leroy December 5, 1775][15]

From this time until the end of the month, "Bostonians" and Canadians came through on their way to Quebec.

December 31st

We heard several times that Mr. Montgomery had summoned Mr. Carleton to surrender and that he had always refused; that he had even addressed himself to the bourgeois of Quebec asking [them] to facilitate his entry into the city, which was likewise refused.[16] Finally, finding no way to enter into the city, he prepared to scale the walls on the first day of the year 1776[17] at four o'clock in the morning, but his only success in this endeavor was to go to the other world seeking gifts for this new year, accompanied by several officers and soldiers. It was reported to us that there were 430 prisoners taken in this action. The royalists only lost two men.[18]

---

15. Benoit Leroy Notarial Records, BAnQ, CN 401, S60, Fonds Cour Supérieure. District judiciaire de Trois-Rivières. Greffes de notaires.
16. (December 31) Montgomery sent several parleys to the city walls in attempts to seek surrender, but they were refused, sometimes being met with musket and cannon fire. He resorted to having Arnold's Sartigan Abenaki Indian auxiliaries fire arrows over the walls with surrender messages attached.
17. The attack actually occurred on the early morning of December 31, 1775. A marginal note, probably Berthelot's, on the manuscript makes this correction.
18. The report of losses was remarkably accurate. Thomas Ainslie, *Canada Preserved: The Journal of Captain Thomas Ainslie*, ed. Sheldon S. Cohen (New York: New York University Press, 1968), 37.

From this time on, "Bostonians" and Canadians returned upriver, some with their heads bandaged, others with their arms in a sling. I met a "Bostonian" who told me that he had left the end of his thumb in Quebec and that he was very happy not to have left more there.

William Goforth Letters—December and 1 January

"Extract of a letter from Montreal, dated December 17, 1775."

New-York Journal, 18 January 1776

[unattributed]

"The companies of the Captains Weisenfelt, Cheeseman, Mott, Varrick, and Quackenbos,[19] are before Quebec; Captains Goforth's and Lyon's are stationed here, under Col. Ritzma.[20] Captain Willet has the command at St. John's."[21]

Letter: William Goforth to Alexander McDougall

Montreal, Jan the first, 1776[22]

Sir,

I have just time to inclose you a letter* I Rec^d from Quebec, it being the highest intelligence we have. [I] Am in great hast[e] [and] Expect

---

19. All originally First New York Regiment companies: Friedrich Weisenfels (First Company), Jacob Cheesman (Fifth Company), Gershom Mott (Seventh Company), Richard Varick's (Sixth Company), and John Quackenbos's (Eighth Company); "SoFR."
20. Captain Lyons commanded the Ninth Company, originally of the First New York Regiment; "SoFR." Lieutenant Colonel Rudolphus Ritzema had been the acting commander of the First New York Regiment in Canada, since Colonel McDougall was in New York City. Ritzema had been ordered to remain in Montreal to serve as a deputy for Connecticut Brigadier General David Wooster, who commanded the rear areas as Montgomery advanced toward Quebec City.
21. Captain Marinus Willett, one of New York City's leading radicals in 1775, commanded what was originally the Second Company, First New York Regiment; "SoFR." See also the reference to Willett's command at Fort St. John's in Goforth's January 19 letter.
22. From AMP, NYHS.

to Morrow to go on a Command in the Country to Visit some of our Country Gentlemen.[23] [I] hope on my Return to give you a good account of them and to Congratulate you on the Reduction of Quebec. I am Sir, with the greatest Respect, yours to serve

William Goforth

[P.S.] your Son is well

[Letter below was enclosed with letter above]

John Lamb to William Goforth,

Du Pre's House near Quebec, 28. Dec. 1775

Dear Sir,
 I was in hopes a few Hours ago to have had it in my Power to date this Letter from the town of Quebec, but have been disappointed;—yesterday Afternoon, the Commanding Officers of the Respective Corps in this Quarter, received the Genl Orders to hold themselves in readiness at an Hours notice; And about 10 O'Clock at Night we all received Orders to Rendezvous at certain Places, at 2 O'Clock in the Morning in Order to Storm, which was complied with by both Officers and men with the greatest cheerfulness and Alacrity. but this Night (contrary to expectation) proving extremely clear, and very Calm, the Genl thought proper to postpone the Attempt, till a more favourable opportunity,[24] which I sincerely hope the Almighty will shortly furnish us with, that we may have it in our power to punish these Miscreants McClean[25] and Carlton for their Villany; Adieu
 I have nothing to add but my Compliments to Coll Ritzema, and all Friends being,

---

23. Around this same time, Simon Sanguinet describes a Continental mission to disarm Tories in the parish of L'Assomption, twenty-five miles downriver from Montreal. It is probably the same event. Verreau, *Invasion du Canada*, 92–93. This would be the second of three loyalist-suppression missions that Goforth refers to in his January 27 letter to Alexander McDougall.

24. For more detail on Montgomery's decision to delay the assault, see Anderson, *Fourteenth Colony*, 192–95.

25. Colonel Allan Maclean and Governor Carleton.

Dear Sir

Your real Friend
& Hon¹ Servant

John Lamb

To Cap^tn Goforth

[*margin*]

Capt Melcher Capt Goforth to forward this to Ritz[ema]

January 1776

1776 January—American Severity

General Wooster published an order to put a stop to all speech against Congress upon penalty of being transported out of the province: this order was published on the church door on the 14th of January.[1]

Every day we are told that a number of "Bostonians" from the Continental colonies will be coming through on their way to Quebec. The hearts of the "Bostonians" or, to put it better, the [Canadian] "Congress supporters" [*congréganistes*],[2] are very happy with this news, but nonetheless, here we are the end of the month of January and only one brigade has arrived.

During the course of this month, Brother Alexis, a Recollet from the Quebec convent, arrived in the city. He assures us that the people of Quebec are not lacking provisions and are only short a very small amount of wood. He was taken prisoner here by Mr. Price, as being

---

1. Command of the Continental forces in Canada devolved to sixty-five-year-old Connecticut Brigadier General David Wooster upon Montgomery's death at Quebec City. Wooster was headquartered in Montreal, where he had commanded the rear areas. On January 6, Wooster issued a proclamation establishing the bounds of tolerable conduct in occupied Canada, a step that was severely derided by both Canadian loyalists and critics in the thirteen colonies. Wooster to Militia Officers, January 6, 1776, in Historical Section of the General Staff, eds., *A History of the Organization, Development, and Services of the Military and Naval Forces of Canada, From the Peace of Paris in 1763 to the Present Time*, vol. 2 (Quebec: King's Printer, 1919), 139–40.

2. The French term *congréganistes* does not have a direct translation, but has been presented as "Congress supporters" throughout this work.

under suspicion; two other Brothers who left Quebec with him were also arrested and all three were taken to Montreal.[3]

Wiliam Goforth Letters—January

Letter: William Goforth to Alexander McDougall

From the Guard House Montreal,
the 5th Jan.y, 1776, 3 OClock morning[4]

Dear Sir,

For particulars From Quebec [City][5] I would refer you to a letter from Col Ritzema to M.r Peter Van Brugh Livingston[6] and another from Capt.n Mott[7] who was in the action, inclosed by his order to M.r Denning,[8] which together with the information you will obtain from Capt.n Melcer,[9] will give

---

3. Badeaux's record does not make it entirely clear when and where the other Recollet brothers were captured. Continental engineer John Pierce, participating in the blockade of Quebec City, mentioned two "fryars," probably Recollets, being detained while trying to depart the capital on January 13; Kenneth Roberts, *March to Quebec: Journals of the Members of Arnold's Expedition* (Garden City, NY: Doubleday, 1938), 710.

4. From AMP, NYHS.

5. See note to Badeaux's May entry for use of Quebec to specifically mean Quebec City.

6. The Ritzema letter provided updated information to the New York Provincial Congress regarding the losses at the Battle of Quebec City, and appealed for more men and money; Rudolphus Ritzema to Peter Van Brugh Livingston, Montreal, January 5, 1776, in *Journals of the Provincial Congress . . . of the State of New York, 1775—1776–1777*, vol. 1 (Albany: Thurlow Weed, 1842), 287. Livingston was president of the first New York Provincial Congress and a delegate to the second (December 1775 to May 1776).

7. Neither of these letters appears to be extant. Captain Gershom Mott (originally Seventh Company, First New York Regiment) was commended for his performance at the Quebec City battle, in an "Extract of a letter from a field officer in the late unfortunate attack at Quebec," *New-York Journal*, 15 February 1776.

8. William Denning was a prosperous merchant and financial backer of the Revolution, a New York City committee member, and delegate to the New York Provincial Congresses of 1776; Rodney Macdonough, "William Denning," *The New York Genealogical and Biographical Record* 30, no. 3 (July 1899): 133–40.

9. Isaac Melchior (or Melcher), a Pennsylvanian volunteer with Arnold's corps, carried word of the catastrophic Quebec City defeat to Montreal. There, General Wooster employed him as town major of Montreal until mid-February, when Melchior escorted loyalist prisoners to the colonies and then delivered updated reports on the Canadian situation to Congress. David Wooster to Philip Schuyler, February 18, 1776, PSP, NYPL; March 7 and 8, 1776, *JCC*, 4: 188, 190.

you as Compleat an Idea of the Situation of our Troops in that quarter as I have myself. In hearing the melancholy documents from below, a Council of war was called and the Question was put whether General Worster, agreeable to Col. Camels [sic] Request,[10] should go to Quebec or stay at Montreal. When the Severe Season of the Year, and the advanced age of the General,[11] that he had now formd Considerable Connections with the Inhabitants, the Importance of his presence might be to Conciliate their Affections, and that it was of the highest consequence that a stand should be made here in case our Brethren should be Under the Necessity to retreat, it was determined he should stay. Our Garrison here is very weak, so many haveing Either Got the St Johns or Quebec feavour or have in other words been bewitcht to go home.[12] A number of our men would not Engage again, their times are now up, no money to pay them. Those who agree to stay refuse to do duty till they are paid—the whole Garrison full of Clamor.[13] The Tories begin to grow. as to the Gentlemen of the Army who are on Parole of Honour, I believe we have little to

---

10. Both Arnold and Colonel Donald Campbell had immediately sent General Wooster word of the Quebec City debacle, describing the army's desperate situation and requesting reinforcements. They also asked that the general join them, since he was now the senior Continental officer in Canada. Campbell was the Northern Army's deputy quartermaster general and served as a chief deputy in General Montgomery's headquarters. After Montgomery's death in the failed assault, Campbell was temporarily in command while Colonel Arnold was hospitalized with a serious leg wound that had forced him to leave the New Year's Eve battle. Donald Campbell to David Wooster, December 31, 1775, PSP, microfilm reel 12, NYPL; Benedict Arnold to David Wooster, December 31, 1775, in Roberts, *March to Quebec*, 103.

11. Wooster was sixty-five years old at the time; David Wooster, "Summary of the Life of General David Wooster," in *Genealogy of the Woosters in America, Descended from Edward Wooster of Connecticut* (San Francisco: M. Weiss, 1885), 88–90.

12. As 1776 began, enlistments ended for the many men who declined to reenlist in November, and a number also simply tried to desert after the failed New Year's Eve assault; David Wooster to Philip Schuyler, January 5, 1776, PSP, microfilm reel 13, NYPL.

13. While Continental and Montreal sources are generally quiet on this disturbance, the rumors that spread across Canada told of a great riot. See March 8 entry in Badeaux's journal. Also on March 8, wild tales reached the defenders of Quebec City, telling of "a quarrel among the rebels," who "fought in the streets," in which "five were killed, and seven or 8 sent wounded to the Hospital"; "Journal of the Most Remarkable Occurrences since Arnold Appear'd Before the Town on the 14th November 1775," in *Historical Documents Relating to the Blockade of Quebec by the American Revolutionists in 1775–1776* (Quebec: Literary and Historical Society, 1905), 125.

fear from them, their honour being sacred.[14] Those who we have most to fear in my opinion are the Inhabitants who bask themselves in ministerial favour, haveing great influence on the Savages and Unlearnt Peasantry. one Regiment of Regulars are in the lake above us,[15] and should we not succeed at Quebec, will doubtless be apt to Visit us in the Spring. But perhaps I have said too much and you may begin to Conclude that we are Intimidated. that is not the Case. we doubt not but our country men who have sent us here will speedily send us Succor, both of Men and Cash. Col Clinton[16] is ordered to Quebec to take Command their [sic], and I believe they will yet be able (altho we cant send them many) to form and maintain a Blockade—we shall take it.

Your son Stephen is in good health and would have wrote but for the Command of the Barrick Guard and no table or Conveniency to write on.[17] he is not wanting in Filial Affection. he is a good Lad, behaves well and with as much prudence and sobriety as must be Expected from a young man.

Perhaps my wife may be frightend with the accounts from these parts. [I] Should be glad you would be kind enough to see her and meet and modify them as may be. I am well and with great Respect, yours to serve

William Goforth

---

14. A number of Canadian loyalist officeholders, militia leaders, and inactive half pay officers were released by General Montgomery on a parole of honor. At the end of November, several New York officers protested this "dangerous" decision to Montgomery, and less than a month later, a number of pro Continental Montrealers expressed concerns about the disruptive influence these paroled loyalists might have in occupied Canada. Richard Montgomery to Philip Schuyler, November 24, 1775, and "The Faithful Union with Liberty" to Richard Montgomery, December 22, 1775, PSP, microfilm reel 12, NYPL.

15. The Eighth (King's) Regiment was deployed in several upcountry forts around the Great Lakes. "Distribution of His Majesty's Forces in North America, 19th July 1775," enclosed in Thomas Gage to Viscount Lord Barrington, July 21, 1775, Clarence E. Carter, ed., *The Correspondence of General Thomas Gage with the Secretaries of State, 1763–1775* (New Haven: Yale University Press, 1931), 2: 690. See also April 24 entry and note in Badeaux's journal.

16. Colonel James Clinton, commander of the Third New York Regiment and the senior New York officer in Canada at the time. He was sent with the very active Montreal patriot James Price to help stabilize the situation outside Quebec City; David Wooster to Philip Schuyler, January 5, 1776, PSP, microfilm reel 13, NYPL.

17. The barracks, or "clever Guard House," in Montreal was "left . . . almost ruin'd" by the British in their evacuation from the city, presumably leaving little useful furniture

[P.S.] I intend in my next to trouble [you] with my notion of the politics of this province and of some things I think necessary to be done by the Congress.

we have no accounts from home since the letter of your[s] date the 19 Novem^r, tho I should be sorry to be troubling, I should be Glad you would write.

Letter: William Goforth to Alexander McDougall

Montreal the 19th [January] 1776[18]

Dear Sir,

I Received yours dated the 4 Noveb^r in which you informd me what money you have paid to Mrs Taylor, Bradley attorney, mrs Conger, Mrs Rickhow, &[?] Mrs Webber, Cookson and Ford.[19] this letter I received by last Post, am glad I Got it, have changed all their acct^s, but as to Mr Paynes[20] account it is not in my power, a ballance being due to me to the First Jan. he has now left me and [is] trying to raise a Company in General Worsters[21] Regiment, So that I have no Lieutenant but your son.[22] Indeed Mr Payne has been so disorderd with one kind of Disorder or other that it has not been in his power to afford me much assistance since he landed at St Johns. I am Extremely obliged to you for your friendly and Polite letter of 12th Dec^r, and think myself happy that my Conduct toward your son has met with your approbation, and cant but

---

behind; November 17 entry, Henry Livingston, "The Journal of Major Henry Livingston of Third New York Continental Line August to December 1775," ed. Gaillard Hunt, *The Pennsylvania Magazine of History and Biography* 22 (1898): 27.

18. From AMP, NYHS.

19. Six of the seven names listed here match a record of payment to wives or attorneys, dated November 4, in AMP, NYHS (Cookson is not included). Most of these names also match soldiers in Goforth's muster roll of September 19, 1775, see Goforth's letter of November 22, 1775. "Muster Roll of Captn Goforth's Compy," 19 September 1775," NARA, M246, rg 93, r65, f1, p33.

20. James Payne, originally Goforth's first lieutenant, but detached to other service around the New Year; "SoFR."

21. Brigadier General David Wooster, Connecticut's senior Continental general; some contemporaries also wrote his name as "Worster" or "Worcester." Here Goforth is referring to a composite unit generally called "Wooster's Regiment," consisting primarily of New England troops reenlisted by General Montgomery at Montreal in November.

22. Lieutenant Stephen McDougall.

be thankfull for the great Compliments you pay me when you say you Chose your son should return home unless I Continued in the Service. you are pleasd to say you Conceive your son too young to take the charge of a company. he is young it is true, however he has now seen something of the nature of Carrying on a Seige from the Experience St. Johns afforded, and he had some time to learn the nature of Camp and Garrison duty, and in my opinion would Cut no mean Figure at the head of a Company. however I Cant say I would advise you to supersede any man for the sake of promoting him or any one, because I am afraid such Maneuvers will be detrimental to the American Cause. I have seen something of this last since my arrival at this place. On the 16th Instant, one Mr Melcher[23] from Philadelphia (one of Colonel Arnolds Vollunteers and who must in point of duty be considered as in the Ranks), was by General Worster jump'd over the head of every Lieutenant in the Garrison and Captn, and made Brigade Major.[24] Perhaps you may say there is not need of such an officer in Garrison where there are so few troops and that it cant be considered in any other point of view than a Feather in his Cap. be it so, I cant see why all the officers in Garrison should be affronted for the sake of Plumeing a Vollonteer. I much question if such an Instance can be found in any historical accounts of Regular Service. I well know that a Nobleman's Son, who has served for some time as a Vollonteer, thinks himself sufficiently noticed and rewarded if he gets a Commission as an Ensign. be it as it may, I find I am not the only one disgusted at this piece of Generalship. I have discussed with several of the officers on the Ground and find their stomachs heave at it. I shook the more freely upon this occasion because I by no means suppose myself to be the Man intitled to it by Military Course in a regular way, however it undoubtedly Strikes me immediately and were it not for the two following reasons (the one is my men made me promise not to leave them when they Reinlisted and also that they should be at liberty to Return the 15 April next;[25] the other is that I could not Reconcile it

---

23. Isaac Melchior—see note to Goforth's January 5 letter.

24. Brigade major was a functional position, also known as town major, responsible for day-to-day management of garrison duties, and the focal point for interaction between the military and the local populace.

25. In mid-November, General Montgomery determined April 15 would be the end of reenlistment service, as it was the best compromise between allowing the men to return home for spring planting and giving the colonies enough time to deliver new reinforcements to Canada.

to my Conscience to raise any Disturbance in the Garrison or turn my back upon the Cause at this Critical Juncture), I would have immediately delivered my Commission to the General. I do not speak from any ill will to the young Gentleman. he is my Townsman[26] and messd with Col Ritzema and myself till his promotion. perhaps it may be said he underwent great Fateague in his march with Col. Arnold, however I much question if it was more than the long Seige of St Johns.[27] Captn Willet[28] was the man whose right it was, who has in my opinion been unkindly treated in another Respect. He was appointed to Command of St Johns by General Montgomery and Removed by General Worster, and a Lieutenant of Colonel Waterberries (a worthy man (but young)) lately made a Captain, Promoted to the Command.[29] Captain Willet has insisted upon a Court of Enquiry, with the Result of which perhaps I may hereafter trouble you.[30]

I am determin'd with the leave of providence to return to my Family after the 15 of April. I hope before that time Quebec will be ours, but if it is we must be Speedily Reinforced with men, Supplied with hard Cash, and furnishd with all the apparatus of war fit[t]ing for a Regular Seige. the Liberation of our poor Brethren below may almost be compared to the Forlorn hope.[31] Inclosed[?] you have as late news

---

26. Goforth was born and raised in Philadelphia, moving to New York City sometime in early adulthood; see William Goforth biography above.

27. Goforth imagines incorrectly here. The well-documented travails of Arnold's Kennebec Expedition resulted in numerous deaths from starvation and accident—the survivors that reached Canada looked "more like ghosts than men"; Morison Diary, November 4, in Roberts, *March to Quebec*, 531.

28. Captain Marinus Willett, originally Second Company, First New York Regiment.

29. Robert Walker, originally a lieutenant in Samuel Whiting's Company of David Waterbury's Fifth Connecticut Regiment. He became a captain and company commander in mid-November when he agreed to continue serving for another five months. Henry P. Johnston, ed., *The Record of Connecticut Men in the Military and Naval Service in the War of the Revolution, 1775–1783* (Hartford, CT: 1889), 64–71; NARA, M804, rg 15, pension S.12072 (Enoch Bailey), p3.

30. Willett's postwar recollections mention his command of Fort St. John's beginning in late November, but tactfully do not mention a court of inquiry and only say, "he remained [in command of the fort] until January, when the term for which his men were enlisted expiring [sic], he was relieved, and again returned to Montreal." William M. Willett, *A Narrative of the Military Actions of Colonel Marinus Willett, Taken Chiefly from His Own Manuscript* (New York: G. and C. and H. Carvill, 1831), 38–39.

31. "Forlorn hope," a body of troops assigned a particularly hazardous assignment or posting.

from Quebec as we have by the letter of Capt[n] Mott.[32] However [I] beg you would not be so Discouraged as to order up the forces from thence, they must be Reinforced. we must yet have the place by Gods leave, and I hope before I Return, and then I shall Return with pleasure to you and my other Friends, and I hope Return your Son in good Health. he begins to get a Belly like an older man. we want some of your 32 pounders, Large Mortars, and plenty of Shells in my opinion.[33] I am Sir, in the mean time, with the greatest Respect, your most obedient and most Humble Servant,

William Goforth

[P.S.] Major Gansevelt[34] is gone down to Quebec and before now join'd our Army there with a Reinforcement of 120 men. Capt[n] Sacket[35] with his Company, and Mr Dow,[36] once our Sarjent Major, is now Lieutenant and only officer of Capt[n] Livingston['s] Company,[37] Sets of[f] tomorrow with his Company[38]____

---

32. Gershom Mott, originally Seventh Company, First New York Regiment.

33. Montgomery's early attempts to shell Quebec City with the available 24 pounders and mortars proved that employing such medium-weight field pieces was futile against the capital's fortifications. "Journal of Robert Barwick During the Canadian Campaign," December 14 entry, William Bell Clark, ed., *Naval Documents of the American Revolution* (Washington, DC: Government Printing Office, 1964), 2: 1398.

34. Major Peter Gansevort Jr. originally of the Second New York Regiment; "SoFR."

35. Probably Samuel Sacket, originally from the Fourth New York Regiment; "SoFR."

36. Second Lieutenant James Dow; "List of Officers of the four Regiments raised in New-York in 1775 (now in Canada) as they rank February 28, 1776, enclosed in Philip Schuyler to Nathaniel Woodhull, February 27, 1776, *AA4*, 5: 331.

37. Captain Henry Livingston, commander of the First Company, Fourth New York Regiment; "SoFR." Captain Livingston had returned to New York in late November 1775, along with troops who did not reenlist at Montreal; "New-York, November 30," *The New England Chronicle or the Essex Gazette* [Salem, MA], 30 November 1775.

38. This detachment was the first sent from Montreal to augment the beleaguered Quebec City blockade after the New Year's Eve debacle; Donald Campbell to Robert R. Livingston Jr., March 28, 1776; LAC, MG23-B40, Robert R. Livingston Collection.

Letter: Willliam Goforth to Alexander McDougall

Montreal, Jan 27th, 1 Clock at night[39]

Sir,

The Remnant of our Regiment are ordered to hold themselves in readiness to march at the shortest notice I expect we shall leave this in a day or two and proceed to three Rivers and Quebec I am sorry to tell you that I must now for a while part with my Lieutenant,[40] as I am for a while to be stationed at the three Rivers in order to Curb the Tories and perhaps for some other Reasons I imagine I shall lay there till the Battering Cannon Arrives, when I Expect to Join the Regiment at Quebec. I hope you will be speedy in forwarding Every thing necessary for a Regular Seige. in my Opinion, nothing less than 32 or 24 pounders will be sufficient to shake the Walls. they laugh at our 18 pounders. your son is in good Health and in as high spirits as need be. I am Sir, with the greatest Respect, your most obedient and most Humble Servant,

William Goforth

[P.S.] Altho I am lo[a]th to trouble you, yet must beg leave to say I am informd one Daniel Shover of Major Weisenfellss Company[41] has left his place and taken away my Best tent and frying pan. [I] Should be glad you would send Your Servant and make him deliver them, at least the Tent. I wish we were once Master of that Dirty hole of Quebec, for I begin to long to come home.

---

39. From AMP, NYHS.
40. Lieutenant Stephen McDougall.
41. The First Company, First New York Regiment, a sister unit of Goforth's; "SoFR." Daniel Shauer is listed on Goforth's September 19, 1775 muster roll; "Muster Roll of Captn Goforth's Compy," September 19, 1775. Shauer must have transferred to Weisenfels's company sometime thereafter. Presumably Goforth's property was taken when Shauer returned to New York from Montreal, before his enlistment expired at the end of December.

"Extract of a letter from Montreal, Jan. 27," *New-York Journal*, 15 February 1776

[unattributed letter by William Goforth]

The remnant of our battalion are to hold themselves in readiness, and expect marching orders tomorrow, I am for some time to be stationed at the Three Rivers, some matters being necessary to be settled with the Tories, who, in different parts begin to be insulting, since our late misfortune at Quebec. This makes the third visit I have had amongst this kind of people,[42] I expect soon to be called down to Quebec.

Your old friend Capt. Mott[43] behaved well in the attempt to storm, and in the retreat, brought up the rear with great reputation.

Our blockade at Quebec is yet maintained. On the 25th instant Capt. Seaborn, from the Massachusetts, the first hero that has appeared to our assistance since the repulse at Quebec, arrived with 27 men.[44] His arrival had a very good effect, for in the morning of the same day was found at the Church door, an anonymous seditious paper, very artfully written, calculated to stimulate the inhabitants to rise and cut us all off.[45] However, I believe few of them had as much courage as the writer had ingenuity. They are now convinced the lakes are frozen, and think the "Bostonians" are coming as thick as the trees in the woods. The Tories now seem quite crest-fallen.

---

42. The first was in early December, when Goforth joined Lieutenant Colonel Ritzema on a mission to Longueuil and Boucherville to investigate alleged Tory conspiracies being led by Luc de La Corne and Joseph Fleury Deschambault; "Montreal, Dec. 2," *New-York Journal*, 11 January 1776, which is an extract of a letter that may have been written by Goforth; Ritzema, "Journal," 104. The second was referred to in Goforth's January 1 letter to McDougall, which was almost certainly a mission to L'Assomption.

43. Captain Gershom Mott, originally Seventh Company, First New York Regiment. See Goforth's January 5 letter and note.

44. Captain Zebadiah Sabin of west Massachusetts volunteers, attached to the Green Mountain Boys; see Appendix 2 and note regarding Sabin.

45. This Tory letter remains unattributed; there were certainly many loyalists who were inspired to propaganda action by both the rebel defeat at Quebec City, and General Wooster's new policies that restricted agitating activity in Montreal and the entire province.

February 1776

The 8th of February, a detachment under the command of Captain William Goforth and his lieutenant, Mr. Macdugall,[1] arrived to take possession of the city. The 9th. They had the barracks prepared and moved in there on the same day.[2]

FIGURE 12. Government House Barracks, Three Rivers, circa 1890. This large stone building served as quarters for Goforth and his company. It stood from 1723 until the city's great fire of 1908. Maison des anciens gouverneurs des Trois-Rivières, Bibliothèque et Archives nationales du Québec, PER M-176 (RS 400).

---

1. Lieutenant Stephen McDougall, "SoFR," also in *AA4*, 2: 1334.
2. See note on the November 8 entry for a description of this building.

Commissions

License to Sell Liquor

The 10th. Captain Goforth sent for me to translate a proclamation into French that he had published on the church door on the 11th, which was a Sunday. He sent one [copy] to each parish. This proclamation ordered all militia officers to hand in the commissions that they had received from General Carleton, and he forbade the retail sale of drink without a license from General David Wooster.[3]

The 12th. The city militia officers turned over their commissions to the commander.

The 13th. The commander, seeing that M. de Tonnanancour had not yet remitted his colonel's commission, sent his lieutenant, Mr. Macdugall, with a letter on his behalf addressed to Mr. de Tonnancour, in which he paid him great compliments and said to him at the end—that he was sending his lieutenant to get his commission from him and that he hoped that he would not refuse to turn it in. Since the letter was in English and the lieutenant didn't understand French, Mr. de Tonnancour had me sought out to interpret. When I had explained the tenor of the letter, Mr. de Tonnancour responded that he did not believe himself obliged to render his commission, understanding it to be something that belonged to him and that was part of his property; and what's more, that Mr. Montgomery had promised to maintain all citizens' property (as it appears in his response on page 17 & 18 [Badeaux is referring to his November 20 entry]). Mr. Macdugalle said that these were his orders and that he would transmit his opinion to the commander. Mr. de Tonnancour had a horse hitched to a cart and went off with the lieutenant to see the commander. The Chevalier de Tonnancour and I followed them. We went to the castle,[4] where Captain Goforth was

---

3. Shortly after becoming the Continental commander in Canada following General Montgomery's death at Quebec City, Wooster issued orders requiring militia officers appointed by Governor Carleton to exchange their commissions for Continental equivalents; David Wooster to George Washington, January 21, 1776, *AA4* 4: 796. In a separate order, Wooster forbade liquor sales unless licensed by his authority.

4. The Castle (*château*) was another name for the Government House barracks. See note for November 8 entry.

lodging. When we got there, Mr. de Tonnancour had me tell the commander that he was mortified at the trouble that Mr. Macdugalle had taken in coming to ask for his commission; that if he had thought that it to be justified, he would have brought it himself, but that not believing himself to be obliged to give up a commission which did him honor, he had remained quietly at home. The commander answered that he had strict orders from General Wooster to take them, and that he could not exempt him from this under any pretext. Mr. de Tonnancour, seeing that he could gain nothing in spite of all the reasons he had offered, told him, "Well then, Sir, as I am of too advanced an age to make the trip to Montreal, I give you my son who I will send to represent my arguments before the General." The commander refused and told him that it had to be he, himself, in person, because it was certain that the general would not exempt him from remitting it and that if he continued to insist that he would have him sent before Congress. He gave him 48 hours to decide either to go or to turn in his commission. In that interval there was abominable weather of snow and great cold, which caused Mr. de Tonnancour to remit his commission to the commander, being unable to extend the deadline.

New Commissions

The 18th. The commander convened an assembly at his quarters for the election of new militia officers.[5] This took place after Mass. As I had no business in this assembly, I went home. I had no sooner arrived there than I saw an envoy from the commander who begged me to go to the castle to be part of the assembly. I could not refuse him, especially in the circumstances in which we found ourselves. I went and the assembly opened immediately. All those present asked that Mr. La framboise[6] continue as captain, which was accorded them. Then

---

5. In late January, General Wooster issued new orders calling for parishes to hold elections for militia officers. David Wooster to Committee of Congress, July 5, 1776, in *AA5*, 1: 6.

6. (February 18) Jean-Baptiste Fafard *dit* Laframboise was a prominent merchant who had also been the city's captain before the militia was dissolved in 1765. Marcel Trudel, *Histoire de la Nouvelle France*, vol. 10, *Le régime militaire et la disparition de la Nouvelle France, 1759–1764* (Montréal: Fides, 1999), 105; Trudel, *Régime Militaire*, 36; UMPRDH indiv. #56210.

they named Mr. Charles Lonval lieutenant and Mr. Pierre Baby ensign,[7] and three sergeants. After which it was a question of naming some for the outlying areas. Mr. St. Pierre[8] who had always been one [a militia officer], said that he was no longer of an age to serve in this capacity and that we could give this charge to someone else. Mr. Baby took the floor and said to him: "What! You served the King of France, the King of England, and you refuse to serve the Congress! Is it not as worthy as the others?" Such idiocy did not receive much approval and, since no one else said anything; he could only applaud himself. After the assembly, I had the honor of being invited to dine with the commander, his lieutenant, Mr Laframboise, Mr. Leproust and Mr. Bellefeuille, the son, and Mr. Freeman.[9] We went to Mr Sills's[10] where we were to dine. During the meal, the conversation was uninteresting and in spite of the "Bostonians," we drank to the health of General Carleton. The commander made a bet that before long he would be in Quebec. We told him that we didn't think that he would get in there at all and that we believed that relief would be coming. So, Mr. Leproust wagered 24 bottles of wine that on the 5th of May there would be ships from Europe arriving in Quebec. The commander accepted the wager; so we are sure to have 24 bottles of wine to drink once the 5th of May arrives; May God grant that it be new wine arriving on those ships![11]

---

7. Louis Charles Fafard Lonval; UMPRDH indiv. #161996. See November 9 entry for Pierre Baby.

8. This appears to be Jean-Baptiste Boulanger *dit* St. Pierre, UMPRDH indiv. #66523, although he was only forty years old at the time. A list of loyalist militia prisoners taken at Fort St. John's included a Boulanger from Three Rivers; "List of prisoners," AA4 3: 1427. Jean-Baptiste was the eldest son of Joseph Boulanger *dit* St. Pierre, who had died in July 1775; UMPRDH indiv. #43142; Pierre-George Roy, "Liste de messieurs les officiers et gentilhommes canadiens . . . ," *Recherche Historiques* 12 (1906): 317.

9. The commander Captain William Goforth and Lieutenant Stephen McDougall; Antoine Claude Leproust (see extended November 21 entry related to Loiseau searching loyalist homes, and note); Antoine Lefebvre Bellefeuille was a loyalist, released by the Continentals shortly after his capture at Fort St. John's; Constant Freeman Sr. was a New England–born merchant, driven from Quebec City by Governor Carleton's November 22 proclamation that required inhabitants to either take up arms for the Crown or leave the city. James Freeman, "Record of the Services of Constant Freeman, Captain of the Artillery in the Continental Army," *Magazine of American History* 2 (1878): 350.

10. Samuel Sills, one of the first Anglo-merchants who settled in Canada following the Conquest. He was postmaster for Three Rivers; *Ursulines*, 3: 416; Sulte, *Mélanges historiques*, 21: 38–39.

11. Mr. Leproust's guess was only off by one day. British relief arrived at Quebec City on May 6. There is no record that Goforth made any attempt to pay off this bet.

The twentieth of February. The commander went to Becancour[12] to designate militia officers. I went with him, as did many of the men from the city. After the election, we had a kind of lunch and returned to the city.

The 21st. Thirty "Bostonians"[13] passed through, no doubt counting toward the two hundred that had been announced.

FIGURE 13. *Ste-Anne de la Pérade Church and Other Buildings*, by Elizabeth Frances Hale. Characteristic of most rural parishes, there was a small cluster of buildings at the center of this northeast Three Rivers District community: the parish church, presbytery, perhaps a couple shops or homes, and possibly the seigneurial manor. The rest of the population was spread fairly evenly in farm plots across the parish's arable riverside land. Library and Archives Canada, Acc. No. 1939-252-13.

---

12. This parish sat on the south bank of the St. Lawrence, about five miles downriver from Three Rivers, along and near the Becancour River (see Map 3).

13. See William Goforth's March 24 letter to Alexander McDougall for details of this and subsequent Continental troop movement through Three Rivers. By the captain's record, this was Captain Samuel Wetherby's detachment of Charlestown, New Hampshire, volunteers; see Appendix 2.

The 29th. Since the commander had asked me to go with him to St. Pierre Lebecquet[14] to interpret for him in the election of the militia officers, I went with Mr. Bellefeuille, the son. We left at 9:00 in the morning. As we were passing through Champlain we learned that they were burying Mr. Morrisseau, the parish priest,[15] and the commander stopped at the church to see the ceremony. After the service we left and got to St. Pierre at 1:00 in the afternoon. Once we got there, we found the habitants split into two parties. Some wanted the assembly to be held at the parsonage, the others wanted it in another house. After having examined the arguments, the commander ordered that the assembly be held in the parsonage according to tradition. When we arrived at the parsonage, several habitants said that they wanted nothing to do with the captain who had been named 8 days before. The commander asked the reason for this. A certain Etienne Chandonnet[16] who (no doubt) represented the others, said to the commander: "Sir, the reason we have for not taking this man as captain, is that he has an English heart and that he accepted commissions from General Carleton, when we refused them" The commander answered them very wisely. He said to them: "Although this man accepted a commission from General Carleton, and he served the King, that is not a sufficient argument; he could be as good a subject of Congress as he has been faithful to General Carleton, but to avoid any difficulties, I will hold a new election." The commander ordered me to open the election, which I did and received the votes, in spite of the noise made by the habitants, who argued against the first captain. Nonetheless, if there had been one more vote, he would have prevailed, but Augustin Brisson was named captain, Joseph Francois Maillet, lieutenant, Augustin Trottier,

---

14. St-Pierre-les-Becquets was the easternmost south bank parish within Captain Goforth's Three Rivers District military governorship, about twenty miles downriver from the city of Three Rivers (see Map 3).

15. François Morisseaux-Bois-Morel, parish priest for Champlain since 1750. Tanguay, *Clergé canadien*, 121.

16. Chandonnet is mentioned in the Baby-Taschereau-Williams Commission report as a particularly active rebel sympathizer, who vexed local loyalists. That government commission toured Quebec and Three Rivers Districts immediately after British forces recovered the province, to identify collaborators and restore government authority. Gabriel, *Quebec during the American Invasion*, 48–49.

ensign.[17] As soon as the assembly ended, we left and arrived in the city at 9 o'clock in the evening, in extreme cold.

William Goforth Letters—February

FIGURE 14. British winter uniform. During their time in Three Rivers, Goforth's soldiers may have appeared somewhat like these men. In November 1775 General Montgomery had promised each reenlisting soldier "a blanket coat, coat, vest, breeches, one pair stockings, two shirts, leggins, socks, shoes, mitts, and cap." Many of these new supplies came from captured British army stores in Montreal. Charles MacKubin Lefferts, Privates, Royal North British Fusileers, 21st Regiment of Foot, Winter Dress in Canada; Object #1921.112, New-York Historical Society.

---

17. The Baby-Taschereau-Williams Commission mentions that Brisson, Maillet, and Trottier accepted Continental commissions, and that Trottier had refused a militia commission from Governor Carleton in the summer of 1775. Gabriel, *Quebec during the American Invasion*, 48–49.

Letter: William Goforth to Alexander McDougall

Three Rivers, Feb the [blank in Ms.—actually 14th or 15th] 1776[18]

Sir,

In my last to you from Montreal, I Informd you that I Expected to part with my Leuitenant, your son. But seizing Mr. Leuitenant Odlam[19] in my Company, as he had none on the Ground, I carried my point with the General to keep him with me at Three Rivers, where we both are at present in good health. Upon my arrival here I Immediately, agreeable to my Instructions, Examind the barracks [and] found them as to the Building very good, but out of repair.[20] I suppose about £300 York Currency[21] would put them in good order. for the present, I shall go to as little Expence as possible. I have put one Large and one Small Room in order for my Men, and one Large and Small ditto in order for myself and Leiutenant, between which I have a fine Large Room for a Store, sufficient to Lard a Considerable Quantity of Provisions. two Rooms I have got fixed upstairs, sufficient to hold a Company, with a stove in it. the Barracks if completed, I Imagine [would be] sufficient to hold five full Companies, with which and the Billets that may be served on the Inhabitants, I Conclude I could Accomodate Six or Seven hundred men Tolerably well. the 8th I arrived at this place. the 10th Instant Issued an Instrument of writing which I had translated into French, and Read in the french Church on Sunday, which was on the 11th in the afternoon.[22] five of the principle Inhabitants came to pay their Respects to

---

18. From AMP, NYHS.

19. Lieutenant Digby Odlam, originally Ninth Company, First New York Regiment; "SoFR." It appears he was assigned as first lieutenant in Goforth's company, replacing the sickly Lieutenant James Payne (mentioned in Goforth's January 19) when the unit was reenlisted in November, for service through April 15, 1776. Goforth indicates here that General Wooster reassigned Lieutenant Odlam to headquarters duty, or other service in Montreal, so Stephen McDougall was Goforth's only lieutenant at Three Rivers.

20. See note to Badeaux's November 8 entry regarding the "Government House" barracks building.

21. Three hundred Pounds York was equivalent to £168 British Pounds Sterling or 750 Spanish milled dollars (the theoretical equivalent of a Continental dollar); Jackson Turner Main, *The Social Structure of Revolutionary America* (Princeton: Princeton University Press, 1965), 289. As a comparison, this equated to three years of Captain Goforth's Continental captain's pay.

22. See Badeaux's entries for February 8 and 10.

me; [the] next day five more, who apologized for their not waiting on me with the other Gentlemen the day before. the officers of the Town have brought in their Commissions Except the Chief Colonel.[23] I have sixteen other parishes in the district to[o], Besides this.[24] Our Election is to be held at my quarters at the Barrack on Sunday, near 11 OClock.[25]—

Dear Friend, I hope you will Credit me when I tell you that the Cause of my Country is still near my heart—But as to Continuing in the Service (altho I make no positive promises) Longer than till the time my Men are engaged is expired, for I dont think I shall. I hope Providence, which has hitherto supported me, will Enable me to Close the Champain [sic] with honour, when I intend to Return and stay with my family. In the mean time, altho I would not by any means undertake to direct in the Appointment or promotion of officers, and altho I have a high opinion of most of our officers, Yet from the Experience I have had of them I would beg your attention while I recommend some who I think would make Excellent Officers in the artillery, and in my opinion, the success of our arms depends much on haveing a good Train of Artillery, and beg you will give it weight or in other words, allow yourself time to Recapitulate the great advantages that must attend our haveing one, and the shabby figure we shall make without one. should it be thought proper to Raise a Regiment of them, I would be glad to see Lamb at the head of them all, for a better peice of shift was never put together.[26] we must have him out of Quebec, yet Mr Wools,[27] the Capt^{ns} Leiutenant also deserves much from his Country. but should you want more Captains, I think I can Recommend some as good as the world affords. First, Jonathan Peircy,[28] who is not only a mechanick but seems to have a Mechanical Turn, is truly brave and has paid considerable attention to that Branch. to my knowledge, he has frequently

---

23. Louis Joseph Godefroy de Tonnancour, the Three Rivers District militia colonel appointed by Governor Carleton. See Badeaux's February 13 entry.

24. See Map 3—Three Rivers District.

25. See Badeaux's February 18 entry.

26. Captain John Lamb, commander of the New York Artillery Company, joined Benedict Arnold's corps in the Battle of Quebec and was wounded, losing an eye, and was captured; Leake, *Memoir*, 131–34. Goforth's "piece of shift" phrase was apparently a reference to sturdy cloth.

27. Captain-Lieutenant Isaiah Wool of John Lamb's New York Artillery Company; Leake, *Memoir*, 109.

28. Lieutenant Jonathan Pearcy, originally in the Eight Company, First New York Regiment; "SoFR."

attended Captain Lamb on the Bomb Battery, Besides doing his duty in his own Regiment. Leutenants Arston, Platt, and Houston,[29] all men in whom the Country may place the highest Confidence. Perhaps you may Inquire whether other officers are not as brave as them, doubtless they are, and I do not mean to lessen others by recommending them. all I mean is that the persons above named are not only Equally brave, but seem to me to be Calculated for that department.

The Colonel above mentioned, Tonnencour, has this afternoon brought in his Commission, and as he is a man of the Greatest property in these parts, and by a Common Consequence of the greatest influence, I Expect all will go Smooth and Easy in other Parishes.[30] I am Sir, with the greatest Respect, yours,

William Goforth, Capt[n] and Commander of three Rivers

Letter: William Goforth to Benjamin Franklin

Three Rivers, 22[d] Feb. 1776[31]

Sir,

I have been informd that it is a Custom in the polite world when about to address a Stranger to Apoligize for so doing. But in order to Evade the Necessity of Such Tedious Business I have only to prove that I am perfectly well acquainted with you, which I Shall Evince by assureing you that a Number of years ago when in Providence and looking out of a window I Saw you Pass by.[32] But Perhaps you may, notwithstanding my good Acquaintance and the great right I have to the freedom, ask

---

29. Lieutenants Aaron Aorson and John Houston, originally in the Fifth Company, and Lieutenant Richard Platt, originally in the First Company, First New York Regiment; "SoFR."

30. See Badeaux's February 13 entry.

31. From Benjamin Franklin Papers, American Philosophical Society, IV, 80. Also published in William B. Willcox, ed., *Papers of Benjamin Franklin*, vol. 22 (New Haven: Yale University Press, 1982), 358–61.

32. "Presumably in July, 1763, when [Benjamin Franklin] visited Providence on business of the Post Office"; there is no extant record of Goforth's purpose for being in Providence at that time. Willcox, *Papers of Benjamin Franklin*, 22: 359n.

FIGURE 15. Benjamin Franklin, circa 1780. Library of Congress, LC-DIG-ppmsca-09853.

why it is that I write. I answer because I understand you are a great man that you Can Turn the Common Course of nature, that you have power with the Gods and Can Rob the Clouds of their Tremendious Thunder. Rouse once more my old Trojan, Collect the Heavey Thunders of the United Colonies and Convey them to the Regions of the North and Enable us to Shake the Quebec walls, or on the other hand inform us how to Extract the Electric fire from the Center—then perhaps we may be able to draw a Vein athwart their Magazene and Send them upwards Cloathd as Elijah was with a Suit of fire. one or the other of these must be done, or we shall be drove to the Necessity of another Frolick of boarding the Town.

As this is now the third time that I have been sent forth after the Tories in this Province[33] the [*sic*] which has gavin me a Small View of the Situation of the Country, as also of the Circumstances Condition and Disposition of the people, An Idea of which I would fain Con[v]ey you. therefore would Just Say, I Apprehend their Disposition is to be for freedom, their Condition and Circumstance in General very poor, being not opulent and very Unlearnt. As to their Situation it is distress'd and Pitiable for Notwithstanding the Breathings that they and all the Human Race must have for freedom, yet from a fear that we Shall either be forced out of the Province by the Ministerial Troops on the one hand, or that we Shall leave them to fall a Sacrifice on the other when we have Carried our point with great Britain they are reduced to the greatest distress. That they may be releived from Slavery, I hope we Shall Soon be in Possession of Quebec and they have members in the Congress and Civil Government Established. I would think it an Excellent Expedient, in order to open their Eyes and raise their Appetite for freedom, that twenty or thirty Protestant Clergymen of Different Denominations Should be Sent into the Province who were orthordox both in Religion and Liberty and whose greater Concern would Rather be to promote the Church of Christ and to Cloath Human Nature with happiness than to gain Customers to Support any Sectarian Purpose. I am of Opinion many of them might get modorate liveings from the people, but what do you think of a few missionaries?—Should you Imploy any, Show no Respect to denominations—As to forms, I think the people have as good a right to Compose now as in Past ages, and if you think that George the third has Sinned the Unpardonable Sin Race [erase] his name out of the Common prayer book and put in the name of the Congress, which I Suppose is as much Connected with Episcopacy as he is;[34] and instead of giveing them a Sallery from the Society in England, give them a Sallery from the Society in Philadelphia and I'll warrent they will promote Whygism.[35] As the Canadians bestow but little Learning on their

---

33. Goforth makes this same reference in his January 27 letter to Alexander McDougall.

34. As a Baptist and founding member of New York's 1769 Society of Dissenters, it is not surprising that Goforth would challenge the king's role in religious practice. See Goforth biography (above) for further details.

35. Although generally tolerant, Goforth showed his religious biases here, very typical for Protestants of that time. He presumes that simple exposure to Protestant practices will convert Quebec's Catholics—and result in a more "enlightened" Canadian worldview.

Sons I would beg leave to Recommend the Sending to this province forty or fifty discreet young men as Schoolmasters—the Consequence will be that the Protestants['] Sons will be qualified for places of profit and Honour, and by a very natural Consequence fall into them. Doctors also are much wanted and might be use full in the Same way—this will be Proselytizing without Persecution. The Regalor Officers[36] are Violent in abuseing the Canadians because they are not true to Tyranny—Our People Seem in Some measure to be quite out of humour with them because Some have Changed Sides, but of this I think no man will think Strange who is in the least acquainted with the history of the Cevil [sic] wars in England. However I think it will be necessary from a number of Considerations to have at least an army of ten thousand men in this Province, to Secure the Province to ourselves and Relieve the people from their fears.

Since I began this letter I have understood that Messers Walker and Price from Montreal have Gone to the Congress who Can give you the best information of this Province.[37] Mr Walker has been maimd for dareing in these Corrupt times to be an honest majistrate and his property burnt for dareing to be a friend to the United Colonies.—Sir I am afraid I have tired your patience and therefore Shall Conclude, wishing you when your time Comes, a Pleasant and Easy Passage into the other world, as I Imajine by the Pursers Books that it Cant be long before you will be under way.

William Goforth

Captain in the first Batalion of the Newyork Forces, Commander of three Rivers, and Father of the Solid Boys[38] in the Northern Army.

---

36. British army officers, frequently impatient and haughty with Canadian habitants.
37. Leading Montreal Whig-patriot merchants Walker and Price were southward bound at General Wooster's request, to visit Congress and present their views regarding Continental policy for the Canadians' Indian trade. David Wooster to Continental Congress, February 11, 1776, PSP, microfilm reel 13, NYPL. See Badeaux's April 10 entry for his perspective. See also Badeaux's November 20 entry on Walker and beginning of December entry on Price, with associated notes, for additional background.
38. Solid Boys is perhaps a reference to the fact that, when duty and necessity called, his men had reenlisted to support the Continental cause in Canada.

[P.S.] Perhaps Sir you will Say you dont know me. I Cant help that it is none of my fault, if you had looked into the window as I looked out, perhaps your acquaintance might have been Simelar to mine. However I must be at you again, I am not without my fears that the Northern Department will yet be neglected (as it has from the beginning of the Champain [sic] in Every Respect Except, that of provisions for which the Congress must have Credit) as I have the Command at this place, it is natural to Suppose I must know what forces are Come to our assistance. Since the defeat at Quebec which I Can assure you, notwithstanding the Bustle you perhaps think you have made, does not amount to more than *[39], Exclusive of the Garrison which were at Quebec, and Some of which have been moveing towards the Scene of action. See the inclosed note. the lakes Sometimes is Impassible [by] 20th march. if we have not the heavey apparatus for a Seige, nor men Enough to Storm, we shall Soon be in very pretty way in this part of the world. 23d feb in the morning.

---

39. Goforth did not include a number, but instead left only an asterisk in his original letter.

March 1776

Accusation against Sir Crévier

The first day of March. Mr. Crévier Deschenau[1] from St. Francois, begged me to go with him to see the commander to interpret for him and so that he could justify himself against the calumnies that Joseph Traversy,[2] captain of St. Francois had made against him. I went with him and asked the commander, on behalf of Sr. Crevier, what the grievances were against him. The commander had statements from several habitants of St. Francois sought out for me, which he then gave me to read. These documents stated that they had heard that Sr. Crévier Deschenau had said that he wanted to march knee deep in the blood of the "Bostonians," Canadians and Indians.[3] After having read these statements, I respect-

---

1. Jean-Baptiste Crevier *dit* Descheneau, thirty-five years old, UMPRDH indiv. #163715 or his father, sixty-four-year-old, UMPRDH indiv. #110911, relatives of the seigneur of St-François-du-Lac.

2. Joseph Traversy was appointed as a militia captain and willingly cooperated with the Continentals to such a degree that he chose to flee Quebec after the invading army withdrew. He would serve as a scout for the Northern Army, and eventually received a pension from the United States Government. Traversy would later cite Goforth as a reference for his dedication to the Continental cause. "Memorial of Joseph Traversy to Continental Congress, St Francois, 26 Jun 76," PSP, NYPL; UMPRDH indiv. #154343; Timothy Bedel to Philip Schuyler, June 22, 1777, Isaac W. Hammond, *New Hampshire Provincial and State Papers*, vol. 17 (Manchester, NH: John B. Clarke, 1889), 133; Board of Treasury, Expenditures for pensions, November to December 1784, NARA, M247, rg360, i141, v2, p219, r154.

3. See translator's notes regarding use of "Indians"; see usage in Goforth's January 5 letter and George Measam's March 31 letter (below).

fully showed the commander that they were insufficient, given that the individuals who had given them did not say that they had heard this from Mr. Crévier, but only that they had heard it said. Consequently, these could only be very equivocal proofs and that Joseph Traversy and his witnesses must appear in person to prove their claims.[4]

The commander said that was fair and asked me to write an order in French commanding Traversy to appear tomorrow at eleven o'clock with his witnesses.

This same day, 30 "Bostonians" passed through on their way to Quebec with about 100 Canadians who had deserted the camp in autumn and that they were taking back with them.[5]

The 2nd. 50 "Bostonians" passed through on their way to the camp.

At two o'clock in the afternoon, I went to the commander's for the business between Sr. Crevier Descheneau and Traversy, who did not appear, his wife having sent Joseph Halard[6] to tell the commander that he had gone moose hunting.

The commander asked for a bond in the sum of 1000 *Louis* sterling,[7] to be kept with Mr. Laframboise as bail, to answer for the good conduct of the aforementioned Descheneau. I explained the content of the obligation in French to all those present. Mr. Descheneau said that he would be more than happy to sign this obligation, but that it would not place him beyond the reach of Traversy's malice, who could simply

---

4. This episode is a fine example of Badeaux's legal and judicial experience, developed as a notary.

5. Captain Goforth records 166 Massachusetts and Pennsylvania troops passing through Three Rivers on this day, but no Canadians. It is unclear whether the Canadian troops that Badeaux mentions were those who deserted from Colonel Maclean's loyalist camp near Sorel (see October 24 entry), or whether they were patriot Canadians who had left the rebel camp, the reference to "autumn" would indicate that they were not deserters from Livingston's regiment at the siege of Quebec City. Perhaps this was one of two companies from Colonel Moses Hazen's Second Canadian Regiment that were sent from the Montreal District to join the capital siege—many of Hazen's men were recruited from partisan veterans of the fall Richelieu Valley campaign. Moses Hazen to Edward Antill, March 26, 1776, Halidmand Papers, Miscellaneous Papers, Orders and Returns, 1756–1780, LAC, MG-21, A-616.

6. Joseph Allard was a forty-one-year-old resident of St-François-du-Lac; UMPRDH indiv. #162272.

7. Badeaux is probably referring to the silver *Louis* coin, also known as an *écu*. It had approximately the same value as the milled Spanish dollar and thus, theoretically, the Continental dollar. One thousand *Louis* was certainly a very sizable sum, more than four years' worth of the supposed value of Captain Goforth's Continental Army pay.

find some rascals to make false reports against him for pay, and that, in that way, he would find himself in the situation of paying this sum even though innocent. The commander told him, "Well then, since you don't want to sign this obligation, wait here until Monday and if your accuser doesn't appear, prepare to go to Montreal to justify yourself to the general," and he bid him leave.

I was in the country on the 3rd, 4th, 5th and 6th of March[8] and could not find out exactly how the Sr. Crevier affair had gone; I only learned upon my return that he was forced to go to Montreal.[9]

The 7th. We learned today that all the "Bostonians" who have come downriver since the month of January only total 530 men.[10] Yesterday, I learned in Nicolet that during the night two people supposedly going to the city of Quebec had passed through[11]. . . . God grant that they be able to get there!

Deserters

The 8th. Three emigrants came through the city who had deserted from Quebec on the pretext that they were mistreated (they say) by Colonel Maclean. They said that in Quebec there is no scarcity of provisions, and that some were even brought into the city every day. When they were questioned as to whether or not the people of Quebec intended

---

8. Badeaux was presumably visiting the Ursuline nuns' seigneuries again, in his role as their agent.
9. In a later incident, presumably in the chaos of May or June, Crévier reported that he was taken prisoner by the Continentals and forced to "give them liquor, powder, guns, and several fuzils." "Second Book of Minutes of the Court of Enquiry of Damages, Occasioned by the Invasion of the Rebels," March 10, 1777, LAC, Fonds Hospice-Anthelme-Jean-Baptiste Verreau, MG23-GV7.
10. This compares with Goforth's account of 601 men transiting Three Rivers over this period, as listed in his March 24 letter, perhaps because this report came from Quebec City before the last few score men had arrived.
11. The two messengers were Joseph-Marie Lamothe and Joseph Papineau, carrying messages from New York's royal Governor William Tryon for Governor Carleton in Quebec City. These messages were covertly transmitted through Montreal's Vicar-General Etienne Montgolfier; "Journal of the Most Remarkable Events," LAC, MG23-B7, p75, LAC; Pierre Foretier, "Notes and Reminiscences of an Inhabitant of Montreal During the Occupation of that City by the Bostonians from 1775 to 1776," *Canada Public Records Report, 1945* (Ottawa: Edmund Cloutier, 1946): xxiii.

to defend themselves, they answered that they intended to do more than defend themselves, since they hoped to beat the "Bostonians."

The Americans in Montreal Refuse to March

We learned the same day that the troops from Montreal had revolted because the general wanted to make them go down to Quebec. They responded that, when they came into this country, they were given to understand that Quebec had been taken and that they were only there to guard the cities and not to fight. Upon hearing this response, the general had six of them put in prison, but since their comrades had beaten down the doors, the officers wanted to get involved and several of them were beaten. Nonetheless, the general had six of the most stubborn whipped and the tumult ended there.[12]

FIGURE 16. *The Forges, River St. Maurice*, circa 1832. This establishment was Quebec's only significant industry in the late eighteenth century, just eight miles up the St. Maurice River from Three Rivers. At the time of the American invasion, Canadian Whig Christophe Pélissier directed the forges operations. Library and Archives Canada, C-004356.

---

12. William Goforth writes of soldiers refusing to do their duty until paid, and of the "whole Garrison" being "full of Clamor;" see January 5 letter. However, there is no other extant Continental record specifically describing a Continental mutiny in Montreal of the scope described here, or at this time.

Today, Mr. Pélissier[13] sent the commander of this city two thousand [pieces] of iron to make, they say, pick axes for the siege of Quebec. The 9th. Today, 105 wagons came through, loaded with firkins & barrels for the camp, with 36 "Bostonians" driving them.

We learned that in Quebec a ship in the harbour had left the Cul-de-Sac.[14] That gave rise to several conjectures. The "Congress supporters" said that it was Mr. Carleton intending to escape with his troops, but those who know the generosity of General Carleton's spirit think otherwise, as do I.

The 10th. Two companies of "Bostonians" arrived, announcing that General Lees[15] has arrived in Montreal and that he should to be going to lay siege to Quebec in very few days.

Today the grand vicar preached a sermon to us. At the beginning of his discourse, he gave a slap in the face to several "Congress supporters" who had ridiculed some expressions he had used in a sermon he gave us on Shrove Tuesday.

We have been assured that the two individuals I spoke of on the 7th who were going to Quebec, are from Montreal and that they were able to get in.

The 11th. Eight "Bostonians" passed through going upriver and returning home, saying that their time is done.

---

13. (March 8) Christophe Pélissier, a French-born Canadian, was Three Rivers District's most zealous "Congress-supporter." He was also the director and majority shareholder of Saint Maurice ironworks, seven miles up the river of the same name, north of Three Rivers. These forges were Quebec's only significant industry. M.-F. Fortier, "Pélissier, Christophe," in *DCB* 4, http://www.biographi.ca/en/bio/pelissier_christophe_4E.html (accessed September 1, 2014); Roch Samson, *The Forges du Saint-Maurice: Beginnings of the Iron and Steel Industry in Canada, 1730–1885* (Quebec: University of Laval Presses, 1998).

14. (March 9) The Cul-de-Sac was Quebec City's harbor area. The first report of a ship departing is dated April 21, when Captain Henri Laforce put a schooner under sail; April 21 entry in "Diary of the Weather kept at Quebec in the year of the siege by the Americans in 1776," *Transactions of the Literary and Historical Society of Quebec*, New Series, no. 22 (1898), n.p.

15. Continental Major General Charles Lee. Curiously, although many had been recommending Lee to be commander in Canada over the past few several months, he was only appointed to this command on February 17. Lee's marching orders, however, would be countermanded on March 1, before he ever headed north. The Continental troops were from Bedel's New Hampshire Regiment and the First Pennsylvania Regiment; see Appendix 2.

12th. Mr. Macdugalle,[16] lieutenant of this city, arrived yesterday evening from Montreal. He reports that three gentlemen[17] from Montreal left for the up country carrying beads to the [Indian] nations, to get them to commit to come downriver in the early spring to give aid to the Royalists.

30 wagons loaded with cannon mounts and bullets, muskets & other tools came downriver; 2 cannons, a 24 pounder & a 12 pounder, also went by.

15th. We learned that the two people of whom we spoke on the 7th of the current month were envoys from General Carleton to the up country, sent to advise Captain L'Arnould[18] to come downriver in early spring with the [Indian] nations.

We hear from Quebec that a certain Macuil,[19] who was close to General Arnold, escaped from the "Bostonian" camp and entered Quebec; that he brought with him all the newspapers from [New] York and the letters from Congress; that four sailors who left Quebec returned there after spending three days in the camp; that the son of Mr. Launière,[20] having left Quebec pretending madness, but really to see what was going on in the "Bostonian" camp, had been caught as he was returning to Quebec; that he is presently bound hand and foot in irons in the camp.

16. Lt. Stephen McDougall. See note to Goforth's November 22 letter.
17. (March 12) The three loyalists were Claude Lorimier, Richard Walker, and Stanley Goddard. See March 31, 1776 letter from George Measam to Alexander McDougall (below) in Goforth correspondence.
18. Captain Richard Berringer Lernoult of the Eighth Regiment, garrisoned at Fort Detroit and conferred with the regional Indians; Reuben Gold Thwaites and Louise Phelps Kellogg, eds., *The Revolution on the Upper Ohio, 1775–1777* (Madison: Wisconsin Historical Society, 1908), 128; William R. Nester, *The Frontier War for American Independence* (Mechanicsburg, PA: Stackpole Books, 2004), 76.
19. Not identified.
20. (March 15) Joseph Launière, twenty-five-year-old son of a Quebec City merchant of the same name, UMPRDH indiv. #119432; see also Badeaux's March 28 entry. Continental authorities reported Launière's arrest "for attempting as a Spy to betray our army to the Garrison at Quebec;" Frederick Weissenfels to Serjeant Westerfield, 26 March 1776, PSP, microfilm reel 13, NYPL. He is probably the same Launière listed among Canadian volunteer prisoners taken earlier when the St. Lawrence fleet was surrendered; "Mr. Walker's Statement of his Arrest and Imprisonment," April 24, 1776, *AA4*, 4: 1176.

It is also said that the people of Quebec had a wooden horse made that they placed on the walls of the St. Jean suburb side of the city, with a stack of hay in front of it and an inscription saying, "When this horse has eaten this stack of hay, we will surrender."[21]

Today 100 wagons loaded with axes, mattocks, picks, cannon mounts, bullets and other tools passed through; there were 50 "Bostonians," two 12 pound cannons and a swivel gun.

The 16th. At two in the afternoon, there was a bolt of lightning, followed by very loud thunder.

The 17th. 36 wagons loaded with firkins for the camp and 120 "Bostonians" arrived.

The 18th. St. Patrick's Day[22] The Irish among the congressional troops arriving in the city yesterday[23] marched through the city with their swords and bayonets in hand, to the sound of fifes and drums. They each had a fir branch in their hats, with the exception of the officers who each had an artificial plume. A silk handkerchief that was pierced through served as their flag. It was attached to the tip of the top of a fir tree; below the handkerchief were two crossed bayonets. They went to give a dawn serenade to the religious ladies crying "hurrah!" three times. From there they went by Mr. de Tonnancour's and, stopping at his door, they began to yell, "Goddamn this house and all that is in it," knowing that Mr. de Tonnancour was a Royalist. Mr. Godefroy, his son, who was at the window of his room when he heard them, answered, "God may forever damn you all!" They retired and went to Mr. Laframboise's who had two buckets of rum delivered to the soldiers and asked the officers to come into his home and regaled them with a half dozen

---

21. The defenders of Quebec City raised an observation tower above Cape Diamond in February 1776, topped by a crow's nest insulated with straw, giving the appearance of a wooden horse. The story of the horse and straw was credited to loyalists at Pointe Lévy, on the opposite shore of the St. Lawrence. "Journal of the Most Remarkable Events," LAC, MG23-B7, 74, 81–82.

22. Badeaux dates this entry March 18, a Monday. St. Patrick's Day was a day earlier. Presumably the entry is dated in error.

23. Goforth's March 24 letter to Alexander McDougall indicates that this was a Second New Jersey Regiment detachment, consisting of 179 men led by Major David Rhea.

flasks of liqueur. This was paying dearly for the honor done him. After noon they went to Mr. Delzene[24] to give him a morning serenade, but I don't know if they were rewarded; there is every reason to presume so, as he is a good "Congress supporter."

Today ten utility sleds loaded with firkins arrived.

The Americans' Misery in Three Rivers

The 19th. The troops asked for charity in every house in the city, saying that they were dying of hunger.[25] I gave them 4 or 5 pounds of salt pork at different times (in spite of myself). Some ten of them went to Mr. de Tonnancour who gave them food, but, not content with that, despite the cook['s resistance], they tried to forcibly take the meat on the spit. Finally they were threatened with [summoning] the commander and they left, striking the walls and doors with their bayonets a few times.

Meanwhile, the grand vicar having fed a few of them and not believing himself to be obliged to feed the whole garrison, had to close his doors so that he could eat in peace.

The 20th. 20 wagons loaded with tools of war and 30 "Bostonians" arrived.

The Americans Demand Free Labor

Today, the habitants of Saint Pierre l'Ebequet[26] arrived in the city with orders to take some baggage to the camp. Several of them came look-

---

24. (March 18) French-born Trifluvien Ignace François Delzenne, father-in-law of pro-Continental Canadian Christophe Pélissier; UMPRDH indivs. #133206 (Delzenne) and #219878 (daughter).

25. Captain Goforth does not make any particular note about starving Continental troops arriving in the city at this time, but the Northern Army was having great difficulty getting provisions (particularly barrels of salt pork) into Canada in 1776 due to mismanagement, logistics issues, and poor troop discipline. Based on Goforth's March 24 letter, it appears these troops would have been Major Rhea's detachment of Second New Jersey troops, the same men who had held their own in the St. Patrick's Day festivities, still lingering in town, see March 18 entry.

26. St-Pierre-les-Becquets (see Map 3).

FIGURE 17. *Sledge and Habitants in a Snowstorm*, by Mary Frederica Dyneley. This sort of utility sled (*traineau*), or a larger equivalent, would have been used to transport supplies at the Continental Army's request. The habitant's hooded gray capot and colorful sash were traditional Canadian winter clothing. Library and Archives Canada, Peter Winkworth Collection de Canadiana, Acc. No. R9266-187.

ing for me to ask me to go with them to the commander and beg him to exempt them from this voyage.[27] "How is it," I said to them, "that last summer, when you received orders from the King, you didn't need anyone else's help and you plainly refused to go! Today you need interpreters to beg for you? Come on, my friends, it is only natural that you suffer the effects of freedom along with us." Thus, seeing me so disinclined to render this service, they left.

The commander sent for me to interpret for him in several affairs and asked me to present his apologies to Mr. de Tonnancour for the

---

27. Habitants had traditionally been expected to perform compulsory labor service (*corvée*) for the government and/or seigneur when called, often to maintain public roads. The Continentals co-opted this custom to call on parishes for free transportation of army provisions, stores, and troops. Harris, *Seigneurial System*, 69–70; Gabriel, *Quebec during the American Invasion*, 50.

insults given by the soldiers at his home and to assure him that he had no part in all that. And assured him that if anything of the sort were to happen in the future, he should let him know and he would put everything in order.

The 21st. There was nothing new, other than a few wagons leaving the city on the commander's order to take food to the camps.

The Americans Don't Pay Their Hauling Fees

The 22nd. An habitant returning from the camp said the "Bostonians" were preparing to fire on the city of Quebec next Monday which would be the 25th, the day of the Annunciation of the Blessed Virgin. The wagons that passed through during the day of the 15th are back and they told us that they had not been paid for their travels.

A person coming from Montreal told us that Lake Champlain & the Chambly River were impassable[28] and that the "Bostonians" had lost 2 cannon that they were taking to Quebec at Pointe aux Fers.[29]

The 23rd. 60 "Bostonians" left this city for Quebec.

The 24th. We learned that Mr. Moses Hazen,[30] previously of the 44th Regiment, having obtained a commission as colonel from the Congress, raised 6 companies of Canadians[31] in the upper parishes and, having

---

28. While used as ice highways when frozen, once the ice began to "break up" with the spring thaw, the waterways became impassible until clear of ice—a period lasting a few weeks.
29. Point au Fer, New York, a large west shore peninsula on Lake Champlain, forming King Bay. It is about five miles south of the Province Line.
30. See previous journal entries on Hazen, and associated notes, May 1775 and September 22. Hazen established himself in the pro-Continental camp after he was imprisoned by Governor Carleton, put aboard a ship as a prisoner when Montreal was evacuated, and then freed by Easton and Brown when they captured Prescott's ships in November 1775.
31. (March 24) On January 2, 1776, Congress appointed Hazen as commander of a new Second Canadian Continental Regiment, with an authorized strength of one thousand men; *JCC* 4: 78. Hazen only succeeded in recruiting 477 of them, attributed primarily to the lack of hard money for recruiting and pay; LAC, MG23-B4, "The Case with Col. Hazen's Regiment," US Revolution Mss. Vol. 4, September 3, 1778.

convinced Gen. Wooster that he needed to go with his troops to meet the Indians who were coming, departed with his force, not with the intention of opposing them, but rather to join them in coming to the aid of Quebec City.[32]

The 25th. 90 "Bostonians" arrived in this city on their way to Quebec and said that there were 15,000 men at la Pointe [Crown Point][33] waiting for it to be possible to navigate the river before going to Quebec and that Gen. Wooster was to come downriver in a few days.

On the 26th, two Indians from Sault-St. Louis[34] passed through saying that there are 5,000 men, as many troops as Indians, waiting for the first possible navigation to come downriver to the aid of Quebec.

We have been assured that there is a French flotilla coming to Canada and that when it encountered some English ships, there was an engagement and the French carried the victory. This news requires confirmation.[35]

Sortie from Quebec

We learned that the ship that had been announced as being under sail on the 9th of this month, went into the lower parishes to take on food, was only traveling for three days and is back in Quebec. It is said that the people of Quebec, having made a sortie of about 400 men, killed

---

32. Although no evidence remains that Hazen was a double agent, several Continentals and "Congress-supporting" Canadians felt he was suspicious and that he did not act with sufficient zeal for the cause. Hazen was particularly notable for repeatedly advocating lenient treatment of loyalists; Sanguinet, 83; William Heywood testimony to Committee of Congress, July 1776, Julian P. Boyd, ed., *The Papers of Thomas Jefferson* (Princeton: Princeton University Press, 1950), 1: 453.

33. Crown Point was the principal southern Lake Champlain embarkation point en route to Canada.

34. (March 26) The Kahnawake (Caughnawaga) Indian mission village sat at Sault St. Louis, southwest of Montreal. Like St-François (Odanak), this community had strong pro-rebel elements, but variously cooperated with, and distanced itself from, both sides at different times during the invasion.

35. There is no factual basis for this report.

10 "Bostonians" and took 5 prisoners, after which they returned to the city.[36]

La Rose

The 27th. 35 "Bostonians" going downriver to Quebec arrived in the city. This same day, Mr. Gugy came to town to get an order from the commander requiring his miller to leave his mill, since he [Mr. Gugy] realized that he [the miller] was not acting honestly. Since he had been told to get out, he [the miller] went to get advice from Laroze, captain of Rivière du Loup, who told him, "Do not leave, because the Congress will take Mr. Gugy's mill away from him and you will keep it." Not that he thought that it would happen this way, but to trap Mr. Gugy and to gain an advantage over him. Because he thought that when the miller insisted on staying for this reason, Mr. Gugy would say something disadvantageous about the Congress and they would have reason to have him arrested, since he [La Rose] had missed his chance the previous December.[37]

The 28th. General Wooster arrived in the city and all the "Congress supporters" went to see him.[38]

Mr. Launière, Jr., who had been taken prisoner with a certain L'Etourneau when leaving Quebec, came through on the way from Quebec.[39]

---

36. Major John Brown reported being ordered to counter a large loyalist sortie on March 14, but the enemy retreated before there was a fight. There are no further details available; Howe, *Colonel John Brown*, 10.

37. (March 27) This was a reprise of La Rose's scheming against the loyalist Gugy; see Badeaux's December 4 entry.

38. General Wooster was traveling from Montreal to lead the forces at the Quebec City blockade. After the Canadian command devolved to him upon Montgomery's December 31 death, Wooster waited many weeks in Montreal—stabilizing that city's political situation, establishing province-wide policies, pleading for reinforcements, and waiting for better weather—before moving his headquarters to the front. See Goforth's January 5, 1776 letter.

39. See Badeaux's March 15 entry and associated note on Launière. There does not seem to be a record of Letorneau, but it may be that this was a nickname of François Robitaille of L'Ancienne-Lorette, who was reported in Quebec City, and was captured by Continentals upon exiting, around the same time as Launière's arrest; Frederick Weissenfels to Serjeant Westerfield, March 26, 1776, PSP, microfilm reel 13, NYPL; "Journal of the Most Remarkable Events," LAC, MG23-B7, p74.

A certain Sergeant Brown, from Connecticut,[40] who had been taken prisoner at Fort St. John's and who had deserted, also passed through. He made it to Pointe de Lévi[41] where he asked a habitant to take him across to the city of Quebec and told him he would give him 5 guineas. The habitant told him that he was going to get his rowboat, but instead warned the "Bostonians" and had him [Brown] taken prisoner. He said that there were 1,000 men[42] below Quebec ready to enter.

30th. General Wooster left for Quebec after stating that if Mr. Carleton did not surrender, he would take the city by force.

Mr. Pélissier gave him his covered carriage and driver, and two horses to take him to the camp.

60 "Bostonians" arrived going downriver and 8 officers going upriver arrived.

American Bad Faith

A few days ago Mr. Laframboise gave a grand dinner where there were several "Bostonians," among whom was a minister.[43] When the time came to sit down at the table, this minister did a kind of monkeying about [*singerie*] while blessing the table. When they left the table, Mr. Laframboise asked, "why didn't he do that ceremony again?" Mr. Sills,[44]

---

40. Brown (first name unidentified), taken prisoner of war at Fort St. John, had apparently been released on parole from Connecticut, as Continental authorities reported his subsequent arrest—"Serjeant Brown of the Royal Artillery, being Found out of the Limits, where his Parole of Honor obliged him to Remain;" Frederick Weissenfels to Serjeant Westerfield, March 26, 1776, PSP, microfilm reel 13, NYPL; and "List of persons taken in Canada, to be sent down to Hartford, in Connecticut," June 25, 1776, *AA4*, 6: 1074.

41. Pointe-Lévy was a well-populated parish and served as the primary ferry point between Quebec City and the southeast bank of the St. Lawrence. In the winter months, there was also a natural "ice bridge" across the river, spanning between that parish and the capital city (See Map 4).

42. In Verreau's published edition, historian Jacques Viger is attributed as noting, "This undoubtedly refers to Mr. Beaujeu's unfortunate expedition." See March 30 entry and notes.

43. (April 30) Based on Goforth's record of units transiting Three Rivers, in his March 24 letter to Alexander McDougall, it is very likely that this was Congregationalist Chaplain Augustine Hibbard of Bedel's Regiment (New Hampshire); F. B. Heitman, *Historical Register of Officers of the Continental Army during the War of the Revolution, April, 1775 to December, 1783* (Washington, DC: 1903), 219; *Lineage Book, National Society of the Daughters of the American Revolution* (Harrisburg, PA: Telegraph Printing Company, 1910), 31: 6.

44. See Badeaux's February 18 entry and notes regarding Sills.

who was part of the company, told him: "if you knew what he said, you would not ask him to repeat it. He said, "God, listen to my prayers; damn all the Canadians and the Royalists, let the fire of your anger fall upon this province." Laframboise began laughing most amusedly.

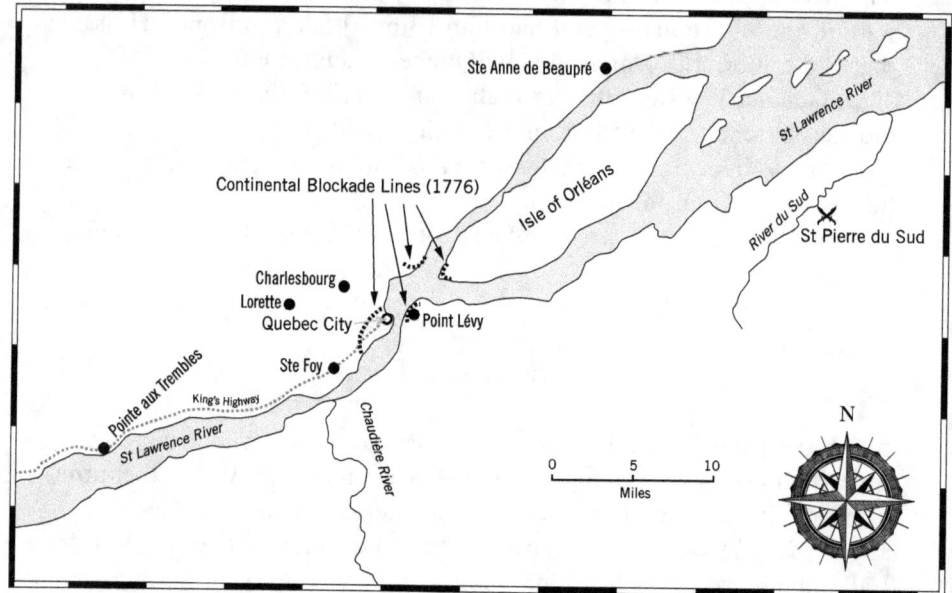

MAP 4. Quebec District.

The Curé Bailly Affair

We learn that the "Bostonians" have attacked several Canadians who had just taken over the guard at the Pte de Lévi, that they killed several, took 30 prisoners and the others escaped into the woods.[45] They say the

---

45. (March 30) Governor Carleton encouraged loyalist elements in the southeast-bank parishes below the capital to rise up against the Continentals. Loyalist seigneur Louis-Liénard de Beaujeu-de-Villemonde led a force gathered from parishes northeast of St. Thomas de Montmagny and marched for the rebel position at Pointe-Lévy. The Continentals received warning of this threat from friendly Canadians and gathered a combined Continental/habitant force to meet it. Loyalist priest, Charles-François Bailly-de-Messein ventured to the parish of St-Pierre-du-Sud to recruit additional support, when he and his detachment were surprised by the Continentals and their Canadian compatriots, resulting in a short firefight. The loyalists surrendered with three dead and ten wounded. De Beaujeu disbanded his force upon hearing of the defeat at St-Pierre, and the uprising ended. See also April 3 journal entry.

priest, Mr. Bailly,[46] and another whose name is unknown, were killed in this action. Since this news is reported in so many different ways, one can give no basis to it until we see the prisoners come upriver.

The Canadians Rise Up against the Americans

We have been assured that a frigate left Quebec going downriver to find several habitants who have revolted. It is said that thirteen parishes have risen against the "Bostonians."[47]

The 31st. Today the one called Lizotte[48] arrived from Montreal on pretext of going to Charlesbourg to see one of his children. He has a passport from Gen. Wooster. He is carrying a document for Gen. Carleton, for which reason he is offering 300 ₶ to whoever will carry it to Quebec. In this document, his Excellency is informed of the Yankees' situation and the number of the King's troops in the Colonies; 2nd, that there are 2,000 troops and Indians ready to come downriver; 3rd, that, in the parishes of la Chine, Pointe Claire and others,[49] there are several hun-

---

46. Priest Charles-François Bailly-de-Messein was not killed, but was seriously wounded. Claude Galarneau, "Bailly de Messein, Charles-François," in *DCB* 4, http://www.biographi.ca/en/bio/bailly_de_messein_charles_francois_4E.html (accessed March 15, 2014).

47. (March 30) The report of thirteen parishes was fairly accurate. After this skirmish, General Arnold sent additional troops to work with "Congress-supporting" Canadians as they pacified the southeast-shore parishes below Quebec City. There were no further skirmishes. There were also no ships operating from Quebec City's harbor yet; see note to March 9 entry.

48. Not positively identified, there are three primary possibilities: (1) There was a merchant Louis Lisot (Lixaute) with children born between 1770 and 1775 in three of the parishes surrounding Quebec City in 1773, and who also apparently enlisted as a private in Colonel Hazen's Second Canadian Continental Regiment in 1777; UMPRDH indiv. #169825; NARA, M881, Compiled service records of soldiers who served in the American Army during the Revolutionary War, 1775–1783, rg93, roll 86. (2) There was a Lisot listed as captain of the schooner *Maria*, captured as part of Prescott's flotilla off Sorel (no further identification), "Return of Military Stores on board the Vessels under the command of Brigadier-General Prescott, bound to Quebeck, November 19, 1775," *AA4*, 3: 1693; and mentioned as a prisoner in Continental correspondence, James Lockwood to Captain Hector McNeill, Camp before Quebec, April 25, 1776; Clark, *Naval Documents*, 4: 1244; and (3) Loyalist journals from Quebec City note the arrival of a "Loiseaux" on April 5, bearing a wealth of intelligence; "Journal of the Most Remarkable Events," LAC, MG23-B7, p92,; Ainslie, *Canada Preserved*, 73.

49. Lachine and Pointe-Claire were on the Island of Montreal, west of Montreal city. A little more than a month later, in May, many Canadians from Pointe-Claire joined the force of British regular troops, Indians, and Canadians that marched on Montreal from the upcountry.

dred men waiting for those from up country to go downriver with them; 4th, that 6,000 troops have wintered in Louis-Bourg, in order to come to Canada;[50] 5th, that his Excellency is exhorted not to surrender, and that the Yankee plan for taking Quebec is made known to him.—1st, they are to have General Carleton summoned to surrender and if he refuses,[51] they are to send letters by means of arrows,[51] to the bourgeois inviting them to surrender, lest their goods be taken, confiscated and sold for Congress's profit. 2nd, they are to send pretended deserters to try to corrupt the citizens of the city. If all that is not enough, they are to attempt an assault; and if they are pushed back, they are to decamp through Sault-de la Chaudière,[52] having provisions from parties in New England coming there to meet them.

This same document says that 4 of the most famous negotiators have come from London to Congress,[53] to get the Colonies to return to their senses, seeing that all of Old England is inclined to make war on them. It also alerts his Excellency, Gen. Carleton to the fact that the majority of the troops will finish their terms on the 15th of April[54] and informs him of the situation of the city of Montreal. I pray the Lord that all this knowledge may find its way to Quebec so as to engage the citizens to hold out.

---

50. There was no such army at Louisbourg, on Nova Scotia's Cape Breton Island. The French fortress, which had formerly helped guard the entrance to the Gulf of St. Lawrence, no longer existed. The British destroyed its massive works after conquering the post in the French and Indian War. William Wood, *The Great Fortress: A Chronicle of Louisbourg, 1720–1760* (Toronto: Glasgow, Brook, 1920), 136. However, a relief fleet carrying more than ten thousand British troops and German auxiliaries was crossing the Atlantic from the British Isles at this time.

51. See note for December 31 entry for previous Continental use of arrows for delivering messages over the capital walls.

52. There was no such Continental supply depot established on the Chaudière.

53. There was no factual basis to this report.

54. (March 31) In 1775, the New York troops had originally been enlisted through December 31, 1775; New York Congress "Instructions to the Officers," June 27, 1775. Shortly after arriving in Montreal, in November, General Montgomery vigorously encouraged reenlistment until April 15; Proclamation to Troops, November 15, 1775, *AA4*, 3: 1683. Many of the New York troops and some New Englanders did reenlist at that time.

William Goforth and Other Letters—March 1776

Letter: William Goforth to Reverend John Gano [forwarded to Alexander McDougall][55]

Three Rivers in Canada, March 24th 1776[56]

Dear Sir,

Since I have been in Canada, I received a Letter from you fifty days afterdate. And a few days ago, I Received your second favour, which you desired me to forward to you[r] Son, which I did by the first oppertunity, both of which I acknowledge and would were it in my power, pay with Interest. I am doubly oblidged to you for the kind Information you gave of my wife and Children. I am glad to hear she has removed to the Country. I was much distressd on her account and the Children[s']; also for my poor old mother,[57] least the Tories should have sufferd a Cannonadeing or Bombardment before they would have got moved.[58] Could I but return home and find my wife and Children well, and a Solid Basis laid for Civil and Religious Liberty,[59] I should not think

---

55. Reverend John Gano, was the head of New York City's first Baptist church, attended by the Goforths. William Goforth and his wife Catharine had been married by Reverend Gano. William Goforth's eldest daughter, Mary, would marry John Stites Gano, one of the reverend's sons. *History of Cincinnati and Hamilton County, Their Past and Present* (Cincinnati: S. B. Nelson, 1894), 480; *Daily Advertiser* (New York), 3 February 1787; Goforth Family Bible.

56. From AMP, NYHS.

57. Goforth's wife Catharine was tending to four children under ten years of age, the youngest of whom was just born on January 20, 1776. Goforth's mother Mary was living with the family, too. Goforth Family Bible; "From records kept by Mrs. Sarah Gano Burt," in Burnham, *Genealogical Records*, 72.

58. The patriots in New York City were in a tense standoff with Royal Navy ships stationed immediately offshore. A catastrophic naval bombardment of the extremely vulnerable city was always considered an imminent possibility that might be sparked by the slightest escalation by either side, and many families moved from the city as a result. Champagne, *Alexander McDougall*, 101–102.

59. Here Goforth returns to the theme of religious liberty, important to him as a Baptist dissenter from the established Anglican Church.

much to begin the world again *De nova*.[60] After our arrival at Montreal, your Son Daniel[61] was taken Sick. our Regiment Receivd orders to proceed to Quebec, which was afterwards Countermanded with respect to Capt[n] Lyons[62] Company and mine. as Capt[n] Varricks[63] Company was about to go for Quebec, to which your Son belonged, he seemd much Distresst that his bad "State of health" would not permit him to go, but at length determind to take Dada Goforth[']s advice,[64] saying he knew his father would be satisfied if he was advised by him. I Immediately told him that he was neither well Enough to go forward, nor to Return home, and therefore that he must content himself as well as possible till his health Should be recoverd, and then follow his Company, with which he complied and was very low, sometime During which period I should have been glad had it been in my power to have afforded him any consolation or assistance. However the fact was that I believe he did not want for Friends, he haveing before been so happy as to have procured the Love and Esteem of all his Brother officers. After he had in some measure recovered his health, on hearing Somethings from the Camp below which respected his Company, he came again to ask my advi[c]e whether or no[t] he should proceed. I told him he was yet weak and the weather intensely Cold, he had better wait a few days till he was better [Reenervated?]. he replied he had formerly promised to take my advi[c]e but he now believed he must be excused and Immediately determin'd and set of[f] for Quebec. I have received a letter from him since, and as I am for the present stationd at this place, being about half way between Montreal and Quebec, I hear[d] from him after and that he is well. This post at which I am stationd is looked upon as but of

---

60. Latin: "anew."

61. Lieutenant Daniel Gano, originally in Richard Varick's Sixth Company, First New York Regiment. Notably, Daniel Gano was only seventeen years old at this time; "A Muster Roll of Captn Richard Varick's Company . . . ," October 6, 1775, NARA M246, rg93, r65, f1, p45.

62. Captain David Lyon, originally Tenth Company, First New York Regiment, "SoFR." Lyon's and Goforth's companies were used to garrison Montreal as the others went to Quebec City at the end of November, see "Extract of a letter from Montreal, dated December 17, 1775," *New York Journal*, 18 January 1776, in William Goforth Letters—December and January 1, above.

63. Captain Richard Varick, Sixth Company, First New York Regiment, "SoFR."

64. As Goforth was forty-four years old at the time of the invasion, he was looked upon as a father figure by the younger officers.

Small Consequence, my business being to furnish Horse Carriages &c for the passing army, and see them supplied with provisions. however, I generally find myself very Busy all day. I have it also in my orders to call in the old Commissions given to the officers of militia in the Seventeen Parishes in the District of three Rivers by the late Governor Carleton, and to have new officers Elected. Some Seem Shy of Receiving the post, being afraid either that the ministerial troops will drive us out of the province or that we, after Carrying the Point with Great Britain, will leave them to fall a Sacrifice. But in General, they Learn to be fond of holding Commissions under the Congress (of which I am very glad). in some parishes, there have been three or four Candidates for the Captaincy, and I Received Information that Bribery and Corruption is already begining to Creep into their Elections. at some, the Dispute Runs so high that I am oblidged to Interfere. at one, I was under the necessity of going about 27 miles and superintend the Pole [*sic*] myself, haveing no way to settle it but by giving them a new Election. however, they have since declared themselves Satisfied.[65] I have Sent up about thirty names to the General in order to get Commissions under the Right Honourable the Continental Congress, which have been newly elected, and expect soon to send more. the people in General, and Especially the men are very unlearnt for which they are Real[l]y to be pitied.[66] However I hope God in his providence is about to open a door for them to Receive Instruction both with Respect to Civil and Religious Liberty. I have been Extremely Sorry that our Forces dont come forward faster. of Late, they have come up faster, but upon the whole I must say I think this department has been Neglected. I have troubled you with an account of all the fresh Forces which have past [*sic*] this post, Exclusive of those who were in Montreal, which have been nearing the seat of action. officers are included in the account.

---

65. See Badeaux's entries for February 20 and 29.
66. Only about 25 percent of the population was literate, with women generally being more educated than men; Roger Magnuson, *Education in New France* (Montreal: McGill-Queen's University Press, 1992), 91. Captain Henry Livingston observed, "Among the common people all the learning is confin'd to the women, who are sent to school when young, which the men seldom or never are not one in 20 of the latter can read;" Hunt, "Journal of Major Henry Livingston," 22.

Jan 31	Captn Seaban from the Bay Government,[67] the first Hero that Came to our assistance	25
31	Captn Smith with	19
Feb 9	Leiutenants Munson and Pettibone with part of two Company's	25
21	Leuit Walker with	17
21	Captn Wetherby with	33
22	Leuit Meacham with	12
24	Captn Hinman with	23
24	Captn Peirce with	25
24	Uzziah Wright, Gentleman Volunteer with	8
26	Leuit Sunderland with	32
26	Serjeant Clark with	20
1	March Leuitenant Loomis with	58
1	Leuitenant Talbert with the first Pennsylvania Company	60
1	Leuitenant [Dean][68] from the Bay Government with	4[8][69]
4	Serjeant Saint John with	15
4	Serjeant Gidion Brenson with	07
5	Captn Goodridge with	35
5	Leuit Frisby with	31
5	Leuit Walbridge with	49
6	Captain Gidion Dowd	48
6	Captain Wright	63
10	Leuit Hughs from Philadelphia with	60
10	Leuit Grant from New England	30
10	Leuit Jenkins from Philadelphia with	45
10	Major Safford of Col Warner['s] Regiment with	60
10	Captain Grosvenor with	42
12	Captn Jenkins with [sic] from Philadelphia, with his company chiefly passed before	08

---

67. See Appendix 2 for identification of the officers and units listed in this letter.

68. Illegible name in original is listed as Lieutenant Deane in a published version of the letter printed as "New York, May 1, Extract of a Letter from an Officer in the Continental Army, dated Trois Riviers [sic], March 24, 1776," *Constitutional Gazette* (New York City), 4 May 1776.

69. Second digit illegible in original. The version printed in the *Constitutional Gazette* (above) lists "40," however forty-eight results in Goforth's total sum of 1362.

12	Captn Colay from New England with	46[70]
16	Leuit Yard, the first of the Jersey forces with an escort with provisions	34
17	Major Ray of the Jersey Batalion	179
20	Captn Carlisle with	29
20	Leuitenant Grant with	14
22	Leuit Stone with	34
22	Captn Wait with	47
22	Leuitenant Stainer with	81

Of new forces . . .   Total amount 1362

about three hundred of Montreal Garrison moved down   300

about six hundred I suppose left after the defeat   600

according to accounts th[at] hear I can obtain Recruited by, or among Canadians[71]   500

You must make allowance for the sick and wounded at the Camp   2762

and Judge for yourself of our Army I suppose it may be among you now as it was before at St John's, you Set at home and Count Large numbers. [*Margin*: "The General's Bagage past [*sic*] this [Ms illegible] yesterday, that is General Worster, hope to Receive him at this Camp."]

---

70. "40" in 4 May 1776 *Constitutional Gazette* version, forty-six supports Goforth's total sum.

71. General Montgomery, with Congressional authority, formed the First Canadian Continental Regiment on November 19, 1775, under Colonel James Livingston. Two months later, Benedict Arnold, without authorization, directed Lieutenant Colonel Jeremiah Duggan to form another Canadian Continental regiment. Unaware of Arnold's action, Congress authorized the Second Canadian regiment later in January and appointed Colonel Moses Hazen to command, who subsequently replaced Duggan; see note to Badeaux's March 24 entry. Richard Montgomery to Philip Schuyler, November 19, 1775, PSP, microfilm reel 12, NYPL; Benedict Arnold to Continental Congress, January 12, 1776, in Roberts, *March to Quebec*, 113; January 22, 1776, *JCC*, 4: 78.

72. The Green Mountain Boys were the first anticipated reinforcements, being closest and receiving an urgent request for relief from General Wooster. The Second New Jersey and First Pennsylvania Regiments, and Porter's Massachusetts Regiment were the first units rushed north by Congressional order on January 19. These units took months to mobilize and equip, much longer than anyone expected (or hoped). Individual companies deployed when ready, leaving the regiments spread piecemeal along the almost four hundred mile route from Albany to Quebec City. Some companies were diverted to garrison Montreal, as well. *JCC*, 4: 70-73.

Perhaps you ask where are the Green Mountain Boys, the 'Bostonians,' [the?] Jersey, the Pennsylvania men?[72] That is a mystery I should be glad to have unraveld by you. I have accounted for all that has past this [post]. I think you may depend on the account and make use of it as you Please. a few officers have passd unnumberd, among which are the Colonels Warner, William, Ervin, Maxwell, Wait, and Major Morris,[73] &c. Perhaps you may think I want to Discourage you; far from it. I would be Glad to give you Every Encouragement in my power. Perhaps you ask me what I think of Quebec, and whether it will be taken or not. my opinion is that it will. I am just informd that three companys are comeing down from Montreal and some more by the River Sorrell,[74] and I expect as soon as they join the forces below, that an assault will be made. if it is taken at all, it undoubtedly must be by storm. as for the Stores Sent forward, I think nothing of them with Respect to a Regular Seige. I flatter myself that we shall take it from the Extensiveness of their works. Were it no larger than Saint Johns, I Should not think one should be able to make our entrance good, but as they are not able to man half their works, I have not the least doubt but some of the Basteens [Bastions] will be Carried with Ease if we are well formd, with Lad[d]er, &c. If you ask me Whether or no[t] we shall be able to hold it, I answer that unless the Congress are more in Earnest than they have appeard to be heretofore, I don[']t believe we shall. the most of the mens['] times for which they inlisted Expire the fifteenth April, and altho in my opinion the people of this province are humane and are Breathing after freedom, yet through the Neglect of payment for their Labour and the forcing paper money upon them, I am afraid the Congress is sinking [fast in?] their Esteem, and no wonder when we Consider that they are insulted by [Ms illegible, due to tear] soldiers in marching through the Country: a priest[']s house was

---

73. Colonels Seth Warner (Green Mountain Boys) and William Maxwell (Second New Jersey), Lieutenant Colonels Thomas Williams (Porter's Regiment, Massachusetts) and Joseph Wait (Bedel's New Hampshire Regiment), and Lieutenant Colonel James Irvine and Major Anthony Morris (De Haas's First Pennsylvania). Williams: John Fellows to Philip Schuyler, January 27, 1776, NARA, M247, rg360, i153, v1, p486; Wait: NARA, M804, Revolutionary War Pension and Bounty-Land Warrant Application Files, rg15, pension W. 2044 (William York), p25; Irvine and Morris: "Roster of Field and Staff Officers," Thomas Lynch Montgomery, ed., *Pennsylvania Archives, Fifth Series*, vol. 2 (Harrisburg: State Printer, 1906), 66.

74. The Richelieu River is also known as the Sorel.

the [other?] day enterd in a Violent manner, his Watch taken from him, &c. at another house they Ran in debt about twenty English shillings, and because the man wanted to be paid, they Ran a Bayonet through his neck. other houses have been enterd in a Violent manner with fixt Bayonets, women and Children terrified. the men, in order to get Rid of them, oblidged to furnish them with horses, Train, &c., without any prospect of pay. I have issued orders to the Captains of Militia on such future a Case to Raise their men and bring these sort of men to me.

FIGURE 18. New Jersey Continental soldier. Second New Jersey Regiment troops passing through Three Rivers in March 1776 would have generally appeared like this illustration, in blue jackets with red facings. Charles MacKubin Lefferts, Uniforms of the American Revolution: Private, 3rd New Jersey Continental Infantry, c.1910; Object #X:379, New-York Historical Society.

[Margin: "tomorrow or next day"]

If you receive this letter in new york, please to wait on Colonel macdougal with it and acquaint him at least with the part of it which Respects the Disorders of the Soldiers. it is high time the Congress should be informed of it. Should it be asked how it Can be prevented, I answer by making the men march in a Body accompanied by Every officer belonging to [the?] Company which on the account of the mens['] being entertaind in a Body Large Enough.[75] Perhaps it may be asked whether the men marched without officers or not. I answer by desiring you to look at the list I have sent you. Perhaps you may ask whether these Leuitenants are not worthy of Commissions. I answer, I think they are fine promising young Gentlemen in the General, but at the same time must say that I don't think there is one officer too many, were [Ms illegible, ink blot] the Companies full, and should be glad [if] the Captains of the Different Companies were orderd to march with them. I would not be understood that no Gentleman should be Captain of a Company who is not able to march afoot at the head of his company; let him Ride is welcome, I say, and he sometimes in front, Sometimes in rear, but always with them when going into night quarters. [I] hope strict orders of this kind will soon be given.

I am at present fat and looked to be hearty, but I have my own feelings. I have taken Several Potent Colds. in a word, I find this Champain [*sic*] has in some measure Shaken my Constitution. I feel it in my Bones and at sometimes am Scarcely able to put that Cheerfull Countenance on matters which good policy Requires. please to Remember me to all Friends, in particular to your Spouse and Children. my Best Compliments to my Daughter in law, Mrs. [Salle?].[76] [I] hope to set of[f] for home [as] soon as Quebec is taken. Please to Correct, I have no time. Excuse length—

Am Sincerely your

William Goforth

---

75. Goforth's sentence appears incomplete, but he is clearly suggesting that units only march in large bodies accompanied by as many officers as they have.

76. The reference to "daughter-in-law" Mrs. Salle (or Sulle, or Solle) is unidentified, and is clearly not a literal relation to Goforth, as his oldest son was not yet ten years old.

"New-York, May 1. Extract of a letter from an officer in the Continental Army, dated Trois Riviers, March 24, 1776," *Constitutional Gazette* (New York) Saturday, May 4, 1776

[unattributed letter from William Goforth—much of the content is similar to previous letter]

My business at this post is to furnish horses, carriages, &c, for the passing Army, and see them supplied with provisions, which business takes up almost my whole time. I have it also in my orders to call in the old commissions given to the officers of militia in the seventeen parishes in the district of Three Rivers, by the late Governor Carleton, and to have new officers elected, some of them seem shy of receiving the post, being afraid either that the ministerial troops will drive us out of the province, or that we after carrying our point with Great-Britain, will leave them to fall a sacrifice; but in general, they seem to be fond of holding commissions under the Congress; in some Parishes there have been three or four candidates for the Captaincy, and I receive information, that bribery and corruption is already beginning to creep into their elections; at some the disputes runs [*sic*] so high, that I am obliged to interfere; at one I was under the necessity of going about twenty seven Miles to superintend the pole [*sic*], and was obliged to give them a new election, with which they were satisfied. I have sent up about thirty names to the General, in order to get commissions under the Right Honourable the Continental Congress, which have been new elected, and expect soon to send more. I have been extremely sorry that our forces do not come forward faster, of late some have come up, but upon the whole, I must say I think this department has been neglected. I have troubled you with an account of all the fresh forces which have past this post, exclusive of those who were in Montreal, who have been nearer the scene of action, officers are included in the account.

[continues with listing of officers and soldiers passing Three Rivers, exactly as provided in Goforth to Reverend John Gano, 24 March (previous), minus "10 Leuit Jenkins[77] from Philadelphia with 45," which seems to have been inadvertently omitted]

---

77. Captain William Jenkins, First Pennsylvania Regiment; Montgomery, *Pennsylvania Archives*, 2: 66.

[last paragraph]

General Wooster's baggage passed through here yesterday, and I expect to receive his Excellency at this garrison to morrow. Passed by this Post also, Colonels Warner, Williams, Irvin, Maxwell, Wait, and Major Morris.[78]

Letter: William Goforth to Alexander McDougall

Three Rivers in Canada, 28th March 1776

Dear Sir,

please Examine at Leisure the inclos'd and believe me to be in great haste and with great

Respect, your

Goforth

Letter: Jonathan Brogden to William Goforth [enclosed in previous]

Camp before Quebec, 26th March 1776

Dr Daddy,[79]

I have just Time to let you know That me and my Family[80] are Arrived at head Quarters on Saturday 23rd Instant in good health, hoping you are in the same.

I am inform'd that 500 hundred [*sic*] Canadians and a few Regulars from the Garrison have Assembled to Gather 12 L[e]agues below Quebec with 2 Twelve pounders and are Getting More Formidable every day, has intersepted sume [*sic*] Provisions of ours. We have sent a party of men after them to take their standerd which the[y] have Errected and

---

78. See note above (March 24 letter to Rev. John Gano) for details of these field officers.
79. See William Goforth to Rev. John Gano (previous) for younger officers' use of "Dada" or "Daddy" when referring familiarly to Goforth.
80. Another familial term applied to fellow officers.

bring it to head Quarters. for my part I dread the Consequence, as our party dose not amount to 100 men, offr^s. included. God and he only can determin our Fate. I Think we have sent our Gundelow and sume armed Batteaux in order to intersept an armed Schooner from Quebec and the[y] are Cutting more out from the Ice, I mean the Regulars.[81] Dr Daddy Excuse hast[e], and I know your Prudence will know how to handle this Dangerous Nuse [news].

Jno Brogden

[Margin] nothing shall Escape my notice to you of all that passes and if you think me worth your notice, let me have your opinion

Letter: George Measam[82] to Alexander McDougall, Montreal

Post-Office Montreal March 31st 1776

Sir,

Since the arrival of your Regiment in this Province I have contracted an acquaintance with Capt Goforth and since his departure from this City to take the Command of Three Rivers have now and then a Letter from him. I yesterday received one from him covering a Letter to you, in which was two Letters from his Friends at the Camp before Quebec of very serious moment. He being in has[t]e and knowing General Wooster to be on his rout[e] from this to Three-rivers in his way to Quebec, enclosed them to me to peruse and communicate to the Commander here. Colonel Hazen's [Ms illegible] I believe was at that time unknown to him, as you will see by his Letter to me which I enclose you, lest you shou'd imagine your Letter has been opened without proper authority. It was opened by the Command^g Officer here, Col: Hazen for the express purpose of knowing the news as you will see by Capt Goforth's Letter to me, it was his intention.

---

81. See Badeaux's March 30 entries and notes regarding the loyalist uprising that culminated in the Skirmish at St. Pierre, and regarding ships rumored to be departing Quebec City harbor.

82. George Measam was an Anglo-Canadian supporter of the Continental cause. General Montgomery appointed him postmaster of Montreal, and later General Wooster appointed him "commissary of stores" in that city; Benjamin Franklin to John Adams, August 2, 1776, and "Petition of George Measam," August 25, 1776, *AA5*, 1: 726, 1157.

I now beg your serious attention, we have been most shamefully neglected; I know not where the fault lies, but we have neither money nor Credit, nor a third part the number of troops we ought to have, this Province must be treated as a Conquered Province for altho the Generality of the Canadians are friendly inclined, their peculiar situation as a People lately Conquered by the Brittis [sic] arms, must now be considered as Conquered by the Americans, tho it may be called a Voluntary Conquest we cannot expect much from them, nor depend on any thing.

They are a People by education averse to the resistance of the Commands of their Sovereign be they just <u>or unjust.</u> they have been wavering in opinion all winter since the unfortunate repulse of General Montgomery, and now I am sorry to see by the enclosed Letters they have, some of them turned the wrong way. Matters have not been politically managed with regard to this Province, a starved war is the most expensive, and dangerous; we now have many enemies among us which may have been made friends to the cause, had a Committee of sensible men been sent up from the Congress with some money, to regulate the po[l]ice[83] of the Country. Shou'd a small reinforcement to the Garrison of Quebec arrive I dread the consequence, shou'd this happen, or they land before Quebec, be assured the greatest part if not the whole of the Inhabitants will join them; for they now, some of them, publickly say they are drawn into a scrape and are neglected by the Congress. Besides this many of the army are returning home, their times are out and I fear they can not be prevailed on to stay; all this is discouraging to those who are inclined to be ever friends and animating and strengthening the Tory party. And besides, three rank tories Goddard, young Dick Walker and one Lorimie[r] are gone into the Upper country with intelligence (it's thought) to the 8th Regiment and the Governor of Detroit to form a body of Savages and come down;[84] something like Conoly's plan.[85] This I doubt not but you are acquainted with, their departure having

---

83. policy.

84. See Badeaux's March 12 entry and note.

85. This is a reference to a failed loyalist plot in late 1775, conceived by Pennsylvanian John Connolly. The intent was to gather Indians and Canadians around Detroit and lead them against the rebels at Fort Pitt, and then join Lord Dunmore in Virginia. John Connolly, *A Narrative of the Transactions, Imprisonment, and Sufferings of John Connolly, an American Loyalist* (London: 1783), 19–21.

been known a month or 5 weeks. This I communicate to you for the service of our cause and Country, and to manifest to you that all that the brave General Montgomery gain'd (with the loss of his life) maybe soon lost. I am a sincere friend to the cause,

fr Your most obedt servt Geo. Measam

Extracts from a Letter of Captain Goforth[86]

[original source unidentified, extract undated]

Reports are various with respect to Indians. Some say five thousand are coming down to cut off Montreal; others say they are to pass Montreal, come to Three-Rivers, and hasten to Quebeck to the relief of their father, (Carleton,) who is now confined within the walls, and must be relieved, or they will lose all their trade. Whether reality or fiction, time will soon discover. Should have written to the General [Wooster] before now about some flagrant abuses that have been committed by the private soldiers on their march to Quebeck, had I not expected to have had the honour to receive him at this place before now. A Priest's house has been entered with great violence, and his watch plundered from him. At another house they run in debt about twenty shillings, (English,) and, because the man wanted to be paid, run him through the neck with a bayonet. Women and children have been terrified, and forced, with the point of the bayonet, to furnish horses for private soldiers without any prospect of pay.[87] I have not had it in my power to discover the offenders, but have issued a proclamation. Captain Stout,[88] of the Jersey Forces, left with me a silver tablespoon, which he thinks was taken by one of his men from some inhabitants of Montreal. Please to advertise, that the owners, sending the marks, may have it again.

---

86. *AA4*, 5: 753-754. This may have been the letter enclosed in George Measam to Alexander McDougall, March 31 (previous).
87. This account is very similar to details provided in Goforth's March 24 letter to Rev. John Gano (previous).
88. Captain Joseph Stout, Second New Jersey; NARA, M246, rg93, r37, f20, p17.

April 1776

On the first of April there is nothing new other than twelve "Bostonians" who came by, beating their drums and playing their fifes.

The 2nd. Today I went to the commander's home to ask him, on behalf of the Ursuline Ladies,[1] for payment for the sick who have been in the hospital since last fall.[2] He answered that no money had arrived. I responded to him, "Sir, what do you want these ladies to do? They advance their money to nourish and heal your soldiers, and they cannot be paid. It is impossible for them to continue to take care of your sick." "Well," he told me, "tell them to have patience and they will be paid." "Well," I told him, "I am going to tell these Ladies to feed your soldiers patience; we'll see how fat they'll be." He started laughing and told me that there would be money before long.

As I was taking leave of him, he asked me why the merchants didn't want to accept congressional bills.[3] I told him that my thought was that they were not yet masters of the land and that the capital city was still the King's, and he alone could change the colony's money, and that I didn't believe that Congress could establish any exchange of money in this province until it was completely conquered. "Well then," he said, "before long we will force you to take them." "In good time," I said, "when we are forced, we'll have to do it."

---

1. Badeaux was the Ursulines' attorney, *DCB* 4, "Badeaux, Jean-Baptiste."
2. See Appendix 1—The Accounts of the Three Rivers Ursuline Nuns.
3. Continental dollars.

FIGURE 19. Ursuline Convent, Three Rivers, aquarelle by H. Bunnuff, 1826. The first convent building—with chapel, hospital, and cloister—was erected here in 1716. It was rebuilt following fires in 1752 and 1806, and was expanded and modernized in subsequent centuries. The Recollet Chapel is the structure in the left background. Bibliothèque et Archives nationales du Québec, E6 Fonds ministère de la Culture et des Communications, S8, SS1, SSS1983.

Prisoners from Mr. Beaujeu's Party

The 3rd. The prisoners from the "Bostonians'" attack we talked about on the 30th of last month arrived today, numbering 24[4] instead of 30 as had been announced. There is nothing worse or more repugnant to nature than to see poor unfortunates led by their compatriots without these latter being affected by it in the least; on the contrary, those miserable people lead them with an incomparable jubilation and as if they were leading people they had never heard of, or their worst enemies.

---

4. This may be 21 or 24 in the manuscript.

These prisoners say that they had received orders from General Carleton to come to the aid of Quebec City and that they were 500 men under the command of Mr. Beaujeu[5] who had sent 50 of them as forward guard (they were of that number); and that the people from Rivière du Sud, having gotten news of their arrival, had arrested them; and that their confessor, the priest Mr. Bailly, had been wounded.[6]

1/2 the Americans Are Sick

A certain "Bostonian" captain passing through with his prisoners and his company had a map of the city of Quebec and said it is impossible for the "Bostonians" to take it (unless it be by starvation), Quebec City being too well fortified on all sides. This captain is returning with his company to New England because he says that it is madness to want to try to take this city, all the more so since half of the "Bostonians" are sick and not in a state to be able to fight.[7]

4th. Mr. Couillard,[8] one of the prisoners, asked Mr. de Tonnancour to lend him some money, which he was very easily granted.

The 5th. 20 "Bostonians" passed through going downriver.

---

5. (April 3) Louis Liénard-de-Beaujeu-de-Villemonde was a fifty-nine-year-old noble who acted as seigneur on the Laurentian island of Ile aux Grues, northeast of the capital. He was a veteran French officer, having served in campaigns ranging from the Mississippi and Great Lakes to Acadia (Nova Scotia); David Daniel Ruddy, "Liénard de Beaujeau de Villemonde, Louis," in *DCB* 5, http://www.biographi.ca/en/bio/lienard_de_beaujeu_de_villemonde_louis_5E.html (accessed March 16, 2014).
6. See notes to March 30 entry for more details on this event.
7. This was hardly an exaggeration. Roughly one-third to one-half of Continental soldiers in Quebec were sick at any time in the spring of 1776. At the beginning of May, General John Thomas reported, "a Few more than two thousand Men, & Twelve Hundred of which are unfit for Duty, with the Small Pox, &c."; Copy of John Thomas to Benedict Arnold [May 2, 1776], PSP, microfilm reel 13, NYPL.
8. Jean-Baptiste Couillard-Després of L'Islet was the military leader of the loyalist detachment, guided by Bailly, that was defeated at St-Pierre on March 25; Louis-Philippe Bonneau, *On s'est battu à St-Pierre* (Saint-François, QC: Société de conservation du patrimoine de Saint-François-de-la-Rivière-du-Sud, 1987), 90–91, 104.

The 6th. nothing new happened.

The 7th. It is rumored that Colonel Maclean tried to desert three times from Quebec and was caught. I only transcribe this news to show the falsehoods that are brought back to us, for I do not believe this one bit; I am far too convinced of Colonel Maclean's bravery.[9]

We were also told that the cannons from atop the walls of Quebec had been turned around to face the city. I also believe this news to be false.

The 8th. Sir Belette, Sr.,[10] passed through coming from Quebec, having been taken prisoner for the second time; he says that the "Bostonians," suspecting that he had been in Quebec, had him arrested.

A courier came upriver reporting that a bombshell fired into the "Bostonian" camp by the people of Quebec had completely dismantled one of their batteries;[11] that two young men leaving the city of Quebec said that the city was not lacking war munitions or food in any way, and that there was absolutely no desire to surrender.

Two Pretend Deserters Were to Set Fire to Quebec to Facilitate the Attack by the Americans

He also reports that General Wooster had sent two of his soldiers into Quebec City, pretending to desert, and had given instructions to set a fire in Quebec; so that, while the people of Quebec were occupied putting out the fire, he could try to scale the walls into the city; that these soldiers did what they had been ordered to do and set the upper city

---

9. There is not the slightest historical support for such rumors questioning Maclean's loyalty.

10. (April 8) François Bellet, the forty-five-year-old St. Lawrence ship captain who commanded the ship carrying Montreal's powder during the flight of Carleton and Prescott. He was noted for dumping all the powder into the river before his ship was surrendered to the Continentals off Sorel in November. Sulte, *Histoire de la Milice*, 44; David Roberts, "Bellet, François," in *DCB* 6, http://www.biographi.ca/en/bio/bellet_francois_6E.html (accessed September 1, 2014).

11. Records from both sides of the Quebec City siege do not reflect destruction of a Continental battery at this time—like much of the news reaching Three Rivers at this time, it seems to be nothing more than hopeful rumor.

and the lower city on fire during the night, and that the "Bostonians" had tried to approach the walls; but that the city had burned so strongly that they had to make a disorderly retreat.[12]

This same day, 20 wagons laden with salt pork for the camp arrived, along with some thirty Yankees.

Hazen

A certain Rainville[13] came through with his wife from the upper parishes on pretext of making a vow to the great Ste. Anne [at Ste-Anne-de-Beaupré].[14] This man carried intelligence into Quebec City for our General Carleton on behalf of Mr. Moses Hazen, current commander of the city of Montreal,[15] and is charged with a letter from Mr. Carleton for the aforementioned Mr. Hazen. The man said that as soon as navigation was open, the troops and Indians from up country were to come downriver, and that Mr. Hazen, with more than three thousand Canadians from the upper parishes, were to join them in going to the aid of Quebec. May God wish it so!

---

12. Although there were deserters and pretended deserters transiting the blockade lines in both directions, this seems to be an event that occurred on March 31. The Quebec City garrison discovered that some Continental prisoners of war planned to break out of their prison and then light fires and create disturbances that would distract the loyalist defenders, to facilitate their compatriots' entry through the city's St. John's Gate. Armed with this information, Governor Carleton tightened the prisoners' confinement, and then emulated a breakout in hopes of drawing the Continentals toward the walls, where they could be fired upon. Despite presenting a fairly convincing façade, General Arnold refused to take the bait. "Journal of the Most Remarkable Events," LAC, MG23-B7, 82.

13. (April 8) Forty-two-year-old Laprairie/St-Philippe resident François-Marie Rainville, UMPRDH indiv. #167945 and family records.

14. Ste-Anne-de-Beaupré had been a significant pilgrimage site since the mid-1600s. Linda Kay Davidson and David M. Gitlitz, "Ste Anne de Beaupré (Quebec, Canada)," in *Pilgrimage: From the Ganges to Graceland: an Encyclopedia*, vol. 1 (Santa Barbara, CA: ABC-CLIO, 2002), 561.

15. When General Wooster left Montreal, he appointed Colonel Hazen as district commander. Many Canadian patriots and Continentals were suspicious of Hazen's loyalties, but there is no extant evidence that he was a double agent. Hazen went on to become a Continental general later in the war. See Everest, *Moses Hazen*.

The 9th. Two 'Bostonian' officers passed through on their way from the camp and said in passing that they were very happy to be away from it and that it was impossible for their people to take the city of Quebec.

We have been assured that the habitants of Varennes[16] have taken uniform and are ready to aid Quebec at the first sign. We learn also that the citizens of the city of Montreal mount the guard every night.

The news going around today touching on the impossibility of taking Quebec and of the aid that must come, greatly troubles "Bostonian" hearts. But it matters little; the few royalists to be found in the city give silent thanks to the Lord for all the news. Grand Vicar St. Ongé declared, and had a salvation sung, for the three Easter feasts in the church of the Ursuline Ladies, asking heaven's blessing upon our arms. The refrain, *Domine salvum fac Regem* [God Save the King], was sung there for three days.

The 10th, a habitant coming from the "Bostonian" camp says that 300 men from Charles-Bourg were ordered forward to carry ladders along the walls of Quebec, but that they refused, saying that it was useless to get themselves killed carrying ladders; that even if they were to be set against the walls, they would never be able to climb up there; and that the "Bostonians," fearing an uprising in that parish, had sent 300 guards there.[17]

This same habitant says that they are preparing a fire ship at Pointe aux Trembles[18] to burn the frigate that is before Quebec; but we are

---

16. This was another false rumor. Immediately after the Continentals' New Years Eve defeat, Governor Carleton had tried to covertly call the Varennes militia to mobilize and march to the capital's relief. That parish had been notably zealous in government service during the fall of 1775. However, Carleton's message was intercepted by the Continentals before it passed their blockade lines, and nothing more came of it. "Lanaudière, Jr. to Magné and Militia Captains, 4 January 1776, Intercepted by Arnold," *AA4*, 4: 855.

17. This appears to be another loyalist exaggeration. The Continentals certainly did not have three hundred soldiers to be committing to any individual parish at this time. Other accounts, including the Baby-Taschereau-Williams Commission report, fail to record such an incident in Charlesbourg (or neighboring parishes); Gabriel, *Quebec during the American Invasion*, 6–7.

18. The Continentals were preparing a fire ship at Pointe-aux-Trembles (Quebec District); Certificate of Charles Lee, April 27, 1780, NARA, M247, r147 i136 v4 p270. The rebels employed it on May 3 and narrowly missed the harbor.

assured that several ships from Quebec are preparing to come to Pointe aux Trembles to destroy the Yankee ships.[19]

Price and Walker

It is said that Mr. Price and Mr. Walker are held up in Congress because they are the authors of the "Bostonians'" arrival in this province, having led Congress to believe that all the Canadians were ready to welcome their troops. But today, when they see the capture of Quebec is impossible, they are blaming them.[20]

The 11th. Nothing new.

The 12th. 22 "Bostonians" who had been in the city for three days made themselves cross the channels[21] to get to the camp.

We have been told that either today or tomorrow the "Bostonians" are to attempt to take the city of Quebec by scaling the walls, due to the fact that the majority of their group complete their time on the fifteenth of this month.[22] The soldiers of this garrison also finish their time on the 15th, but Captain Goforth does not wish to let them leave until Quebec has been decided.

"Lord, God of the armies,[23] protect the city of Quebec and preserve, please, those who defend it. Great St. Joseph, you to whom God

---

19. The Quebec City defenders sent their first naval scout out in a canoe under Canadian Captain Henri Laforce, on April 17; "Journal of the Most Remarkable Events," LAC, MG23-B7, 99. The first ship did not raise sails until April 21; see note to March 9 entry.

20. General Wooster had asked Walker and Price to go to Philadelphia and present their views to Congress. See Goforth's February 22 letter to Franklin. The two Canadians were not detained in any way; however, they were never formally called to speak to Congress, either.

21. Badeaux uses the word *cheneau* here, literally channels or gutters. Presumably he is referring to points on the King's Highway where high water, slush or deep mud made traveling difficult, as a result of the progressing spring thaw.

22. See note to March 31 entry regarding the end of the New Yorkers' enlistments.

23. Note that Goforth coincidentally uses the same term "God of Armies" in his April 21 letter.

confided the care of this province by making you its patron,[24] allow them, through your intercession, to be delivered from the enemies who surround them and preserve those who support their defense, for the sole motive of God's glory and the faithfulness of our King: We beg this of you and we ask you by the love that you had for Jesus and Mary and that Jesus and Mary had for you to protect it in this moment when the enemy of our religion would make itself its master. Deign to listen to our prayers and accord us the grace that we ask of you."

The 13th. There has been nothing new. We are impatient to receive word of Quebec's fate. The lake [St. Pierre] broke-up at three in the afternoon and left nothing but a lot of noise to be made by ice chunks.

Arnold

The 14th. Absolutely no news from anywhere. At six in the evening, General Arnold arrived from the camp on his way to Montreal.[25] As soon as he arrived, he sent an express messenger to the [St. Maurice] Forges looking for Mr. Pelissier,[26] who arrived at 8:30 and dined with him, accompanied by Mr. Laframboise, Mr. Courval, Mr. Delzene[27] & others.

The 15th. General Arnold went to dine at the Forges and before leaving, hurried off an express messenger to Montreal. We have no idea why.

---

24. Saint Joseph had been patron saint of New France (now of Canada) since the early days of the Jesuits. The more commonly known Saint John the Baptist (*St. Jean-Baptiste*) was not declared patron saint of Quebec until 1908.

25. Shortly after General Wooster arrived at the Quebec City siege, General Arnold departed camp to take command of the Montreal District, relieving Colonel Hazen.

26. The St. Maurice Forges served as a center of pro-Enlightenment, Whig sentiments with both director Pélissier and inspector Pierre de Sales-Laterrière actively supporting the Continentals' republican agenda. See March 8 entry and note, Pierre Dufour and Jean Hamelin, "Sales Laterriere, Pierre de," in *DCB*. 5, http://www.biographi.ca/en/bio/sales_laterriere_pierre_de_5E.html (accessed November 24, 2013); and Pierre de Sales Laterrière, *Mémoires de Pierre de Sales Laterrière et de sus traverses* (Quebec: L'Evenement, 1873).

27. (April 14) Joseph-Claude Poulin Courval Cressé, inspector of the St. Maurice Forges during the British military regime and son of Claude Poulin Courval de Cressé; UMPRDH indiv. #162420; Samson, *Forges du Saint-Maurice*, 287, 403, 437. See note to February 18 entry for Laframboise; note to March 18 entry for Delzene.

FIGURE 20. Benedict Arnold. Library of Congress, LC-USZ62-68483.

Joseph Jutras,[28] otherwise known as The Spud, quite artfully concluded that Quebec must be taken, because, says he, there will be no relief. Mr. Baby, with his big nose, felt that no relief would come from downriver, because the King sent all his forces into the Colonies. This news is necessarily disconcerting to us, coming from two such good politicians.

We have learned that the Yankee batteries were toppled by the cannons of Quebec City.[29]

The 16th. General Arnold left for Montreal this morning at 9 o'clock. He had himself taken by canoe to Pointe du Lac, the water being too high to go by land.

The 17th. The city garrison, having finished its time the day before yesterday, left this morning at 7 o'clock, with great rejoicing.

His lordship tells us that someone from Montreal came through last week going into Quebec City and that he was carrying instructions to General Carleton, containing fourteen articles, which he put in a trouser button for fear of being caught and searched. We are impatiently awaiting this person.

It is said that Mr. Pélissier received a commission as colonel-general of the Canadian militia from General Arnold yesterday.[30]

On the 18th, a courier arrived from Montreal with a packet of letters sent in all haste by the commander to Mr. Pélissier. The same day the "Bostonian" minister, who had been at the Ste Foy camp,[31] arrived on his way to Montreal. We are told that a lot of "Bostonians" have arrived at St John's waiting to cross the lake [St. Pierre] so they can go downriver.

---

28. Probably Joseph-Claude Jutras Vallée; Roy, *Famille Godefroy de Tonnancour*, 115; UMPRDH indiv. #151889. See note to November 9 entry for Pierre Baby background.

29. Like the April 9 entry, there does not seem to be any record substantiating such effective counter-battery fire by the Quebec City defenders.

30. In November, General Montgomery appointed new militia colonels for Montreal District (François Cazeau) and Quebec District (Regnier de Roussi); Anderson, *Fourteenth Colony*, 163. Three Rivers District apparently did not have a Continental-approved militia colonel until Pélissier's appointment.

31. By context this may be the same rude chaplain mentioned in Badeaux's April 30 entry—his only previous comment on a Continental minister (probably Augustine Hibbard, of Bedel's New Hampshire Regiment).

We have been assured that General Howe has left Boston and is coming to Canada.³² The "Bostonians" say that he has left Boston, but that no-one knows where he has gone. All this is only meant to put the Canadian people to sleep; one must hope that once awakened, it would take a lot of rocking to put them back to sleep.

The 18th, a certain Brindamour,³³ a captain in Mr. Levingston's regiment, arrived from Quebec. He says that General Carleton has asked the citizens of Quebec to hold out until the 22nd of the current month and has said that then, if no help arrives, he will surrender the city. He also says that the people of Quebec have nothing but a half pint of wheat to eat each day. Since this news comes from a very unreliable source, we put no faith in it.

19th. No news from anywhere. It has been announced that a large number of "Bostonians" are coming by boat. There must truly be a considerable number since we are told that there are 500 Catholic priests with them, because, they say, the majority of the army is Catholic.³⁴ Now we're in business; there'll be no shortage of parish priests any time soon.

I forgot one event from the 14th. Mr. Courval,³⁵ after dining with General Arnold, returned home, but since the water had risen a great deal, he was unable to get there. It did no good for him to call to his servants to come get him by canoe; it was useless, everyone was asleep. He returned to Sills' to ask for a bed. Upon seeing him, the commander and a few others asked why he had come back. He told them why. Then they said: "we need to go see how high the water has risen." They went down to the shore; they grabbed Mr. Courval under the arms and dragged him through the water to his house and left him on

---

32. British General William Howe evacuated his force from Boston by sea on March 17, 1776. Howe's corps reorganized at Halifax before joining the attack on New York later that summer.

33. Jean Ménard *dit* Brindamour, who served under James Livingston as a partisan lieutenant in 1775 and then as a captain in Livingston's First Canadian Continental Regiment. In the spring of 1776 he was sent back to the Richelieu Valley to recruit for the Second Canadian Continental Regiment. Jean Menard *dit* Brindamour Memorial, n.d., NARA, M247, r41 i35 p163; Moses Hazen to Edward Antill, April 3, 1776, Haldimand Papers, LAC, MG-21, A-616.

34. There is no indication of where such a wild, exaggerated rumor originated.

35. Joseph-Claude Poulin Courval Cressé, see April 14 entry.

his doorstep to wait for someone to open the door and they left. That's the way they joke with the friends of the 'common cause.'[36]

23rd. Two couriers from the Ste Foi camp arrived within an hour of each other, coming to advise Captain Goforth to go downriver to Quebec with the rest of the soldiers here.[37]

The 24th. 200 "Bostonians" passed through by boat on their way down to the camp. They say that 2000 will go downriver tomorrow.

Regiment in the Up Country

We have learned that the King's Regiment[38] and the Indians that were in the up country have arrived at the Lake of the Two Mountains and that they are awaiting news of the flotilla arriving from lower down before coming downriver.[39] We have been assured that General Carleton has received news of the reinforcement coming to him.

The "Bostonian" Canadians[40] say that General Howe was captured when leaving Boston with 1,500 men and 15,000 piastres. We don't believe a bit of it.[41]

25th. 3 ships arrived carrying 76 "Bostonians," heading downriver. I went down to the shore to see them arrive. One of them asked me the news

---

36. Badeaux adopts the patriots' own terminology. The "Common Cause" was a popular expression in the thirteen colonies to describe their united resistance to perceived British misrule. A characteristic example of contemporary use is: "The Defence and Maintenance of our Rights and Liberties is the common Cause of every American . . . ," *Boston Post Boy*, 13 December 1773.
37. See Goforth's letter to Alexander McDougall, April 21, 1776, April 24 postscript, for Goforth's description of his orders from General Wooster.
38. (April 24) The British Eighth Regiment, also known as The King's Regiment, was stationed amongst the numerous upcountry posts beginning at Fort Oswegatchie (Ogdensburg, New York) and ranging from there around the Great Lakes.
39. Although Claude de Lorimier was traveling around the region above Montreal, no forces were actually assembled until early May, and they departed from Fort Oswegatchie (La Galette) on May 12. Lorimier, *At War*, 48–49; Andrew Parke, *An Authentic Narrative of Facts Relating to the Exchange of Prisoners Taken at the Cedars* (London: T. Cadell, 1777), 21–22.
40. Note that Badeaux now refers to "Bostonian" Canadians, rather than "Congress-supporters," perhaps indicating a higher degree of Canadian commitment to the Continental cause.
41. Another completely false rumor.

from Quebec. I told him that I didn't know anything at all. But that got me talking. I asked him if he was taking a lot of their men downriver. He asked me how I could expect there to be a lot when they hadn't been paid at all. "It's been 7 months since we were taken on, no-one had given us a penny and several of our people have even deserted. We left sixteen men from our company in Carillon."[42] "But," I said to him, "are you thinking of taking Quebec?" —"Even if," he said to me, "we were to take it, we would surely not keep it for long since there is a flotilla down below coming to the aid of Quebec." "Well then," I said to him, "what, then, is your plan?" —"My faith," he said, "I know nothing about it, we are given to hope that we will have Quebec on the 10th of May and that's all." I left him then, seeing that he had no good argument to give me.

Mr. St. Ongé, the vicar general, announced a novena[43] this morning, to ask God for his holy blessing on this province and for the preservation of our religion. This novena is to begin Sunday the twenty-eighth of the current month. The religious ladies are to join in with a communion novena.

The friends of the common cause make fun and laugh at our prayers, but we don't worry about it much. We hope that God will hear and that he will favor the King's armies; if, in any event, it pleases him to not do so, we will always have the honor and the glory of saying that we were faithful subjects of his Majesty until the end, and that we have never given our soul to the devil by becoming rebels against our King under a false pretext of oppression, as a number of our co-citizens have done.

26th. The 76 men who arrived yesterday left today for the camp. All those of "Bostonian" hearts went to see them off with much jubilation, as if they expected the success of those people to make their fortune. Since I was down at the shore, Mr Freeman, Jr.[44] came to ask me if I

---

42. Carillon was the French name for Fort Ticonderoga.
43. See note to Badeaux's October 2 entry for novena.
44. Constant Freeman Jr., son of Constant Freeman Sr. (mentioned in Badeaux's February 18 entry), offered his translating services to Captain Goforth, as soon as the New York troops arrived to establish the garrison at Three Rivers. Based on Badeaux's account, it appears Goforth elected to rely more on the notary than Freeman, although the younger Freeman reported that Goforth used his interpreting services "until the post was abandoned." After Captain Goforth declined General Wooster's offer to take on an additional duty as a commissary officer (see Goforth's letter to Alexander McDougall, April 6, 1776), the younger Freeman accepted this position. Presumably Freeman was using the "three boats" to transport army provisions. Freeman, "Record of the Services of Constant Freeman," 349–51.

could recommend someone to pilot his three boats to Quebec. I told him yes, I showed him a man who is deaf and mute and I left him. He went to ask him, but he saw that I was making fun of him, because he could never get him to understand a thing.

Mr. Hart[45] arrived from Montreal. He brings with him verification that General Howe has retreated from Boston: he says that the "Bostonians" sent ships to find out which route he took and that if he comes to Canada that General Washington is ready to come to this province with 10,000 men.[46]

At seven in the evening, a certain La Couture,[47] a courier for the "Bostonians," arrived from the camp. He says that they have armed a schooner that is going upriver and that it is now in Champlain and headed for Montreal. He also reports that Joseph Papillon[48] has been taken prisoner and put in the bottom of a ship's hold bound hand and foot in irons; he doesn't say why.

27th. A certain Blondeau[49] has arrived from Montreal saying that above Montreal there is an uproar caused by the Indians who are with the King's Regiment and that every day one can see that many people are missing from the city; they are going to join them.

We are told that two men from Montreal have entered Quebec in a rather funny way. These men had been in the "Bostonian" camp for three or four days dressed as beggars. On the last day they went up the last guard post; there they cooked a piece of salt pork. When it was cooked, one of them took it and started running away, the other

---

45. Aaron Hart, see December 4 entry and note.

46. On March 25, the Continental Congress ordered General Washington to detach four battalions (regiments) from his camp at Cambridge, Massachusetts, as reinforcements for Canada. These men would become General John Sullivan's brigade, which began arriving in June. It is not clear if Hart's intelligence was related to these orders. None of Congress's orders regarding troop movements were contingent upon Howe's destination. *JCC* 4: 236.

47. Perhaps this was Ignace Couture of Pointe-Lévy in the Quebec District, who actively cooperated with the occupying Continentals. Gabriel, *Quebec during the American Invasion*, 67–68.

48. Most likely Sir Louis-Joseph Papillon of Pointe-aux-Trembles (Neuville), UMPRDH indiv. #148778; Gabriel, *Quebec during the American Invasion*, 27.

49. Possibly Maurice-Régis Blondeau, a Montreal fur trade merchant; François Béland, "Blondeau, Maurice-Régis," in *DCB* 5, http://www.biographi.ca/en/bio/blondeau_maurice_regis_5E.html (accessed September 1, 2014).

ran after him, caught him and they pretended to squabble. The one who had the salt pork escaped and the other one went after him again. When he arrived at the last sentinel, he told him: "do me the pleasure of holding my bag so that I can run after my comrade who stole my salt pork." The sentry took the bag and so my man started running after the other one. The sentry believed him: "Run, run, you're going to catch him." Indeed, they ran so well that they ran right into Quebec, the salt pork in hand. It was quite an inventive ruse.

28th. An officer has arrived from the camp reporting that seven ships are on the way upriver and that they are on their way to pick up artillery in Montreal, in order to breach the wall in Quebec. We hope that before their battery can be readied, we will have some help.

Today our *curé* announced a grand Mass to be sung Tuesday in honor of Saint Joseph,[50] patron saint of this province, begging him to take it under his protection.

A courier from Montreal just arrived reporting that General Thomas[51] has arrived there with 2,000 men and that they will be coming downriver any day now. We will believe it when we see it since they have told us so many lies that we can't believe one word of what they say.

General Thomas

29th. General Thomas has arrived in the city. As soon as he arrived he hurried off an express letter seeking Mr. Pélissier, but just as he was leaving, Mr. Pélissier showed up. The General left immediately for the camp; he announced that 3,000 men were to come downriver.[52]

---

50. St. Joseph's Day occurred a few weeks earlier, on March 19. (See April 12 entry and note).

51. Major General John Thomas, a veteran Massachusetts provincial officer who had served under Washington in the Boston siege; Charles Coffin, *The Life and Services of Major General John Thomas* (New York: Egbert, Hovey and King, 1844). On March 6, Congress appointed Thomas to command the army in Canada, as a long-awaited replacement for General Montgomery; *JCC*, 4: 186.

52. Thomas had a brigade of four Continental battalions following him, commanded by Brigadier General William Thompson. Although the authorized strength of these units totaled 2,912—very close to the number quoted from Thomas, when they headed to Canada they mustered only 2,177; Return of the Regiments Going on Command to Canada, 17 April 1776, Horatio Gates Papers, NYHS.

30th. 13 ships arrived carrying 250 men and two 24 lb. cannons according to what we are told, but I saw them and they are 9 pounders and nothing more.

We learn that someone from this city gave the commanding officer a list of the royalists of the place, that is:

At Mr. de Tonnancour's	3	
Father Isidore and Brother Adrien	2	
The grand vicar	1	
Mr. Leproust	1	
Mr. Bellefeuille	1	16
Mr. Maillet	1	
Badeaux	1	
Stansfeld, Fraser & Morris	3	
Sir Niverville & Sir Normanville	2[53]	

This person did not give a correct list since I know many others that I will only divulge when it is necessary.

---

53. (April 30) The Loyalists listed were:

Tonnancour: Louis-Joseph and sons Pierre-André and Chevalier Charles-Antoine; Roy, *Famille Godefroy de Tonnancour*, 59; UMPRDH couple #27458;

Recollet Father Superior Charles-Antoine Isidore Lemire *dit* Marsolet and Recollet Brother Adrien, and Vicar General Pierre Garreau *dit* St-Ongé. For biography of Brother Adrien Pelletier *dit* Antaya, see Odoric-Marie Jouve, *Dictionnaire biographiques des Récollets Missionnaires en Nouvelle-France, 1615–1645 et 1670–1849* (Montréal: Éditions Bellarmin, 1996), 775.

Antoine Claude Leproust (see extended November 21 entry regarding Loiseau's searches and seizures, and note).

Presumably seigneur François Lefebvre Bellefeuille, father of Antoine Lefebvre Bellefeuille (see September 10 entry and note); UMPRDH indiv. #138819; David Lee, "Lefebvre de Bellefeuille, François," in *DCB* 4, http://www.biographi.ca/en/bio/lefebvre_de_bellefeuille_francois_4E.html (accessed September 1, 2014).

Notary Louis Maillet, see November 17 entry and note.

Joseph Stansfield, merchant and possibly seigneur.

Malcolm Fraser, merchant, see November 17 entry and note.

William Morris, merchant, who had joined Badeaux on his Montreal trip to visit General Montgomery, see extended November 9 entry and note.

Chevalier Joseph Boucher de Niverville, see November 17 entry and note.

Seigneur Joseph Godefroy de Normanville; Roy, *Famille Godefroy de Tonnancour*, 105.

Someone came to tell me this, telling me that I was of the number. I answered that that didn't bother me a bit; on the contrary that the name royalist did me honor and that I would be mortified if anyone thought differently of me.

We just learned that 8 days ago, Colonel Maclean made a sortie from Quebec with 18 armed boats; that he attacked the Foulon guard,[54] pushed it back and took 9,000 rations from the enemy; that will help them survive until help comes.

45 "Bostonians" who had finished their time came upriver. They said that two men had deserted from their camp in Quebec and that Captain Pepper[55] was to have surrendered to Quebec with a boat filled with supplies, but as he had been found out, the "Bostonians" had taken him prisoner.

Belette's schooner[56] came through at 6 o'clock in the evening on its way to Montreal. There are several "Bostonians" aboard who have finished their time and are returning to New England.[57]

---

54. Neither Continental nor loyalist records indicate that any raid occurred around this time. The landing point of Anse au Foulon, below the Plains of Abraham, was also known as Wolfe's Cove. The only related activity around this time occurred on the evening of April 21, when Canadian militia captain Henri Laforce hauled out a provincial schooner from its winter storage, drawing fire from the Continentals; see note for March 9 entry.

55. Captain Samuel Pepper commanded the schooner *Polly*. He had been coerced into British service in 1775, and his family stayed in Quebec City, while Pepper sailed the St. Lawrence. After the ship was captured off Sorel on November 19, 1775, the Continentals employed Pepper as a captain, as well. General Wooster had plans to give Pepper more prestigious naval commands in the spring of 1776, until the captain was caught sending his son into the capital with intelligence, and was arrested. Christopher Prince, *The Autobiography of a Yankee Mariner: Christopher Prince and the American Revolution*, ed. Michael J. Crawford (Washington, DC: Brassey's, 2002), 38–39, 73–74; April 10 entry, "Journal of the Most Remarkable Events," LAC, MG23-B7, p96.

56. (April 30) The Continentals were using the schooner *Magdelaine*, property of Captain François Bellet, which had been captured in government service by the rebels at Sorel in November. See April 8 entry and note.

57. With many men's enlistments expiring on April 15, General Wooster enforced strict orders to control their departure and enforce discipline on their return march, including a requirement that they wait for ships to transport them upstream to Sorel or Montreal; April 14, 15, and 18 orders, Doyen Salsig, *Parole: Quebec, Countersign: Ticonderoga, Second New Jersey Orderly Book, 1776* (London: Farleigh Dickinson, 1980), 76–77, 80.

William Goforth Letters—April

Letter: William Goforth to Alexander McDougall

Three Rivers in Canada, 6 April 1776[58]

Dear Sir,

I received your favour of the 8th February, by which I found myself under several new obligations to you and first for the great Care and kindness Shewn to my wife and family in perswading them to move at the time it was expected the Town would have been attacked by the men of war[59] &c., and for every Species of Intelligence, Such as that Ten Batalions were orderd for this Province,[60] The arrival of the Salt Peter, Powder and Arms &c. Since my arrival at this place, I have lived Considerable happy among the people in this District and made Considerable progress in calling in Commissions, given out by the Late Governor Carleton and also in geting new officers Chosen for the Different Parishes of Militia. Some have been Served with new Commission and would more of them had it not been for the multiplicity of business which Crowds upon the General. As He has no press,[61] he

---

58. From AMP, NYHS.
59. See Goforth's comments in his March 24 letter to Rev. John Gano, and notes.
60. By Congressional resolution, nine regiments (battalions) were directed for Canadian defense. Three were already in Canada: Livingston's First Canadian Regiment and two new regiments that would be formed from the remnants of the 1775 Northern Army. The First Pennsylvania and Second New Jersey were ordered to speed north as expeditiously as possible, while New York, Connecticut, and New Hampshire were to send one regiment each, and Pennsylvania was to send a second regiment as well. After news of Montgomery's defeat reached Philadelphia, Congress directed General Washington to send an additional regiment to Canada from his camp at Cambridge, Massachusetts, and also authorized the second Canadian regiment that Arnold had already started to recruit. However, Congress gave command of the new unit to Colonel Moses Hazen; 8, 19, and 20 January, *JCC*, 4: 39-40, 70, 75.
61. Among other headquarters duties, General Wooster's small staff was forced to hand-print all the new militia commissions; the only printing press in Canada at the time was in Quebec City. Congressionally supported French immigrant Fleury Mesplet arrived with his press in Montreal on May 6; Jean-Francis Gervais, "Brown, William," *DCB* 4, http://www.biographi.ca/en/bio/brown_william_4E.html (accessed September 27, 2014); Claude Galarneau, "Mesplet, Fleury," *DCB* 4, http://www.biographi.ca/en/bio/mesplet_fleury_4E.html (accessed September 27, 2014).

has not half Clerks Enough. I believe we shall soon take Quebec (altho I am Sorry no more forces are come forward) but I take for granted that we shall take it, I also take it for granted that we soon shall have ministerial Troops arrive here and therefore am of opinion it may be [Ms illegible] Great advantage to have the malitia well settled and put under the direction [of] good Field officers.

    I shall now make bold to hint Some things to you which I think absolutely Necessary to be done. and upon the Supposition that we get Quebec, I am of opinion it will be necessary to have a number of Bomb proofs in different parts of the Town, by means of which the men may be Secured, and also that it will be Necessary to have a magazene with warlike Stores and provisions Sufficient to Stand the Seige till the Severity of the Season forces a retreat. Besides this, it will be Necessary to have Such a Respectable army that we may be able to Sally out, other wise the Enemy will make themselves master of some advantageous peices of Ground by means of which they may be able to keep footing in the province and Terrify and Gall the Inhabitants to such a degree that all Communication between the lower Colonies and our Army may be entirely Cut-of[f.]

    It is Generaly looked upon that Quebec is a place of Such Strength that it is a Barrier Sufficient to prevent any Vessels of war from comeing up the River, but it must be rememberd it has been passd and may be again. and from the best accounts I can obtain, I think from the Consideration of the h[e]ight of of [sic] the works from the Surfice of the water, that it would be no great Risque with a flowing Tide and fair wind to attempt it in a dark night. Should Such an Event take place, I must inform you it would be in the power of one single twenty Gun ship to destroy the Towns of Montreal and Three Rivers, together with the most of the Vilages on each side of the River for above one-hundred and Eighty miles—or Subject the people to any Contribution they please to call for, Either of men or money. perhaps, you Enquire how this shall be remedied?; I [c]onsider very Easily by Erecting a Battery of about twenty peices of heavy Cannon at Rich[e]lieu Rapids[62]—a place about forty five miles below this, the Channel is very narrow and near the shore, and So difficult that it must have day light or a very Clear night

---

62. The Richelieu Rapids confined St. Lawrence passage to a very small corridor, for a long stretch near Deschambault, about thirty miles above Quebec City (see Map 3).

to pass it. here the Tide never sets up, at most only by Swells, and in Common Requires a Breeze of Six or Eight knots to Stem the Current. The Channel Runs on both Sides of the River before this Town, that is three Rivers, but about a League and a half at a place called Cape Magdaline, they both Unite and fall in near the North Shore where a Battery might also be usefull. a few days since, the Captain of malitia for this Town[63] and a number of other Gentlemen who are, as I believe, our hearty Friends, took a walk to Shew me the Channels, and are very desirous that Something of this sort should be done for they are greatly affraid of falling a Victim to ministerial Vengence and Especially those who are noted for haveing taken Commissions under the Right Honourable the Continental Congress.

Montreal is the highest that the men of war Can pass up the River. it is a Large Town fenced with a thin stone wall Sufficient if well man[ne]d to keep of[f] any number of musketry, but would be little more than an Egg Shell Before the Guns of a Sloop of War. here are no Warfs and the Channel is so near that the Shiping lays with their Heads to the shore to unload. here a battery might be built to great advantage (in my opinion) between the wall and the water Edge, which might be well Coverd by a breast work man[ne]d with mus[ket]ry on the high Land in the Town.

I hope you will Excuse my being so tedious and make allowance for all Erasements and interlineations. I have not time to Coppy. I hope you will not take these hints amiss, perhaps you may say it does not come from the proper Channel, that is should come through the medium of the General, and that I ought to have used my influence with the general and that the information should have come from him. think of my Distance. I spoke [to] him when he passd Here the 30th March.[64] I believe he Does not Disapprove of it, but his great haste would not permit him Leisure from my arrival the 9 Feb to the 30th march. I had from my duty to attend Disputed Elections, to Supply the passing army, the Care of the barracks, and being obliged to do the Duty of a Quarter master and Commissary. [I] had imploy Sufficient and my share of Toil and no assistance but your son, who is a good Lad. However,

---

63. The Three Rivers city militia captain was Jean-Baptiste Fafard *dit* Laframboise, frequently referenced in Badeaux's journal.

64. See Badeaux's entries for March 28 and 30.

on the General[']s arrival I thought my self greatly rewarded to have his approbation, and perhaps finding I stood well with the people, he in order to keep me in this post, offerd to give the additional pay of Commissary.⁶⁵ I thanked him and I told him I should not leave the Garrison suddenly, but hoped when Quebec was taken, [*sic*] hoped to Return with his approbation. [I] told him also that I made it a point never to ask for any post. that I had never ask[ed] to Come here, nore I should not ask to go away, but if his honour should be pleased to order me down, I should be proud to wait on him. he very merrily told me he was a going down to try if he could not take Quebec, and that if he found he could not take it without me, he would send for me. I had the honour to spend the Evening of the 29th March with him, and in my turn was calld on for my Toast, which was that the General might speedily enter the Gates of Quebec with Tryumph, which he did not fully agree with, Saying for his part he was determined to go over the wall. — Give an Extract of a letter from the Camp below from a particular Friend. You'll please to observe, that by the General's Return of the Army, Canadians included, we have

	2475
of them Sick	786
	1689

Six hundred and odd fit for duty, the Remainder of them at different posts 30 and 40 miles Distant. in this account he says the officers are included.⁶⁶

Just now, young Mr Maccord⁶⁷ arrivd from Camp and brought your letter to [interlineation] 7th march with one inclosed to your son with

---

65. Before leaving Three Rivers, Wooster appointed patriot refugee, Constant Freeman Jr., as the "Issuing Commissary;" Freeman, "Record of the Services of Constant Freeman," 350.

66. Probably from fellow New York captains Gershom Mott or Jonathan Brogden, both of whom had previously sent Goforth intelligence from the camp at Quebec. In Goforth's letter to John Jay two days later (April 8), the captain refers to the source as a "brother Captain."

67. Jonathan McCord or one of his sons. The Northern Irish–born McCord was one of the principal leaders of Quebec City's antigovernment "British Party" committee, and was exiled from the capital by Governor Carleton's November 22 proclamation that required armed service for the city's defense against the rebels. Anderson, *Fourteenth Colony*, 169.

a bill of Credit. the Gentlemen informd me that in a Return made by Colonel warner,[68] he had but 92 men fit for duty in his Regiment. I dont tell you this to Discourage you Respecting the Expedition, but to shew the necessity of pushing on the fresh Troops. the Camp is Generally healthy Except the small pox.[69]

Mr Maccord left Quebec Wednesday and says the batteries were just ready to open,[70] and notwithstanding every Discouragement, they were in high Spirits. I hope it will not belong [sic] before I shall leave the Ground with Common Credit, but in the mean time [subscribe?] myself as in Reality I am with the utmost Respect your most obedient, and most humble Servant,

William Goforth

[Enclosure] An Inventory of the Effects belonging to Capt Jacob Cheeseman,[71] Deceasd, taken at Holland House Head Quarters before Quebec, January 11th 1776

Present:
Major Zedtwitz, Capt Mott, Lieut^s Aorson, Platt & Vanwagenen,[72] viz.
Cash Twenty One half Joes, 21 pr of twelve Coprs} £ 67.6.10
                                                 Being }
One silver Table & six silver Tea spoons

---

68. Colonel Seth Warner, Green Mountain Boys.

69. Again, this is quite an understatement by Goforth. According to a report made on April 6, the same day as this letter, about 800 of an estimated 2500 total troops in the Continental Quebec camp were sick, most of smallpox. Samuel Chase to John Adams, April 21, 1776, *LoD*, 3: 568.

70. With the ground frozen solid by the time Montgomery's army arrived outside Quebec City at the beginning of December, Continental soldiers had been unable to dig earthworks for proper artillery batteries until the thaw began.

71. Cheesman, originally from the First New York Regiment had served as an aide to General Montgomery, and died from the same cannon blast that killed his commander in the December 31 attempt on Quebec City's Lower Town.

72. These were all officers originally from the First New York Regiment who had joined General Montgomery's corps traveling from Montreal to blockade Quebec City at the

One pr silver shoe, & One pr paste Knee buckles
One Pack of Blank Tickets
One Bundle of Packets unexamin'd
One Red Morroco Pocket Book Containing sundr
One Green Regimental Coat
One Beavour Hat with a Gold Band, Button Hoop
Three pr Woollen stockings
two pr. Woorsted D°
One pr New Leather shoes
seven White Shirts
One pr White Breeches
three thin Vest coats
Three Black silk stocks
Eight White stocks
One Red silk sash
four pr. silk stockings
Three pr. thread D°
two Diaper Table Clothes
two Diaper Napkins
four white Linnen Night Caps
two Pillow Cases
two White Sheets
A suite of Check Camp Curtains
One pr. of Boots, Spurs &c.
One Brown surtout Coat
One Cutteuax de shase, the property of Commodore Smith,[73] said
    Commodore having Capt Cheeseman's

---

end of November: Major Herman Zedwitz; Captain Gershom Mott (originally Seventh Company); First Lieutenant Aaron Aorson (originally in Cheesman's Fifth Company); Second Lieutenant Richard Platt (originally in First Company—Weisenfels); Gerrit Vanwagenen (originally Eighth Company—Quackenbos); "SoFR."

73. *Cuteaux de chasse,* or hunting knife belonging to James Smith, captain of the sloop *Enterprise* on Lake Champlain, who signed as "Commodore Smith" in his August 1, 1775, letter to General Schuyler; "Paper delivered Major-General Schuyler by Captain Smith," *AA4,* 3:14. Smith probably traded or loaned his presumably better knife to Cheesman, who would be going ashore in Canada.

FIGURE 21. John Jay. Library of Congress, LC-USZ62-95399.

Letter: William Goforth to John Jay[74]

Three Rivers in Canada, April the 8th 1776[75]

Honoured Sir,

I Haveing been orderd by his Excellency General Wooster on the 2d Feb. with a Small party to take the Command of this place, I have hereby had an Opportunity to take an Exact account of all the Fresh

---

74. John Jay was one of New York's delegates at the Continental Congress, and Goforth previously served with him in New York City's Committee of Sixty and Committee of One Hundred; Thomas Jones, *History of New York During the Revolutionary War*, vol. 1 (New York: New York Historical Society, 1879), 479, 488.

75. The Papers of John Jay, Columbia University, Butler Library, Rare Book and Manuscript Division, Jay Papers ID: 5611. Available online at http://wwwapp.cc.columbia.edu/ldpd/jay/item?mode=item&key=columbia.jay.05611 (accessed October 10, 2014).

Forces which have passd this place Since the defeat at Quebec, which I make bold to transmit you, as also what I Supposed a few days ago to have been the number of our Army at the Camp before that place.

Fresh Forces officers included, which past this Post Since the defeat..	1772
I Imajined those which moved from the Garrison at Montreal before I arrived here to be................................	400
and that the Number of well, sick and wounded after the defeat to be..	500
and the new Recruited Canadians to be according to the best accounts I could get to be..............................	<u>500</u>
Total.	<u>3172</u>

But on receiving a Letter from a Brother Captain[76] a few days ago, I was oblidged to Conclude I was wrong Somewhere, or else that great Numbers must have died, an Extract of which I send also, and is as follows; You'll please to observe says he that "by the General Return of the army, Canadians included, we have 2475. 786 of them Sick, six hundred and odd present fit for duty, the Remainder at different out posts, Some of them 30 & 40 miles Distant; this is the State of our army, officers included," and after mentioning Some other things, he says "To insure Certain Ruin, the officers of the Different Provinces, are Continually Stigmatizing Each other.[77] And again Seventy odd men less this day fit for duty than there was two days ago." I mean not to Reflect and was I disposed so to do, I know not on whom I should lay the Reflection, but Cant help Saying I am Extremely Sorry this department had not had greater attention paid to it, and been better Supplyd with men. had we had the number of Men which it was reported we had last Summer, the Bussiness would have been finishd. But instead of the talked of thousands, I believe Colonel Fleming,[78] the D.A.G., Can tell you that when he wanted men he could not Sometimes Call

---

76. Probably Jonathan Brogden or Gershom Mott. See note to Goforth's letter to Alexander McDougall, April 6, 1776.

77. Whenever the Northern Army faced a combination of stress and inactivity, New Englanders and New Yorkers chafed on each other. There were episodic reports of such interprovincial tension for the entire invasion, from the earliest stages of the Richelieu campaign through the siege of Quebec City and the withdrawal from Canada (and beyond).

78. Colonel Edward Fleming, Deputy Adjutant General of the Continental Army; September 14, 1775, *JCC*, 2: 249.

on more than Eight hundred fit for duty. Had we been properly succoured this Spring, the Town of Quebec might have been Stormd without Risque of great Loss. However we have heard Ten Batalions are Comeing for this place and perhaps by this time you may have heard they are arrived. But where they Stay I know not. It may be, you ask, where are the Pensylvania men, the Jersey men and the three thousand Green Mountain Boys? thats a question I Cant Answer, but this I Can tell you that on the sixth Instant, young Mr. Maccord,[79] on his way from Camp to Montreal, Calld to see me and told me a return was made of the Green Mountain men under Command of Colonel Warner and that only 92 were Returned fit for Service. Upon a Supposition that Quebec Should not be taken before the arrival of the Ships of War,[80] I Should on that Score be much Concernd for our little Army and for the poor Canadians who have taken part with the United Colonies, for in my Opinion there would be great Danger of the Communication being Cut off between the Southern Colonies and this, in Consequence of which our little neglected Army must fall into the hands of our inveterate Enemies and the poor Canadians [sic] and if so the Poor Canadians must by a Natural Consequence fall a Victim to Ministerial Vengeance of which they are greatly affraid. But upon the Supposition that Quebec Should be taken (which I would rather Choose to believe) I hope you will not then Conclude that all is over and that this Country is then fully Secured. I well know that Quebec is Generally looked upon to be a place of Such Strength as to make it a Barrier Sufficient to prevent any Vessels Passing by it. but it Should be rememberd that it has been pass'd by Vessels of war and may be again. And Should one Single twenty Gun Ship Get up the River, it would be in the power of the Commander to destroy the Towns of three Rivers and Montreal, together with most of the vilages on both Sides [of] the River Saint Lawrence for one hundred and Eighty miles On the one hand, the Towns and Vilages must be destroyed, or on the other, the People must [be] Subject to any Contributions Either of men or Money that might be Calld for, not a Single Battery being Erected for the defence of any of the Towns or Vilages. At Montreal

---

79. See note on McCord in William Goforth to Alexander McDougall, April 6, 1776.
80. The Royal Navy was expected to bring a British relief army into Canada as soon as the St. Lawrence was clear for navigation, estimated to occur around the first week of May.

a Battery might in my Opinion be Constructed for its own defence. The Channel Before this Town of three Rivers puts down on both Sides of the River, but at Cape Magdline, about one League and a half below ther[e], the[y] Unite and the Channel Sets Close in with the North Shore, where a Battery might be So Constructed as to prevent any thing perhaps from Passing. But the best place in the River is at Richleiu Rappids, a bout 45 miles below this place, there the Tide never Sets up, at most only Swells. the Channel is narrow and near the Shore and is so difficult that they must have a good Pilot and day light or a very Clear night to pass it and what would make that place more advantageous is that the Rapids Sets down So Strong that it requires a Breeze from 6 to 8 Knots to Stem the Current. if a Battery was well Constructed at this place of about 20 peices of heavey Cannon and put under the Command of a good Officer and men Sufficient to defend the works, I allow it would answer Every purpose for all places above it and in my opinion be a greater Security to the upper parts of the Country than Quebec. Again if Quebec is taken, of other things, Will Immediate Call for you[r] attention, a printing Office is much wanting, which if put under the direction of a prudent man that understands French and English and orderd to publish Every thing in both Languages would, I doubt not be of great use to the Cause of Liberty.[81] the different Posts for Indian trade will [want] for your direction also, and Cant help thinking the Supplying the Indians this Summer is a matter that deserves Serious consideration. on the one hand if they are Served with Amunition they may Use it against us, on the other, if they have it not they have been so long out of the use of Bows and Arrows that they must Starve, which doubtless they will try in time to prevent.[82] and if possible Something ought to be done to divert the trade of the merchants in Canada, for altho the most of them are as fond of freedom as you are below and have petitioned against the

---

81. Coincidentally, on February 26, Congress authorized French immigrant Fleury Mesplet to travel from Philadelphia to Montreal with his printing press and complete shop, to serve as a printer in support of the Continental cause; *JCC*, 4: 172.

82. General Wooster decided to prohibit the upcountry Indian trade for military reasons, but also encouraged Montreal merchants to consult Congress for its approval. They sent Benjamin Frobisher with a petition as their sole representative, received in Congress on March 4; Philip Schuyler to President of Congress, February 20, 1776, *AA4*, 4: 1215; *JCC*, 4: 182.

Quebec Bill, yet they [cannot] be easily taught to Sacrifice their trade, as our friends below have done, and you may depend upon it one great Reason why we have so many Tories is Because the dread to Shut their Stores.[83] The Establishing Regular Courts of Justice is much wanted and ardently Calld for by many of the best people.[84] It may be you might be willing to have my Candid opinion Respecting the taking [of] Quebec. I believe we Shall take it and I as Candidly must tell you that I believe we Shall as Soon lose it if we are not better Reinforced with men. if we do not take it, it will be for want of men and if we do not keep it will be for want of Secureing the Passes of the River. I had the Honour to Spend part of the Evening of the 29th March with General Wooster and in my turn was Calld upon to give my Toast which was that the General might Speedily Enter the Gates of Quebec with Tryumph; with this he did not Seem fully to agree and Said for his part he determin'd to go over the Walls. Seemd in high Spirits and on being informd of the Rumpus with the Tories below,[85] Seemd not to regard it and gave me Express orders if any difficulty Should arise in this district to Stop as many men as I thought proper, Saying he was afraid of haveing too many men below. I have Stop[ped] none yet, neither Shall I till he is better Supplied, unless the necessity Should be very pressing. this District Laying between the army of Quebec and Montreal I Conceive to be the Quietest part of Canada at present. on the fourth Instant Lieutenant Witcom[86] arrived here from Chamble,

---

83. As early as the spring of 1775, Montreal merchants had already made it clear that they could not participate in the United Colonies' Continental Association non-importation/non-exportation restrictions on British trade; Committee of Montreal to Committee of Safety of Massachusetts, April 8, 1775, *AA4*, 2: 305–306.

84. General Montgomery's November 12, 1775, response to Montreal's proposed articles of capitulation promised, "Speedy measures shall be taken for the establishing courts of justice upon the most liberal plan, conformable to the British Constitution;" *AA4*, 3: 1598. Preoccupied with military concerns, Montgomery and Wooster never succeeded in establishing a functional Canadian civil government, to include courts of law.

85. Goforth is referring to de Beaujeu's uprising and the Skirmish at St-Pierre-du-Sud. See Badeaux's March 30 and April 3 entries and notes.

86. Lieutenant Benjamin Whitcomb, Captain Samuel Young's Company, Bedel's New Hampshire Regiment; NARA, M804, rg 15, pension R.863 (John Bishop). In the summer of 1776, after the Continental withdrawal back to Ticonderoga, Whitcomb would achieve some notoriety—and earn a promotion to Major—for fatally wounding (or some said "murdering") British Brigadier General Patrick Gordon, whom he encountered while on a scouting mission behind enemy lines on the upper Richelieu River. Cubbison, *Northern Theater Army*, 177–78.

by the way of the Parish of S^t ours,[87] and acquainted me that the Captain of the malitia of Said parish desired him to leave a Small party of men there, that he was endangerd by Executing orders in favour of the Congress. this was Confirmd by our Express who arrived last night with another party, with the addition that the Tories were as privately as they Could, inlisting men in order to fall in with the Tories if we faild at Quebec. this parish of St Ours Laying in Colonel Hazens District,[88] I Immediately Sent a letter to inform thereof, who I doubt not will Soon give a good account of them. the Minds of the Canadians Seems to be fret[t]ed and wavering and begin to think our hand full of men not Sufficient to protect them from Ministerial Vengence. as to fighting for us, we need not Expect them any further than they think we dont Stand in need of them. if we Should miss takeing Quebec depend upon it, they will be panic Struck, and to Save appearances, Secure their Estates and prevent their families from being Butcherd, Join in helping to drive us out of the Country. I hope you will Excuse Every freedom I have Taken. I only mean to Give you a true State of facts. I hope also you will not Consider any thing I have Said as intending to Discourage the Carrying on the war in this province. So far from any thing of that Sort, that I am of Opinion it would be better for the back Settlers in the Lower Colonies to Support the war in this province by a Special tax on themselves than to lose it as a Barrier. I hope Quebec will Soon be ours, that I may get permission once more in an honourable way to Return to my family. I[n] the meantime Beg Leave to Subscribe myself as in Reality I am your most obedient and most humble Servant

William Goforth, Captⁿ in the first Batalion of the New York Force

[P.S.] one thing I beg as a favour of the Congress and that is that as Soon as the Season is proper they would Issue forth a decree ordering

---

87. St-Ours Parish on the Richelieu River, was about ten miles from the St. Lawrence (see Map 2). This report was particularly concerning to Continental leaders since that region had provided strong support to their cause in 1775.

88. When General Wooster departed Montreal to join the Quebec camp, he appointed Canadian Continental Colonel Moses Hazen to command the Montreal District. David Wooster to Moses Hazen, March 23, 1776, NARA, M247, r71 i58 p389.

all the Doctors in America to propose to New england and Anoculate all its inhabitants for the Small Pox, the want of which being done has almost Broke up our Army and Cost many a brave man his life.[89] otherwise the Camp is tolerable Healthy.

Letter: William Goforth to Alexander McDougall

Three Rivers in Canada April the 21 1776[90]

Honoured Sir,

By this Opportunity I hand you my best Respects, and what I expect will be more pleasing, Return you your baby Son. hope you may both Meet in good Health. We have lived happy together and when I think of parting and Especially at this time, it gives me some feelings that are not the most happy. However, when I Sympathize with his Filial Effection and Reflect on several strokes in different letters which I have had the Honour to Receive from you, by which I know you Expect him about this time, and the frequent Intimations which I which I [sic] have given him of my determination to Return the 15 April. My men['] s times being now Expired and I thereby Reduced to the Necessity of Stop[p]ing a Party of men (for which I am fully Impowered by the General to any Number which may appear to me to be Necessary) to Garrison this place, and knowing it to be good Policy to stop an Officer with them, have upon the whole thought it my Indispensible duty to advise him to Return without me, which I have done without any Importunities from him. I shall again give you an account of what by my Calculations should be the state of our Army below.

Fresh Troops that have past [sic] this post since the defeat 1794
Supposed to have moved from the Garrison at Montreal
    before I arrived here 400

---

89. As Goforth notes in his next letter (April 21, 1776), smallpox and other diseases affected 786 of 2475 Continental troops at Quebec. See also Ann M. Becker, "Smallpox in Washington's Army: Strategic Implications of the Disease During the American Revolutionary War," *The Journal of Military History* 68, no. 2 (April 2004): 381–430 and Elizabeth A. Fenn, *Pox Americana: The Great Smallpox Epidemic of 1775–1782* (New York: Hill and Wang, 2001), 39.

90. From AMP, NYHS.

Supposed to be left on the Ground after the defeat of well, sick and wounded	500
Supposed to be inlisted of Canadians from the best accounts I could obtain	500
Total	3194

But on receiving a Letter from a friend dated at Head quarters before Quebec the 31st march, I was oblidged to Conclude Either that I had been wrong in my Calculation some where or that a Considerable Number must have died, an Extract of which I give you and is as follows. You will please to observe that by the General Return of the army, we have 2475; 786 of them are Sick. Six hundred and odd are present fit for duty, the Remainder at different out posts, some of them 30 or 40 miles Distants. (since the date of the above letter at Quebec, only 76 men have past this post and they are included in the above number of 1794. my Frend goes on to say, this is the state of our Army, officers included, and to insure Certain Ruin, the officers of the Different Provinces are continually stygmatizeing Each other. in the latter part of his letter, [he] Says 70 odd men less this day fit for duty than there was five days ago. And I must inform you that what promises to add to our misfortune is that the minds of the Canadians are much sowerd. some of them think they have been insulted by the Vagabond part of our Soldiery, in which there is too much truth. Notwithstanding, I doubt not but that all the officers of the different Colonies detest the Hatefull Idea, and when they have heard of it, have done every thing in their power to detect the perpetrators and make Reparation. they think also that they are not paid for their Labour. as to paper money they treat it with the utmost Contempt and indeed prefer a Certificate that Evinces that they have done the Labour and are intitled to payments if acknowledged to be good by a proper Person, Before paper money, for they are then in hopes of get[t]ing what they Call money sometime.[91] And our enemies dont forget to tell them that they will lose their trade, that when Great Britain

---

91. A multitude of reports from Canada mentioned the universal disdain habitants held for paper currency of any sort. This was an immediate legacy of the French and Indian War when France paid for their North American campaign expenses using notes that were progressively devalued, and eventually defaulted on, after the 1763 Peace of Paris; "General Murray's Report of the State of the Government of Quebec," 5 June 1762, in Shortt and Doughty, *Canadian Archives*, 1: 49.

had command of the Province, they could get a Dollar a Bushel hard money for their wheat, &c. Numbers of them begin to think we have pusht them into action only to divert Great Britain And from the Motely Appearance of our Army,[92] they Conclude That we are not able, and indeed that we dont intend to Protect them from Ministerial Vengence. hence probably has arose the Commotion in the District of Quebec of which you have already heard. They in order to Ingratiate themselves once more into favour to save their property and to prevent their families from being Debauched and Butcherd, are preparing to make their Peace with Administration. On the 5th Instant I was informed by Leiutenant Witcomb[93] who arrived by the way of the Parish of St Ours in the District of Montreal, that the Captain of Militia of said parish had applied to him for a Small Party of men, saying he was in danger of his life for Executing orders Received from officers under the Congress, which account was Confirmd on the 7th by Ensign Webster,[94] who arrived with another small party (the last that have past this post); with this Addition, that the Tories were as privately as they Could in listing men to fall on our Troops if we faild at Quebec. This Parish of St Ours laying in the District of Montreal, I Imbraced the Earliest Opportunity to transmit the account to Colonel Hazen at Montreal, who Commands there, and who I make no doubt will give a good account of them. In order to Convince you that I dont desire to throw a greater Gloom on affairs than necessary, I shall give you an Extract of a letter I received from a Gentleman of Character and an undoubted friend to the United Colonies,[95] dated at Montreal, 11th April. We have been most shamefully Neglected—where the fault lies, I Cannot tell. we ought to have arrived 7000 Men and by the middle of may 10000.[96] This Province ought never to be trusted with less; Beg you

---

92. See Badeaux's perspective on the troops' appearance in his May 5 entry.

93. Lieutenant Benjamin Whitcomb. Goforth conveyed this same information in his April 8 letter to John Jay.

94. Ensign Amos Webster, Captain Edward Everitt's Company, Bedel's New Hampshire Regiment; NARA, M804, rg 15, pension W.14913 (Ebenezer Blodget).

95. This is almost surely George Measam, who wrote a letter to Alexander McDougall on March 31 with many of the same points and phrases.

96. The seven Canadian-bound regiments and six artillery companies that Congress authorized in January would have totaled fewer than six thousand, even if they arrived at full strength. Goforth's calculations may have been inflated based on differences between 1775 regimental establishment and the new, smaller 1776 regimental size.

would write to your friends to this purpose, telling them their Neglect to this Province has Changed the Minds of the Canadians Amazeingly; and that it ought to be Considerd, and I fear must [be], as a Conquerd Province; where as if we had been well supported, the Province almost to a Man would have been for us. A starved war, says he, is the most Expensive and dangerous. I shall make hold also to transcribe a part of a Letter which I received from Montreal of the same date from a principle officer in our Army.[97] The Conduct of the Canadians is much Changed, in General to our Disadvantage, Partly from the Indefatigable pains of our Enemies, and partly from their being harassed on the Publick Service as yet unpaid, and through fear of want of sufficient force to protect them, more Especially as Quebec is not yet Reduced. And again we Can only keep a good strict watch and obtain Every intelligence in our Power of their underhand Mechanations So as to prevent Effectually their put[t]ing them into Execution by Secureing the Principles. And again he says: In short it appears to me of the utmost consequence to our Cause a Constant and Regular intelligence being kept up between the Camps three Rivers and montreal. we are at Present in the most Critical Situation here, from Certain Intelligence we have got. And again Was anything Inemical to be attempted, for which Numbers are Ripe, the Consequences might be very fatal.

I am well Convinced our officers and men before Quebec are not wanting in Courage and ardor to Risque another Escalade. if they do, it must be left to him who is the God of Armies as well as the Arbiter of the world. The Important Crisis is near at hand if they Risque it. I believe you will allow (when you Consider the men at the Posts of Point Levey and the Island of Orleans)[98] that we have not More men without than they have within, if so many. if we miscarry a second time, it is quite probable the Canadians will, for the Reasons before given, fall upon our Army with great Vengence. if they do not attempt it and Regular Forces arrive, they will doubtless [Ms illegible] that as our

---

97. This letter from "a principle officer in our Army" at Montreal is not extant, and its author is not certain. However, the content seems characteristic of information that Canadian Continental Colonel Moses Hazen was disseminating at this time. Goforth mentions writing to Hazen in his April 8 letter to John Jay.

98. These posts, separated from Quebec City by the St. Lawrence, were not mutually supporting, but were important for blockading the capital.

Army be oblidged to Decamp and perhaps if not Succourd speedily, find Enough to do to make their Retreat good, —why are we neglected—is there no more men in the Colonies—does the Congress want activity and Resolution, or are you so beset on Every side that you can spare us no more. if so, I forgive you. or is it oweing to the Tardy marches of the troops sent forwards? I was in hopes before this that a formidable Reinforcement would have arrived, that I should have been honourably Discharged and on my way home to my Family, but for the present the pleasing thought must be laid aside. I trust both [Ms. illegible, and the General?] are satisfied with my conduct at this post. at least they have for the Present desired me to Continue in it. The Principle French Inhabitants of the place who appear to be our Friends, on hearing I was orderd to some other Post, waited upon the Captain of malitia[99] to know the fact, and Expectd some Uneasiness on the Occasion, and have since several of them pressd me to Stay. Several of our English Friends who have their property in Quebec have Importuned me to stay, and have gone so far as to say that they were of Opinion that from the Consideration of the Connection I had found, and the good Understanding I had with the People, it would be of more Consequence (in Case of a Disaster to our Army below) that I should be here alone than that my place should be supplied by an officer (who was a stranger) haveing a Party of men and had no acquaintance and no Connections formd with the People, and that if I removed, they had little more to do than get out of the Province. It may be feard I have said to[o] much of myself, that my letter and that account may become Fulsom to the sensible minds; However I hope your known Charity and Candour will not admit so unkind an Interpretation. I by no Means suppose myself of more importance than other officers had they been here and had time to have formd Equal Connections and to Cultivate an acquaintance with the People. I have been Naturally led to say what I have in [or]der to give you an Idea of the State of the Province and affirm the Reasons why I dont Return to my Friends and Family according to assertions in my Letters. I assure you I have no Views of profit or preferment. General Wooster, in order [to] induce me to stay, offerd to add the pay of a Commissary, as I had done the duty of one, to my former pay, which I Refused in order to be at Liberty to Return. as to my promotion in the

---

99. Jean-Baptiste Fafard *dit* Laframboise, frequently mentioned in Badeaux's journal. See note on Badeaux's February 18 entry for background on Laframboise.

new Regiment below (which was from a fourth Captain to a second),[100] I have absolutely Refused it for the same Reason. the People have said so much to me that they have almost persuaded me that I can at least for the present serve my Country as Effectually here as any w[h]ere. I hope in a bout a month to set of[f] for home.

One Mr Palliseir,[101] a Man of figure and Fortune, and perhaps of as Extensive influence as any French Gentleman in the Province which is in our Interest; Gentleman of prompt abilities, a Liberal Education and an Enterprising Genius, well versed with Theory and in some measure with some of the practical parts of War, has been prevailed upon to take a Commission (by General Arnold) of Colonel of Militia for this place, or District of three Rivers.[102] This District at present I apprehend to the be the quietest and best Disposed part of Canada, oweing as I Imagine to the to the [sic] happy influence of Some of [the] French Gentlemen Gentlemen [sic] in and about this Town, and to its Laying between the Armies of Quebec and Montreal. for farther Particulars, I Refer you to my Leiutenant.[103] I hope you will not Conclude that I want to Discourage you with Respect to Carr[y]ing on the war in this Province, far from it. I think it would be better for the Back inhabitants of the Different Colonies to support the war in this Province by a special Tax up on themselves, than to lose this province as a Barrier. Excuse my being so tedious and

---

100. Goforth is referring to the new 1776 composite regiment which Congress ordered formed from the remnants of the various New York units deployed into Canada. He calculated he would be second captain in seniority if he chose to stay, although an earlier list showed he would have remained fourth; "A List of officers of the four regiments raised in New York in 1775, now in Canada, as they Rank," February 28, 1776, NARA, M246, rg 93, r78, f181, p230.

101. Christophe Pélissier, see Badeaux's March 8 entry and note. Pélissier eagerly embraced the Continental cause, met with General Montgomery in early December, and was providing advice directly to the President of Congress by early January. Christophe Pélissier to John Hancock, January 8, 1776, and July 20, 1776, in *AA4*, 4: 60 and *AA5*, 1: 466–67.

102. General Montgomery had appointed Canadian Militia Colonels under Congressional commission—not to be confused with regular Continental service—for Montreal District (François Cazeau) and Quebec District (Regnier de Rousi) in late 1775. The Three Rivers District position was unfilled to this point. "Indemnity for Losses Sustained by Francis Cazeau of Montreal," in *American State Papers Documents Legislative and Executive, of the Congress of the United States. Class IX. Claims*, ed. Walter Lowrie (Washington, DC: Gales and Seaton, 1834), 517; "Memorial of Regnier Derousi," February 22, 1777, NARA, M247, r51 i41 v8 p260.

103. At this point, Goforth assumed Lieutenant McDougall would head home with the troops when enlistments expired on April 15.

believe me to be with the utmost Respect your very Effectionate Friend and at the same time your most obedient and most Humble Servant—

William Goforth

[P.S] 4 O Clock in the afternoon Just arrived a Serjeant and six men (who were in listed to 15 april) on their Return home. the news the Serjeant Brings is that the army are in high Spirits, that the most of the York forces had reinlisted for a year, that Colonel Warner[']s men, whose time Expired, had Generally agreed to stay one month, and Major Brown[']s men for ten days;[104] that we have two Batteries Just Ready to open, besides the one at Point Levy;[105] and by what I can learn in General, it is Imagined that the General intends to feteague the People in the Garrison incessantly for Eight or ten days, and if they dont in that time Surrender, then to attempt to Carry it by Storm, Calling in the Canadians, which I am sorry he is obledged to do for this only Reason: that so sure as he does, the River being Open, the news will by the means of our Enemies get into Town of [the] time the attack is to be made.

[P.P.S] April 24th 1776 at 8 O Clock at night. Received A Letter from General Wooster ordering me to Quebec to take charge and Command of a Privateer.[106] Suits me [as true accounts are in?], I am tired of marching; other hope to get some [Spoils?]. your Son was Just setting of[f] for home, but on finding I was orderd down, determind to go with me. [I] hope to see you soon and have a good packed powder and Ammunition.[107]

---

104. To keep a sufficient number of men in camp, despite hundreds of enlistments expiring on April 15, Wooster was moderately successful in encouraging short-term extensions (until adequate reinforcements had arrived), and adeptly adjusted orders delaying the others' departure from the camp. 13–18 April General Orders, Salsig, *Parole: Quebec*, 75–80.

105. General Arnold had directed the construction of a new battery on the Plains of Abraham opposite Quebec City's St. John's Gate, and another one north of the city, across the Charles River.

106. Since the armed vessels captured by the Continentals in November 1775 had not been adopted for naval service by Congress or any of the colonies, Wooster chose to man them with his soldiers and employ them as privateers under his authority.

107. Goforth's replacement was Lieutenant Peter Castle, of Easton's Massachusetts Regiment (1775), then "Wooster's Regiment" of re-enlisted men (1776). See note to May 12 entry in Badeaux journal.

May 1776

The first of May we had a heavy snowfall.

Mr. Pélissier must start making 13, 9 and 7 inch bombs for the Yankees today;[1] the English blacksmiths say that these bombs won't explode and that what's more, they won't be ready for 5 weeks. So they think that this will serve the King rather than the Yankees. I hope so.

We have learned that the "Bostonians" in the camp revolted due to lack of food and that they told the general that if he doesn't feed them better, they will abandon their service.[2]

We have been assured as well that the row galley and the *Gaspé*[3] have been sunk to the bottom.

---

1. Immediately after the failure of the New Year's Eve assault on Quebec City, Christophe Pélissier, director of the St. Maurice Forges (see March 8 entry and note) had promised Colonel Benedict Arnold that the forges could produce munitions for the Continentals starting in April; Benedict Arnold to David Wooster, January 2, 1776, PSP, microfilm reel 13, NYPL.

2. There was widespread discontent in the Continental camp, but no major troop revolts. The largest protest appears to have occurred on April 17 when "about 40 of the Yorkers" threateningly demonstrated, seeking permission to head home; Adjutant Russell Dewey Declaration, in Louis M. Dewey, *Life of George Dewey, Rear Admiral, U.S.N.; and Dewey Family History* (Westfield, MA: Dewey Family, 1898), 270. General Wooster made considerable efforts to manage his troops and extend their service as long as possible while awaiting reinforcements.

3. In May 1776, a row galley and the captured British brig H.M.S. *Gaspé* were operating in Continental service on the St. Lawrence. They were scuttled at the approach of Royal Navy vessels shortly after the relief of Quebec City. Cubbison, *Northern Theater Army*, 84; Charles Douglas to Philip Stephens, May 8, 1776, Clark, *Naval Documents*, 4:1452.

We've been told that Captain Maclean,[4] having left Quebec to go looking for supplies on the Isle of Orleans, was captured by the "Bostonians" and taken to General Wooster who asked him how he dared to have supplies brought into Quebec. The captain asked him how he dared ask such a question. And said that he should know that he was doing his duty by serving his prince, which he [Wooster] was not doing, he being nothing but a rebel, along with his whole flea-ridden troop. "But," he said to General Wooster, "the time will soon come and the day is not far when I will see your hair lifted off your old 'carcass'"[5] The general had him placed in irons in the camp.[6]

Today 50 Yankees passed through, going upriver: these poor unfortunates are all the more pitiful as they are all naked and sickly.

We learn from the New York gazettes that there are 80,000 men at sea, as many headed for Canada as for the other provinces and that they are to arrive in Halifax to take orders for each of their posts. The gazette is dated the 15th of April. There is also mention that the King's ship *Glasgow* has beaten a Yankee frigate commanded by Captn. Hopkins.[7]

At 7 o'clock in the evening, 17 ships arrived in which there are 340 Yankees from Pennsylvania heading downriver to Quebec.[8] They

---

4. Almost certainly Lieutenant Neil McLean, who was on the officer returns of the Royal Highland Emigrants but apparently was not yet serving with the regiment. Describing the circumstances leading to his imprisonment after his initial arrest, McLean related an encounter with a rebel "General, who disgorged at me the vilest expressions of scurrility and abuse, and because I had not patience to bear such treatment with becoming submission," was ordered "to be put in irons and to be carried in that manner to Albany"; Return of Officers of the First Battalion of His Majesty's Regiment of Royal Highland Emigrants, Isle aux Noix, 15 April, 1778, in J. F. Pringle, *Lunenburgh, or the Old Eastern District, Its Settlement and Progress* . . . (Cornwall, ON: Standard Printing House, 1890), 422; Neil McLean to Robert Morris, November 5, 1776, *AA5*, 3: 515–17.

5. The phrase "hair lifted off your old 'carcass'" implied scalping.

6. This exchange about "flea-ridden" troops is very similar to one that loyalist Claude de Lorimier recorded in his memoirs, during a Montreal meeting with General Wooster. Lorimier, *At War*, 44.

7. It is not clear which newspaper Badeaux is referring to; the details do not seem to match any available papers with that date. The 15 April 1776 edition of the *New-York Gazette* mentioned Captain Hopkins's April 6 battle with the *Glasgow*—however, the short description offered no definitive outcome, and certainly did not imply that the Continental navy had suffered a defeat. The next week's edition of the same newspaper mentioned a total of 33,000 troops sailing for North America; "Extract of a letter from Portsmouth, Jan. 6," *New-York Gazette*, 22 April 1776.

8. Probably the main body of the Second Pennsylvania Regiment, Colonel Arthur St. Clair.

say that they met Belette's schooner[9] in the lake and, believing it to be a royalist ship, they made a long detour to avoid it.

4th. Two boats full of yankees from the province of Connecticut arrived numbering 40 men.[10] When disembarking from their ships they asked if they had anything to fear from of the royalists. Their people told them no. Then, they asked for news of Quebec and how it was fortified. One of the men who had returned from the camps answered that the people of Quebec shot like devils and that it was impossible to take the city, unless it be by famine, which would not be long coming since they are short of supplies and there is a great deal of sickness in Quebec, according to the report of one of their people who deserted from there not long ago.

It's impossible to express how much the riffraff rejoiced over these people passing through. It's as if each brigade brings them a fortune. Nonetheless, they must see that their interests are hardly being advanced, because today they started chimney fires in the guardroom and the barracks, and they didn't take the trouble of putting them out. On the contrary, they each left with his pack, without bothering with the rest. Had it not been for Mr. Tonnancour, Mr. de St. Ours[11] and a few other Canadians that would have been the end of the barracks.

5th. 240 men have arrived.[12] I don't know which nations they come from, because there are negroes, Indians, *pani* Indians,[13] mulattos. . . . I think they have gone through hell, as black and dirty as they are.

The 6th. 300 men arrived, coming back from the camp and who are returning there. One of them told me there was a French ship with 70 cannons 40 leagues from Quebec, but I think that is false.

---

9. See note to April 30 entry.
10. From Colonel Charles Burrall's Connecticut Regiment.
11. Paul-Roch St-Ours-Deschaillons, who would wed Louis-Joseph Godefroy de Tonnancour's daughter Marie-Josephe in July; UMPRDH indiv. #131464.
12. Probably more of Burrall's Connecticut Regiment.
13. French Canadians used the term *Panis* (Pawnee), for enslaved Indians, which had often been taken from their homes in the eastern Great Plains; William Renwick Riddell, "The Slave in Canada," in *Journal of Negro History* 5 (Washington, DC: 1920), 264.

7th. At 3 o'clock in the afternoon, Mr. Coll[14] arrived from the camp, announcing the arrival in Quebec of a warship of 74 guns and four transports. This news alarms many of the "Bostonian" hearts, but we are as joyous about it as they are distressed.

This same day, 104 "Bostonians" came downriver in 5 boats.

Captain Watts[15] and Mr. Painter[16] were down at the shore when they arrived and they asked if they were in Boston when General Howe left there. They said yes. "Well then," they said, "he was more diligent that you, for he is in Quebec and you are still only here."[17] The poor unfortunates turned colors at that news.

At 8 o'clock, 8 boats and 160 men arrived on their way downriver. One of them approached me and asked if I had heard the news that had spread about ships having arrived in Quebec. I told him yes and that there were 16 more that should be arriving any time. He gave me a *god damn* and said "Now we are really screwed. It would be a lot better to give that up. Nonetheless," he told me, "there are enough of us for them."—"That's true," I told him, "but you aren't paying attention to the fact that General Carleton can mobilize the Canadians from up country."—"Oh, *by God*," he said, "that's true, we're going to find ourselves caught, like in a cage."

At ten o'clock, three couriers arrived, one after the other, reporting that as soon as the King's troop arrived in Quebec, they made a sortie against the "Bostonians," massacred them, took all their supplies and their cannons and that two frigates are on their way upriver with two transports.[18]

---

14. Probably Jean-Baptiste Colle, UMPRDH indiv. #149555.

15. Possibly Captain Jason Wait of Bedel's Regiment, who had transited downriver on March 22, Goforth's letter to Alexander McDougall, March 24, 1776; he may have been returning upriver to rejoin the rest of the regiment around Montreal.

16. Quite probably Captain Elisha Painter, originally from James Easton's Massachusetts Regiment. In November 1775, he agreed to extend his service for another six months and served at the siege of Quebec City in the composite unit under Major John Brown; Elisha Painter Petition to Congress, June 24, 1776, NARA, M247, rg 360, I42, r55, p124a.

17. The relief force that arrived at Quebec City was actually led by General John Burgoyne. Howe's force evacuated Boston in March 1776, and reorganized in Halifax before proceeding to New York in the summer of 1776.

18. When a combined force of the newly arrived troops and the Quebec City garrison marched out of the capital's gates on May 6, the Continental army hastily fled, in a near panic. The British force did not aggressively pursue them, eliminating the opportunity for any actual "massacre."

Wooster

The 8th.[19] A courier from the camp brought orders [telling] those arriving yesterday to return upriver and he says that the rest from lower down are on the way back upriver. No doubt General Wooster has taken the lead, since he arrived here yesterday evening.[20]

Upon receiving news of the royalist successes, the Ursuline ladies sang a *Te Deum*[21] this morning during Mass.

The "Bostonians" have received orders to remain in the city until further orders.[22]

At two o'clock in the afternoon, Colonel Campbelle[23] arrived reporting that nearly the whole "Bostonian" army had been taken prisoner and that the rest were on their way upriver.

The 9th. The "Bostonians" who had come from upriver the day before yesterday returned there today. They say they will dig in at Sorel.[24]

More than 900 departing Yankees passed through today. They admit to having been terribly afraid.

10th. 12 boats filled with Yankees passed by. One must hope that we will soon see the end of this since they are clearing out quickly.

---

19. Badeaux does not mention the birth of his son Jean-Baptiste, who was baptized this day; UMPRDH couple #41876.

20. Since General John Thomas had relieved General Wooster of command at the Quebec City siege, Wooster departed on the evening of May 5, in advance of the main Continental retreat. David Wooster testimony concerning the Canadian campaign, July 4, 1776, Boyd, *Papers of Thomas Jefferson*, 1: 445; "Journal of the Most Remarkable Events," LAC, MG23-B7, p111.

21. *Te deum* praise hymn: see note to October 2 entry.

22. (May 8) At this time, the Continentals were maintaining their main defensive position at Deschambault, about forty miles downriver from Three Rivers, near the Richelieu Rapids mentioned in Goforth's letter to Alexander McDougall, April 6, 1776.

23. Colonel Donald Campbell, deputy quartermaster general for the Northern Army, who had served as a principal aide to General Montgomery. After the failed New Year's Eve assault, Campbell served as second-in-command to Benedict Arnold.

24. At this time, General Thomas had determined that it would be most advantageous to withdraw the entire army to Sorel. John Thomas to Committee of Congress, May 15, 1776, NARA, M247, r71 i58 p253.

11th. Four Indians from Sault St. Louis[25] arrived in the city, saying they have letters from General Washington that they are carrying to General Thomas who is still in Dechambault,[26] informing him that there is a tremendous reinforcement of "Bostonians" at la Pointe,[27] and telling him to dig in at Sorel to await their arrival.

Some Englishmen told me this morning that the last brigade of the "Bostonians" coming upriver was supposed to put fire to the barracks, the guardroom and the powder stores. This news made us very unhappy.

12th. Mr. Bonfield[28] arriving from Quebec tells us that there are 15,000 [British] troops for this province and 50,000 for the American Colonies. So, one must hope that the [number of Yankees] will be reduced.

We were alarmed to see 14 boats coming downriver, thinking that it was the "Bostonians" returning. But our pain changed very quickly when we learned that these boats were on their way to pick up the rest of the "Bostonians" from downriver. The "Bostonian" hearts were very happy and they cried and clapped their hands: ha! ha! we knew that the "Bostonians" would return and that their going upriver was but a feint.

Around two o'clock in the afternoon, Mr. de Tonnancour's farmer came to warn him that the "Bostonians" had pillaged his home. I went to the commander's[29] with the Tonnancour men to complain. The com-

---

25. A number of the Caughnawaga Indians of Sault St. Louis supported the Continentals in various capacities during the invasion. See March 26 entry and note.

26. See note to May 8 entry.

27. "La Pointe" was another name for Crown Point. The additional reinforcements mentioned here are presumably General John Sullivan's brigade.

28. (May 12) John Bonfield, an Anglo-Canadian supporter of the Continental cause. He served as a commissary agent for the occupying army.

29. (May 12) The commander at Three Rivers was now Lieutenant Peter Castle, as Captain Goforth had departed on April 24 (see April 23 journal entry). Castle was an officer of the troops reenlisted from Easton's Regiment to serve as "General Wooster's Regiment" on January 1, 1776. Castle appears to have been given the brevet rank of captain while serving as the military governor at Three Rivers. "Petition of Captain John Stevens," n.d. July 75, *AA4*, 3: 305; "Memorial of Captain Elisha Porter to the Board of War," June 24, 1776, *AA4*, 6: 1048; NARA, M804, Daniel Beeman, rg15, pension W.17295; see also Appendix 1, where he is listed as "Pierre Cassel," and associated note. His garrison force consisted of Lieutenant Jacob Poole and twenty-four men that Colonel Elisha Porter detached from his Massachusetts Regiment on its way to Quebec. Elisha Porter, "Diary of the Canadian Campaign, January-August 1776," *Magazine of American History* 30 (1893): 191; John Beeman pension application, NARA, M804, rg15, pension W.23563.

mander said he knew nothing about those who had pillaged and that he couldn't send anyone because, he said, his men were tired. Masters Tonnancour said to him: "Well then, sir, we will take some people and go after them. We will make them return what they took." The commander spoke again, saying: "Those people could fire on you."—"Well then," said the Masters Tonnancour, "we are men like they and if they fire on us, we can return fire." So, the commander, seeing their resolve, told them that he would write a letter and send his lieutenant with them to go after the men and make them return what they had taken, begging them to not take other people with them because that would cause a big stir. They left to meet up with Mr. Normanville[30] whose home they had also pillaged.[31]

13th. Mr. de Tonnancour and Mr. Normanville have returned. They caught the thieves and made them return a mirror, two horses, embroidered clothes and napkins, a canopy bed and other articles. The unfortunates were getting ready to go pillage Mr. Gugy's[32] in Machiche, but since they were caught in this parish, we think they must have gone straight through.

Yesterday two "Bostonians" came to ask me to put them up. Since all the houses were full, I took them in and questioned them as to their rout. They told me that they didn't know what had chased them, that they had seen almost no-one and that there was something supernatural in their having been made so afraid, that the fear had come over them in a strange way. I asked if they planned to entrench in Sorel. They responded that, speaking for themselves, they were going to entrench at home. It was the third time they had been pushed back

---

30. Joseph Godefroy-de-Normanville. The region's leading seigneurs seem to have been specifically targeted—whether due to their loyalist position, or perhaps just because they had the most prominent wealth. See list of Three Rivers loyalists in April 30 entry.

31. A government court of enquiry documented some of the property losses that both Tonnancour and Normanville experienced. Tonnancour also reported that he had lost a seventy-five ton schooner, burned by the rebels—it is not clear which ship this may have been. "Second Book of Minutes of the Court of Enquiry of Damages, Occasioned by the Invasion of the Rebels," March 10, 1777, Fonds Hospice-Anthelme-Jean-Baptiste Verreau, LAC, MG23-GV7.

32. Seigneur and legislative councilor Conrad Gugy faced persistent harassment from local Canadians who supported the invading army. See December 4 and March 27 entries.

from Quebec: the first when they arrived by way of St Igan,[33] the second in Mr. Montgommery's action and then this chase. They don't seem to be very happy with the service of the Congress since they damned it all to hell.

Mr. Gugy was in town and he got the idea that the habitans of Machiche had stirred up the "Bostonians" and persuaded them to go pillage his place. That they had done that this morning at ten o'clock.

Mr Jon Bonfield,[34] coming in from Montreal, reports that the "Bostonians" have 8 regiments on the way and four generals to go downriver to Quebec. This news makes the "Bostonian" hearts jump for joy.

A creditable person assures us that an Indian came by last Thursday carrying news to General Carleton that the King's Regiment, the Indians and 700 Canadians are in la Galette and that they await his orders to come downriver.[35]

Canadian Excesses

The habitants of Machiche (we are told) are planning to have Mr. de Tonnancour and Leproust junior seized.[36] Our situation must be judged by the sight of so many unfortunates rushing to the loss of this miserable province. We are between life and death since the rise of the Canadian

---

33. Writing "St. Igan," Badeaux presumably meant Sartigan, the tiny frontier settlement at which Arnold's corps first entered Canada, also implying that these men participated in the Kennebec expedition.

34. See May 12 entry and note. Bonfield would serve as a key Canadian civilian advisor to General Thomas during this phase of the campaign. John Thomas to Committee of Congress, May 15, 1776, NARA, M247, r71 i58 p253.

35. While the size of the combined force of soldiers, Indians, and loyalist Canadians was greatly inflated, the character of the report is correct. On May 12, Captain George Forster of the Eighth Regiment led this force from Fort Oswegatchie (Ogdensburg, New York)—La Galette was a nearby Indian village. Five days later, when they received word of the relief fleet's arrival at Quebec City, they increased the pace of their march toward Montreal. Parke, *An Authentic Narrative*, 21–22.

36. Yamachiche was the northern end of a region on the north shore of Lake St. Pierre that had several significant episodes of pro-Continental Canadian activity. It included Rivière-du-Loup, home of the agitator La Rose (see December 4 entry), and extended to Berthier-en-Haut where Captain Merlet had independently acted against government forces (see October 12 and November 19 entries). Note again, the apparently specific targeting of prominent loyalists, at least among those incidents that Badeaux related.

rabble. They are like crazy people and only seek pillage and murder.[37] May the Heavens grant that we soon be delivered from their hands.

14th. Mr. Gugy,[38] who had been in town for some days to get away from several rascals who wanted to have him taken, left today to return home after obtaining an order from the commander saying that his enemies are not to harm him in any way.

G. Thomas

15th. General Thomas arrived with the rest of the army that had remained in Dechambaut.[39] We were hopeful that once they had gone through we would be done with them, but our hope was in vain. Since they are staying here and they are still waiting for people from higher upriver, all the empty houses had to be taken to billet his army. He took Sir Stansfield,[40] who had left for Quebec taking news to General Carleton (they say) with him.

It is said that Mr. Pélissier went to the Sorel camp to get the generals to commit to returning back downriver. That may well be.
16th. General Thomas left by boat for Sorel. He left about 600 men billeted in this city. We know nothing of their plan.

---

37. On May 15, General Benedict Arnold reported, "Many persons in the country are seeking for private revenge under pretence of concern for the publick safety." Canadians were not only marauding on their own, but were calling on the Continentals to help in punishing various individuals for their allegedly loyalist characters. Benedict Arnold to Samuel Chase, May 15, 1776, *AA4* 6: 580.
38. On May 28, in a court martial, four First Pennsylvania Regiment soldiers would be found guilty of pillaging Gugy's residence. They reportedly would also have burned down Gugy's house if they had not been stopped by other soldiers. Given the scale of Continental and rebel Canadian marauding at this time, this was a notable development. Benedict Arnold reported that these soldiers would "be made an example of." However, in the end, their punishment was only a public reprimand. Salsig, *Parole: Quebec*, 117; Benedict Arnold to Samuel Chase, May 15, 1776, *AA4* 6: 580.
39. The Continentals found they were unable to keep their troops properly supplied at Deschambault, and General Thomas ordered them to consolidate at Three Rivers. John Thomas to Committee of Congress, May 15, 1776, NARA, M247, r71 i58 p253.
40. Joseph Stansfield, merchant and possibly seigneur, who had been included in the list of the region's loyalists provided in April 30 entry.

A habitant from Sorel says that no reinforcements have come for the "Bostonians," that at most there are 7 to 8 hundred men entrenched there and that they only have 6 cannon.

There has been a lot of news about the absence of Mister Leproust, Jr.[41] and Mr. Paradis.[42] Some said that they were taken prisoner by the "Bostonians" and that Mr. Leproust has broken an arm; others said they were prisoners in the boats, bound in irons on both feet and hands; but finally we learned from a sure source that they have been returned to Quebec.

Sir Stansfield, who left the city to go aboard ship and was taken prisoner when returning, was set free today, the Yankees having found no proof against him. He told me that on the 11th of this month, the "Bostonians" had pillaged all they could find from Lotbinière's mill, wheat, flour, &c.[43]

17th. A certain La Liberté from Bécancour[44] coming from Montreal to get reimbursed for the effects the Yankees took from him last fall in Quebec, says he passed through La Prairie and that there are no more than 200 men there, that in Sorel, of all those going upriver, almost all continue on to New England, that he saw no evidence of entrenching. He was not paid.

17th. Three Hurons[45] coming from Quebec said that nine transport ships filled with troops had arrived there. We hope that with the first wind from the north we will see them arrive here.

---

41. (May 16) Militia officer Louis-Joseph Leproust, see September 27 and subsequent entries.

42. Jean Augustin Paradis, UMPRDH indiv. #102369.

43. Probably the seigneurial mill in south shore Lotbinière Parish, opposite Deschambault, although there appears to be no other extant record of such an incident. This seigneury belonged to Michel Chartier de Lotbinière, who was among the noble Canadians captured in the surrender of Fort St. John's. The Lotbinière family also held seigneuries west of Montreal. Marcel Hamelin, "Chartier de Lotbinière, Michel-Eustache-Gaspard-Alain," in *DCB* 6, http://www.biographi.ca/en/bio/chartier_de_lotbiniere_michel_eustache_gaspard (accessed September 6, 2014).

44. Joseph Viau Laliberté, UMPRDH indiv. #161011.

45. (May 17) Jeune Lorette, west of Quebec City, was a Huron Indian mission village (see Map 4).

It is said that two habitants of the parish of St Denis[46] in the Chamblie River came by on the south shore going to Quebec to plead for General Carleton's mercy. I hope they get it, at least then the other parishes might come back to their senses.

Mr Gugy, fearing that the enemies that caused the pillage at his place might attack his person, came to stay in town until the rest of the congressional troops go by.

18th. Mr. Pélissier, arriving from Montreal, reports that there are ten thousand men at Sorel ready to descend on Quebec.[47]

19th. We noticed a schooner coming downriver and, since Mr. Pélissier had reported the above news, we thought that it was carrying people or supplies, but our fear was short lived since we could tell that it was light and that it was coming to pick up the baggage of the officers who are in this city.

20th. Letters from Montreal say that last Wednesday 150 "Bostonians" left the city going to The Cedars to meet the King's Regiment, the Indians and the Canadians who are there and that Thursday several cannon shots were heard, from which we presume that there was an action.[48]

Some people from town who went to Montreal to get bark canoes and have returned today, report that there are not more than one hundred "Bostonian" men in Montreal.

Today Sirs Proust and Paradis, returning from Quebec, returned there for fear of being taken prisoner by the "Bostonians" since many people saw that they were back.

---

46. St-Denis parish, twenty miles south of Sorel on the Richelieu River (See Map 2). Of note, on September 18, 1775, there had been a related incident in St-Denis, when representatives bearing an amnesty from Governor Carleton were captured by Continentals and rebel Canadians.

47. Pélissier was presumably referring to Thompson's brigade, which was already in the province, and John Sullivan's brigade, which had not yet started crossing Lake Champlain. Even at authorized strength, these would only have totaled slightly more than six thousand men.

48. (May 20) The fighting around The Cedars (Les Cèdres) actually began with minor skirmishes on Saturday May 18, and the main fighting at the rebels' Fort Cedars began the following day. Major Henry Sherburne led a detachment of Continental reinforcements from Montreal on Thursday, May 16. Parke, *Authentic Narrative*, 7, 23.

21st. A boat from Sorel arrived at 10 o'clock this morning bringing news that the royalists had retaken Montreal and killed all the "Bostonians" and "Congress-supporting" Canadians who were found in the city. As soon as this news arrived, the "Bostonians" prepared to leave for Sorel.[49] They left the city at three o'clock in the afternoon.

We are impatiently awaiting the King's troop from downriver.

General Carleton's Proclamation

Since there were four officers remaining in the town hospital too sick to be able to follow the army, on the advice of Mr. Bonfield, the "Bostonians" had planned to take four of the city's most notable people with them as hostages for their sick.[50] Mr. Pélissier, finding himself with them when they were discussing this, advised them that this would be very bad, that they would irritate the rest of the nation against them. This advice was accepted and they took no one. The sick were reassured when we showed them General Carleton's proclamation. They couldn't say enough what a great, generous and humane man Mr. Carleton was.[51]

24th. The announcement of the taking of Montreal was found to be false, but it is certain that there was an action at The Cedars and that

---

49. General Thomas had decided to withdraw all the troops to Sorel and Berthier-en-Haut on the previous day, passing orders for New Jersey Colonel William Maxwell, commander of the troops remaining in Three Rivers, to join the main camp at Sorel. John Thomas to Commissioners in Canada, May 20, 1776; *AA4* 6: 592. See May 24 entry and note regarding the threat to Montreal.

50. These sick Continental officers are unidentified, as they are not included in the Ursuline nuns' accounts in Appendix 1. One of them may have been Captain Samuel Watson of Colonel Arthur St. Clair's Second Pennsylvania Regiment, who died at the Three Rivers convent that very day, May 21, 1776; 2: Montgomery, *Pennsylvania Archives*, 2: 111; NARA, M804, rg15, S.41826 (Thomas McKeen), 8.

51. Governor Carleton's May 10 proclamation told his militia officers to find all rebel troops left behind, and provide necessary care at government expense. He also promised the rebels "that as soon as their health is restor'd, they shall have free liberty to return to their respective Provinces." Proclamation in Ainslie, *Canada Preserved*, 95.

the Royalists were victorious. The "Bostonians" are sending lots of people there, to stop the King's troop from getting through at that place.[52]

This morning at 8 o'clock, four "Bostonians" arrived in town from upriver. They said they were coming from Pointe de Levi, but we think they are spies coming to see what's going on here. Another one showed up from downriver, armed. He says he's a deserter from Quebec. It's too bad that there are no troops here to take them.

Cedars

Some Lorette Hurons,[53] coming from upriver, tell us that the Royalists have killed and taken prisoner the entire "Bostonian" party that had been sent to The Cedars and that they were to attack them this morning at 8 o'clock in the entrenchment they had made at la Chine. In the action at The Cedars, the Royalists took two cannons from the Yankees.

27th. This morning at daybreak, two boats carrying 24 armed "Bostonians" arrived wanting to surprise the Royalists. They first took themselves to Mr. Leproust's in order to capture his son.[54] Having been warned of their quest, he went out a window without socks or shoes and retired to the woods. They nevertheless invested the house, but he got away without being seen. Perceiving that they would not find him at his father's house, they went to Mr. Bellefeuille's and searched everywhere, without success. Finally they got tired of looking for Sir Leproust. They went to the hospital to get the four invalids, took them onto their boats and left.[55]

---

52. (May 24) British Captain Forster exploited his advantage after the Battle of the Cedars, leading his force onto the Island of Montreal on May 22. However, two days later, he decided to withdraw in the face of deliberate defenses established by Benedict Arnold. Parke, *Authentic Narrative*, 29–31.
53. See May 17 entry and note regarding Lorette Hurons.
54. See May 16 entry regarding Leproust.
55. Probably the same officers described in May 21 entry and note.

At 8 o'clock in the morning we saw twelve ships coming upriver at Champlain; that changed our fear to joy. The Royalists who found themselves at the water's edge—upon seeing the ships, cried out "Long live the King." Mr. Leproust and Mr. Paradis, who were in the woods, were told and returned around eleven. We did not have the consolation of seeing the ships arrive, the wind from the northeast having fallen.

Affairs at the Cedars and La Chine

The General's Proclamation

28th. Sir Baril Duchainy[56] was arrested by a party commanded by Mr. Godefroy de Tonnancour as being suspected of spying for Mr. Merlet, since he served him all winter. He was sent to the frigates that are at Champlain. At two o'clock in the afternoon, I saw two people arrive in a coach coming from upriver. I immediately advised Mr. de Tonnancour of this and he sent Captain Laframboise with me to Mr. Sills' to find out what was going on. We recognized it to be two Royalists from Montreal who told us that the "Bostonians" had lost two parties of 500 men each, both at The Cedars and at la Chine. They advised us as well that there was a fully equipped "Bostonian" entering the city. Mr Marchand of Batiscand[57] and I had him seized. He turned himself over willingly. He told us he had deserted from Sorel with four others, two of whom had crossed to the south and the two others were following behind him. He said he had been sick for several days. Mr. Laframboise had him put in the hospital in accordance with General Carleton's proclamation.

Mr. Monin's[58] boy arrived from Rivière du Loup around two thirty, coming to tell him not to go home since a detachment of 40 "Bostonians"

---

56. Pierre Baril-Ducheny, seigneur of Carufel in Maskinongé parish, adjacent to St-Cuthbert and Berthier-en-Haut. Clement Plante, "Notes on the Baril-Ducheny Family," *Je Me Souviens* (American-French Genealogical Society) 9, no. 2 (Winter 1986), 33.

57. Batiscan Militia Captain Alexis Marchand, commissioned by Governor Carleton in 1775. Of note, the June 1776 government Baby-Taschereau-Williams commission removed Marchand from his militia post based on accusations that he had zealously served the Continentals during the invasion. Gabriel, *Quebec during the American Invasion*, 36–38.

58. Seventeen-year-old Jean-Baptiste Monin, son of Hugues Monin of Pointe-du-Lac, UMPRDH indiv. #183716.

and Canadians had come the previous night to take him, along with Mr. Baucin,[59] that they had been to Mr. Gugy's in Machiche and that he thought they had pillaged there. He said he had heard them tell the "Bostonian" Canadians that they were planning to come to town this evening. We will be on our guard.

We learned with joy that last week 40 ships filled with troops arrived in Quebec.

Affairs at the Cedars and La Chine

29th. Mr. Fargusson and two other people from Montreal who had escaped passed by today to go on board the ships that are at Champlain. They confirmed the loss of the two "Bostonian" parties upriver and they told us that the Indians who are with the King's party behave very humanely toward the prisoners that they take.[60]

30th.[61] Several people from Pointe aux Trembles of Montreal [District] arrived in town escaping from enemies trying to capture them. It is said the Mr. Cuthbert,[62] from Berthier, was taken prisoner and that they took 3000 minots of wheat from him.

---

59. French-born Michel Beaucin, merchant and militia captain of Rivière-du-Loup. See June 23 entry and note, and December 4 entry.

60. Continental authorities annulled the surrender cartel agreed to after The Cedars, due to alleged Indian atrocities. However, Captain Forster's Indian allies seem to have behaved considerably well; there are nothing more than generic accounts relating to "murders" of prisoners; the worst documented incidents involved theft and harassment of the surrendered Continentals. Samuel E. Dawson, "Massacre at the Cedars," *Canadian Monthly and National Review* 5 (January-June 1874): 305–23. Fargusson, or Ferguson, is unidentified.

61. Badeaux does not mention the death of his nineteen-month-old daughter Marie-Joseph, who was buried on this day; UMPRDH couple #41876.

62. James Cuthbert, retired British army officer, seigneur of Berthier and St-Cuthbert, and one of Governor Carleton's legislative councilors. He was arrested by the Continentals, perhaps at the time Badeaux reported, and was sent to Albany. However, according to General Arnold, both Cuthbert and Gugy willingly sold wheat to the Continental army (albeit in compromised circumstances). Jean Poirier, "Cuthbert, James," in *DCB* 4, http://www.biographi.ca/en/bio/cuthbert_james_4E.html (accessed September 7, 2014); Benedict Arnold to Samuel Chase, May 15, 1776, *AA4* 6: 580.

31st. Mr. Lavalterie[63] and several other gentlemen coming from Montreal tell us that the "Bostonians" have made an agreement with the Royalists from upriver, that is, that they have promised to send back the prisoners taken at St. John's last fall and the Royalists have committed to returning the prisoners they took at both at The Cedars and La Chine. What's more, the Royalists proposed that they [the "Bostonians"] withdraw into Montreal and that they [the Royalists] would pull back to la Galette, otherwise, they would continue to harass them.[64]

Mr. Belisle, interpreter for the St Francois Indians[65] just arrived. He had gone to take orders from General Carleton two days ago. Arriving at St. Francois, he was warned that they [the "Bostonians"] were looking for him. The Indians told him: "Never fear, we will defend you if they come to take you." But, having discovered when he was in the village that he was surrounded by 300 "Bostonians," he picked up a stick and, pretending to play a game, he passed through his enemies without being recognized. Once through, he took to the woods and came out at la Baie[66] and from there came here.

The Conclusion of William Goforth's Canadian Service—Summary

The "Privateer" mentioned in the April 24 postscript to Goforth's last letter was the schooner *Maria,* one of the vessels surrendered to the Continentals off Sorel in November 1775. On General Wooster's orders,

---

63. Pierre-Paul Margane-de-Lavaltrie, seigneur of Lavaltrie, north of Montreal. Pierre Dufour and Gérard Goyer, "Margane de Lavaltrie, Pierre-Paul," in *DCB* 5, http://www.biographi.ca/en/bio/margane_de_lavaltrie_pierre_paul_5E.html (accessed September 7, 2014).

64. There was a prisoner of war exchange cartel, but it did not include any specific agreement regarding withdrawals, only a four-day ceasefire. Text of cartel, Parke, *Authentic Narrative*, 32–34, 37–38.

65. Basile Germain *dit* Belisle was an interpreter among the St. Francis Abenakis. LAC, Finding Aid 2122, July 1997 for MG199-F 35, Superintendent of Indian Affairs; UMPRDH indiv. #249658. The village, St François-du-Lac (Odanak), was another Abenaki mission village, south of Lake St. Pierre.

66. The parish of La-Baie-du-Febvre, halfway between St. Francois-du-Lac and Nicolet; about a ten mile hike.

Goforth led the ship on one fruitless mission. His task was to search for vessels hidden on remote stretches of the St. Lawrence, where loyalists had reportedly loaded them to supply blockaded Quebec City. The captain's maritime adventures ended shortly after the British relief fleet arrived at the capital on May 6. A Royal Navy warship was sent upriver to find and pursue any ships in rebel hands, resulting in an encounter on the eighth. As Goforth later reported to General Israel Putnam, "the frigate gave him chase; he crowded all sail possible, but found it in vain; he then quitted with his crew, save a son of Colonel McDougall's,[67] and one more, who were so obstinate they would not leave the vessel, and were taken prisoners." By another officer's account, there were not even any shots exchanged in this river chase. Goforth ran his ship aground and futilely tried to hole it, as he abandoned it near Point-aux-Trembles (Neuville). From there, he met with some senior Continental leaders who dispatched him as an express messenger[68] to General Philip Schuyler back in New York, concluding his tour of duty in Canada sometime in mid-May 1776.[69]

---

67. Israel Putnam to George Washington, May 21, 1776, *PGWRWS*, 4: 358–60. The "son of Colonel McDougall's" was Goforth's long-serving lieutenant, Ranald McDougall. McDougall is included in a June 1776 list titled "Officers taken December 31, 1775," in which he is listed as "Randolph S. McDougall," with a note "May 7, 1776," the date of his capture. Simeon Thayer, *The Invasion of Canada in 1775, Including the Journal of Captain Simeon Thayer, Describing the Perils and Sufferings of the Army Under Colonel Benedict Arnold, in the March Through the Wilderness to Quebec*, ed. Edwin M. Stone (Providence, RI: Knowles, Anthony, 1867), 40–41.

68. The reader will note that Badeaux's journal did not mention Captain Goforth visiting Three Rivers on his way back to New York.

69. David Wooster to Hector McNeill, April 26, 1776, Charles Douglas to Philip Stephens, May 8, 1776, Clark, *Naval Documents*, 4: 1452; "Memorial of Richard Platt," NARA, M247, r51 i41 v8 p190–91; Israel Putnam to George Washington, May 21, 1776, *PGWRWS*, 4: 358–60.

June 1776

June 2nd, the ships that were in Champlain for the past 8 days came by today. As they passed the city, the volunteers saluted them with three rounds of musket fire while shouting three times, "Long Live the King!" The ships responded with four cannon shots. The "Bostonian" hearts only looked at them sidewise. They are not as happy as when their brothers come downriver in boats.

3rd. Today, a party of the King's troops arrived in town and a ship passed by saluting the city with seven cannon shots, while shouting "Hurrah." The people of the city responded by shouting "Hurrah" as well.

4th. Today was the King's birthday. All the troops came into town, fired three shots from their muskets and the ships did the same with their cannons.

We have learned that there are 600 Yankees in Nicolet[1] that were looking for some habitants of the parish. They wanted to capture

---

1. On 1 June, Brigadier General William Thompson ordered a composite force of six hundred men to march to Nicolet, along with eighteen bateaux, establishing a new forward position on the south shore for potential counterattacks on the slowly advancing British. Nicolet was approximately thirty miles downriver from Sorel, at the far downstream end of Lake St. Pierre. Thompson was acting commander at this time, as General Thomas was terminally ill with smallpox. The force was primarily drawn from Arthur St. Clair's Second Pennsylvania Regiment, William Maxwell's Second New Jersey Regiment, and John Philip de Haas's First Pennsylvania Regiment. William Thompson to George Washington, June 2, 1776, *PGWRWS*, 4: 429; 1 June orderly book entry, Salsig, *Parole: Quebec*, 122.

Mr. Bellearmain,[2] the militia captain, his father-in-law and two of his brothers-in-law, but they escaped through the woods and came into town.

The Americans Still Advance

Several Montrealers who had abandoned their homes came here for refuge. They say that the Yankees are pillaging everywhere in Montreal.[3]

The 8th. At four o'clock in the morning, Mr. Landron,[4] the militia captain from Pointe du Lac, came to town warning that a large party of Yankees had landed intending to come here. Colonel Fraser[5] immediately had the general alarm sounded and assembled his people, numbering 7,000. Several guards were sent to different places where the Yankees could get through. Around 8 o'clock they appeared on the edge of the woods behind Mr. Laframboise's land. Our troops kept up a non-stop fire for two hours from cannon, muskets and ships, forcing the Yankees to pull back into the depths.[6] We only had about 12 wounded; no dead, thank God. This party was led by the aforementioned La Rose and

---

2. While awaiting further orders, Colonel St. Clair's men decided they would purge some of the Nicolet loyalists. Local Canadian patriots presumably identified the Carleton appointed militia captain Pierre Bellarmin Brassard as a worthy target, along with his relatives mentioned in Badeaux's entry. Bellarmin had earlier been a merchant ship captain. His father in law was Jean Baptiste Pinard. According to local tradition, Bellarmin's wife Marie, who was left behind and anticipated that her house would be pillaged, hid some clothing in the bottom of a cart outside so that she could be sure that her children would have something to wear after the poorly disciplined troops were done. Bellemere, *Histoire de Nicolet*, 153–54; UMPRDH couple #218245.

3. On May 12, the Committee of Congress in Canada, Samuel Chase and Charles Carroll, authorized the army to confiscate whatever provisions were needed; Commissioners to Canada to John Thomas, May 12 1776, *LoD*, 3: 666. By all accounts, General Arnold used great skill and energy in directing his men in Montreal to execute this task.

4. Some secondary accounts, including the associated Pointe-du-Lac historical marker, refer to the captain as Guay *dit* Landron. However, the UMPRDH database does not include any parish records with that name. The militia captain may have been Jean-Baptiste Landron or André Guay, UMPRDH indivs. #127949 and #154010.

5. General Simon Fraser commanded the lead British brigade that had advanced as far as Three Rivers, both on land and by ship on the river.

6. This engagement is known as the Battle of Three Rivers. The local militia under Joseph Boucher-de-Niverville participated in the initial skirmishes, buying additional time for the regular British troops to form and maneuver. The battle was a significant defeat for

Dupaul[7] who had forced Antoine Gautier[8] to lead them through the woods, but he had done so in such a way as to give our troops time to prepare for combat, cavorting about in the woods and pretending not to know the way, without which, they would have surprised us before daybreak.

At three o'clock in the afternoon, we learned that our troops had taken 20 boats, 28 firkins of salt pork and between 2 & 3 hundred men prisoners, and 8 cannon from the Yankees. Our volunteers did wonders.

At 6 o'clock, General Carleton arrived from Quebec accompanied by his brother and Mr. de Lanaudiere. He left immediately for Pointe du Lac.

9th. The prisoners that were taken yesterday arrived in town, among whom was General Thompson,[9] his aide-de-camp, and a colonel, who had been taken at the Pointe du Lac by a certain Rainville[10] from La Prairie and a certain Chabot.[11] Also among these prisoners was a certain L'Anglois,[12] a militia captain from Cap Santé.

We also learned that Mr. Laforce,[13] who is in the lake with his ship, took several prisoners who had come on barges loaded with ammunition for the Yankees.

---

the Continentals, at a point when they hoped to regain the initiative. After the Battle of Three Rivers, the Continentals largely resigned themselves to withdrawing from Canada.

7. François Guillot *dit* La Rose, see December 4 entry and March 27 entries and notes regarding La Rose and his radical pro-Continental stance. Pierre Dupaul was a merchant from Yamachiche; UMPRDH indiv. #166008.

8. Local hero Antoine Gauthier was a habitant in his mid-fifties at the time; UMPRDH indiv. #150475. Gauthier's wife, Marie Josephe *née* Girard, is credited with rushing to warn Militia Captain Landron of the Continental advance toward Three Rivers. In combination, Gauthier's delay of the American advance, and Landron's early warning to the British at Three Rivers are credited with making a decisive difference in the course of the battle.

9. Brigadier General William Thompson, who commanded the Continental attack, Pennsylvania Lieutenant William Bird, one of the general's aides-de-camp, and Colonel William Irvine, commander of the Sixth Pennsylvania Regiment. "Return of Prisoners taken above Three Rivers the 8th & 9th of June 1776," NARA, M246, rg93, r135, f4, p101.

10. François-Marie Rainville, see April 8 entry and note.

11. See October 18 entry and note.

12. Pierre L'Anglois, had zealously cooperated with Benedict Arnold and other Continental leaders, serving as a patriot militia captain. Gabriel, *Quebec during the American Invasion*, 28.

13. Captain Henri Laforce, merchant captain before the war. He commanded an artillery company in the defense of Quebec City. Governor Carleton gave him command of a schooner when the ice broke in the spring of 1776. Biographical notes to Fonds Hippolyte et Pierre LaForce, P128, BAnQ. See also note to March 9 entry.

12th. We learn from the habitans of Machiche that, ever since the battle given on the 8th, wounded "Bostonians" are coming out of the woods and that several have died. Consequently, a party of Canadians from this city went into the woods to hunt for wounded men and to bring them to town.[14]

---

14. In addition to General Thompson and Colonel Irvine, the Canadians and British captured nine junior officers, a chaplain, a surgeon, and 236 men during and after the battle. According to British Lieutenant William Digby, who was present at the battle, more than fifty Continentals were found dead in the woods between Three Rivers and Rivière-du-Loup, exact casualties were unreported. "Return of Prisoners taken above Three Rivers the 8th & 9th of June 1776," NARA, M246, rg93, r135, f4, p101–108; William Digby, *The British Invasion from the North: Digby's Journal of the Campaigns of Carleton and Burgoyne from Canada, 1776–1777*, ed. James Phinney Baxter (Albany: Joel Munsell's Sons, 1887), 108.

Notes on the Provenance of Badeaux's Journal

Jean-Baptiste Badeaux's manuscript journal is held at Library and Archives Canada in the Amable Berthelot Collection, MG 23-B35. Its provenance is explained in a letter included in that collection, kept with the journal:

Alfred Garneau to archivist Douglas Rymney, 1 June 1876

This manuscript, which I have had in my possession since 1866, is original. It came to me from my father,[1] to whom it had been given, with Foucher's journal,[2] around 1846, by the now deceased M. Amable Berthelot of Quebec, who had received it himself as a gift from his brother-in-law, Mr. Joseph Badeaux, son of the notary Jean-Baptiste Badeaux.

The indication of the name of this latter after the title was added by my father and the small annotations in the margins are from Mr. Berthelot.

When Abbot Hospice-Anthelme Jean-Baptiste Verreau transcribed the journal for publication in 1870, Jean-Baptiste Badeaux's authorship

---

1. François-Xavier Garneau, Pierre Savard, and Paul Wyczynski, "Garneau, François-Xavier," in *DCB* 9, http://www.biographi.ca/en/bio/garneau_francois_xavier_9E.html (accessed August 29, 2014).

2. Notary Feu Foucher composed another journal of the invasion, focused on the siege of Fort St. John's, published as Feu Foucher, "Journal Tenu Pendant Le Siege du Fort Saint-Jean, en 1775, Par Feu M. Foucher, Ancien Notaire de Montréal," *Le Bulletin des Recherches Historiques* 40 (1934): 135–59, 197–222.

was still in dispute. Verreau presented the argument made by his fellow Canadian historian, Jacques Viger, as follows:

PALMAM QUI MERUIT . . .[3]

Mr. Amable Berthelot, of Quebec, is the owner of the original manuscript that I am copying here and whose title is very simply: "Journal begun in Three Rivers, the 18th of May in the year 1775"—with no indication of the author's name. I have heard the paternity of this writing attributed to Mr. Foucher, Notary, and to Mr. Badeaux, also Notary. Authority, tradition.

I have read this journal most attentively and I am convinced—1) that it must have been written by an inhabitant of Three Rivers; 2) by a Canadian (see the word compatriots used on page 164, line 14); and 3) by an Agent of the Ladies Community of Three Rivers. . . . Once I had formed this conviction, I searched in Montreal and in Three Rivers, and I found, with the help of the notarial records and parish registers on the one hand, then of the families, the former acquaintances of the notaries, Foucher & Badeaux, and of the Religious Ladies of Three Rivers,[4] on the other: 1) That

---

3. "Laurels to those who merit them."

4. From Verreau's *Invasion du Canada* (translated): "The agents for the management of ordinary business for our community since its founding, and of those of our seigneury of Rivière du Loup, are in the following order as noted in notarized deeds, although the precise dates of their nomination are unknown to us because of two fires in which all the papers of our house were destroyed by the flames:

Master Poulin, the first, continued until 1726.

Master Petit, from 1726 to 1730.

Masters Pressé and Pillard, from 1730 to 1748.

Master Leproust, from 1748 to 1758.

Master Pillard, a second time, from 1758 to 1767.

Master Badeau, from 1767 to 1794.

Master Badeaux is found to be mentioned as agent for the seigneury of our community in various deeds. The first he did for the said seigneury is dated the 12th of November, 1767 and the second, the 17th of July, 1714 [sic]. Certified to be true, on this 18th of November 1846.

(Signed), Sister Ste-Helene, Superior

Provided to me in Three Rivers, at my request on the aforementioned day and year, returning from Quebec to Montreal. J.V."

Mr Antoine Foucher, born in France around 1716, died in Montreal at the age of 85, on the 15th of February 1801, after having practiced there as a notary from the year 1746 to the year of his death: some time in Terrebonne, never in Three Rivers. His notarial record states that in 1775 and '76 he was working in Montreal. I also found 2), That Mr. J.-Bte. Badeaux, born in the District of Three Rivers,[5] around 1741 (his family was not able to tell me exactly where) died the 12th of March 1796, at 55, in the city of Three Rivers, where he had married on the 29th of October 1764, and where he practiced as a notary from 1767 until his death. His notarial record is there. He was the agent for the Ursuline Ladies of that city from 1767 to '94, which surely includes the years 1775 and '76. After all of that, must not Mr. J.-Bte. Badeaux, and not Mr. Foucher, be recognized as the true author of the interesting journal that we are going to read?

J. V.[6]

A French-language transcription of Badeaux's record titled "Journal des opérations de l'armée américaine, lors de l'invasion du Canada en 1775–76, par M. J. B. Badeaux, notaire de la ville des Trois-Rivières," was first printed in the 1870 *Revue canadienne*. The Literary and Historical Society of Quebec subsequently reprinted this transcription, and in 1873, Abbot Hospice-Anthelme Jean-Baptiste Verreau included it in a published collection of journals, memoirs, and letters related to the American invasion of Canada, titled *Invasion du Canada par les Américains*.[7]

---

5. Actually Quebec City, UMPRDH indiv. #161861.

6. Verreau, *Invasion du Canada*, 161. This appears to be one of the many notes that Verreau incorporated from the collections of historian compatriot Jacques Viger (J.V.).

7. Verreau gave historian Jacques Viger principal credit for the material in his *Invasion du Canada* collection, Verreau only claimed responsibility for providing the finishing touches; Verreau, *Invasion du Canada*, xix. *Revue canadienne* (Montréal) 7; Literary and Historical Society of Quebec, *Historical Documents*, 3rd ser., no. 2; Thérèse Hamel, "Verreau, Hospice-Anthelme-Jean-Baptiste," in *DCB* 13, http://www.biographi.ca/en/bio/verreau_hospice_anthelme_jean_baptiste_13E.html (accessed August 29, 2014); Jean-Claude Robert, "Viger, Jacques," in *DCB* 8, http://www.biographi.ca/en/bio/viger_jacques_8E.html (accessed August 29, 2014).

Regarding the manuscript itself, it appears that Jean-Baptiste Badeaux probably rewrote an earlier version of the journal. The portion prior to September 6, 1775, was written as a summary, rather than a daily journal, and the character of Badeaux's reflections over this period imply that it was written after the invasion had already been defeated. Additionally, the author's handwriting was remarkably consistent through the first half of the journal, with only slight variations over the course of several pages. Only as the reader reaches the mid-March entries is there any noticeable change in manuscript pen strokes. The author's rare interlineations and insertions were employed for minor editing, or to add amplifying detail. These are all indicators that the Library and Archives Canada manuscript is not the original daily record that Badeaux kept.[8]

Alfred Garneau's letter addressing the journal's provenance, quoted above, summarized the few manuscript additions that were clearly provided by different hands. François-Xavier Garneau added "and kept at Three Rivers by M. Badeaux Notary" to the manuscript title. Amable Berthelot provided marginal content summaries and date annotations on the manuscript copy. This translation incorporates many of Berthelot's descriptive headings as section breaks in the journal.

---

8. Bernard Andrès, *La Conquête des Lettres au Québec (1759–1799): Anthologie* (Québec City: Laval University Press, 2007), 138; and the editor's manuscript analysis.

Appendix 1

The Accounts of the Three Rivers Ursuline Nuns

Background

In his 2 April entry, Jean-Baptiste Badeaux discussed the generous care that the Ursuline Nuns provided for sick soldiers in Three Rivers, and the issue of the Continental Army's nonpayment for their services. This appendix consists of the nuns' postwar claims made on the United States for hospitalization costs, and two personal claims from Badeaux and Louis-Joseph Godefroy de Tonnancour. Pennsylvanian, and Canadian campaign veteran, Isaac Melchior forwarded the accounts on behalf of these Trifluviens, having received them while traveling in Canada on business.[1] The originals are found in the Papers of the Continental Congress.

While the Continental soldiers were undoubtedly very happy to receive dedicated medical care, the hospital must have been a very foreign environment for the men. The alien experience must have been exaggerated to varying degrees, by Protestant biases, unfamiliarity with Catholic religious orders, and preconceptions against women's roles and

---

1. See note to Goforth's January 5 letter regarding Melchior. Following his military service in Canada, Melchior served with the army at Ticonderoga, then as Pennsylvania's barracks-master general. His final military position was barracks-master general for the Continental Army, which he filled from 1777 through the end of the war. In his letter accompanying these claims, Melchior advocated for repayment, noting that "these people who furnished provisions, goods &c. to your Army when in extreme distress they merit your immediate attention—who nursed your sick—who confided in your money almost to their utter ruin—it is these people who have suffered," NARA, M247, rg360, i35, r41, p121–24.

abilities in medical care. Although there do not appear to be any extant records of the hospital experience from those soldiers that received care from the Ursuline Sisters, there is a fine description from an Irish gentleman traveling through Canada in the mid-1790s:

> The [Ursulines'] hospital, which lies contiguous to the chapel, consists of two large apartments, wherein are about twelve or fourteen beds. The apartments are airy, and the beds neat and well appointed. Each bed is dedicated to a particular saint, and over the foot of it is an invocation to the tutelary saint, in large characters, as, "St. Jacque priez pour moi, [St. James, pray for me]" "St. Jean priez pour moi," &c. The patients are attended by a certain number of the sisterhood appointed for that purpose.
>
> The dress of the Ursulines consists of a black stuff gown; a handkerchief of white linen tied by a running string close round the throat, and hanging down over the breast and shoulders, being rounded at the corners; a head-piece of white linen, which covers half the forehead, the temples, and ears, and is fastened to the handkerchief; a black gauze veil, which conceals half the face only when down, and flows loosely over the shoulders; and a large plain silver cross suspended from the breast. The dress is very unbecoming, the hair being totally concealed, and the shape of the face completely disguised by the close white head-piece.[2]

Jean-Baptiste Badeaux's Cover Letter to the Ursuline Nuns' Accounts[3]

The Nuns of three Rivers in the province of Quebec, shall be verimuch obliged to Colonel Melcher of philadelphia to procure them the

---

2. Isaac Weld Jr., *Travels Through the States of North America and the Provinces of Upper and Lower Canada during the Years 1795, 1796, and 1797*, vol. 2 (London: John Stockdale, 1799), 15–16.
3. NARA, M247, rg360, i35 r41, p119.

FIGURE 22. Ursuline nun. This is an example of the Ursuline nuns' habits, which were essentially unchanged between the order's Canadian beginnings in 1639 and the Continental Army's arrival in Three Rivers. Portrait de la Vénérable Mère Marie de l'Incarnation, 1677. Library and Archives Canada, R5027-1.

Payement of three accounts amounting to £ 26-3-6 hallifax[4] for soldiers of the Continental army, who had been Sick in their hospital in the year 1776.[5]

Mr. de tonnancour & Badeaux of the Same Place hope that Colonel Melcher will be so good as to take notice of their inclosed accounts.

[signed Badeaux P.N.]

3 Rs the 23th Mars 1784

First Ursuline Account,
December 5, 1775 to March 7, 1776[6]

State of the invalid soldiers from the continental army who were cared for and medicated at the Ursuline hospital in 3 Rivers and their expenses.

---

4. The Ursuline nuns' accounts were originally kept in Canadian *livres*. In 1777, Halifax Currency became the official standard for the Province of Quebec, thus the 1776 expenses were converted for these 1784 claims. The total of the three Ursuline accounts was 629 ℔ 12ƒ in Canadian *livres*, which converted to the equivalent £ 26-3-6 Halifax Currency provided by Badeaux. This was based on a conversion rate of twenty-four *livres* per Halifax pound. Halifax currency £ 111/2/2.67 was equal to £100 sterling, and £4 Halifax also equaled one Spanish dollar. A. B. McCullough, "Currency Conversion in British North America, 1760–1900," *Archivaria* 16 (Summer 1983): 84, 92.

5. In 1777, Badeaux had also submitted a claim to a Quebec government board of enquiry, claiming a loss on behalf of the Ursulines of £31-9-8. This claim specifically mentioned that it was "signed for by William Goforth as Commandant of Trois-Rivieres." The £5-6-2 difference from the 1784 claim submitted to Congress is not explained by any available records. "Second Book of Minutes of the Court of Enquiry of Damages, Occasioned by the Invasion of the Rebels," March 10, 1777, Fonds Hospice-Anthelme-Jean-Baptiste Verreau, LAC, MG23-GV7.

6. NARA, M247, rg360, i35 r41, 113/113a. Another version titled "Copies des comptes des Dames religieuses des Trois-Rivières, les américains—1792," is available in Jean-Baptiste Badeaux Notarial Records, BAnQ, CN 401, S5, P4140, Fonds Cour Supérieure. District judiciaire de Trois-Rivières. Greffes de notaires (microfilm M146/36). Badeaux certified the BAnQ version as a proper copy from the Ursulines records, September 10, 1792, although expenses were recalculated and recorded in Halifax currency, and three of the four account pages were translated to English. The 1792 BAnQ version also provides some details not included in the earlier NARA copy (such as individuals' unit assignments). The version presented below is a translation of the NARA documents.

N 1 Samuel Rocks[7] Entered the hospital 1st of December
1775, left 1st of January following, making 3[1] days
room and board at 20ſ per day   31lt
for remedies and bloodlettings   12lt   43lt[8]
N 2 Joseph Casavant[9] militiaman from the
congressional troops of Colonel Leveston
Entered the hospital 5th of December 1775.
Left 4th of January following, making 30 days
room and board at 20ſ   30lt
for remedies   6lt   36
N 3 Waller West[10] Entered the hospital 5th of
December 1775, left 4th of January following,
making 30 days room and board at 20ſ   30lt
for sundry remedies   14lt10ſ   44ſ10
No 4 Nicolas Titcomb[11] Entered the hospital 12th
of January 1776, left 15th of February following,

---

7. The BAnQ version lists this individual as "Samuel Roks," in "Captain Robert wrights Company" (Livingston's First Canadian Continental Regiment). Probably Samuel Rock, originally from John Graham's Company, Second New York Regiment. Reenlistees were allowed to join any unit they wished. Rock would have been admitted to the hospital while traveling from Montreal to Quebec City. "Copies des comptes des Dames . . . ," BAnQ, CN 401, S5, P4140; NARA, M881, rg93, r98, p2; "Muster Roll of Captain John Graham's Company of the Second New York Troops," September 12, 1775, Isle aux Noix; NARA, M246, rg93 r0067 f19 p15.

8. The original accounts were kept in Canadian *livres* (lt). There were twenty sols (ſ) per *livre*.

9. Joseph Casavant *dit* Ladebauche, Livingston's First Canadian Regiment, from the parish of Verchères, UMPRDH indiv. 29370. Admitted while traveling to Quebec City.

10. Walter West, Captain Israel Curtis's New Hampshire volunteer company, originally attached to Bedel's Rangers. Curtis and thirty-four of his men agreed to continue serving in Canada through the winter. They were then part of the composite unit led by Major John Brown. West would have been admitted while traveling to Quebec City. "Petition of John House and Daniel Clap," NARA, M246, rg93 r49, f49, p72; NARA, M804, rg15, W.21377 (John House).

11. Nicholas Titcomb, Samuel Ward's Company of Arnold's Corps. The BAnQ version of the accounts specifically identifies him as being "in Colonel arnolds Regt." "Copies des comptes des Dames . . . ," BAnQ, CN 401, S5, P4140; Stephen Darley, *Voices from a Wilderness Expedition: The Journals and Men of Benedict Arnold's Expedition to Quebec in 1775* (Bloomington, IN: Author House, 2011), 227. Reaching Three Rivers at this time, Titcomb was probably a deserter. Arnold kept his New England troops from leaving the camp at Quebec, even though their enlistments expired on January 1. It is highly unlikely Titcomb would have been sent south on orders, particularly before any reinforcement had reached the camp at Quebec.

making 34 days of room and board at 20ſ   34₶
for assorted remedies and ointments   13₶   47₶
No 5 McDannell[12] Entered the hospital 19th of
January, left 25th of February making
37 days of room and board at 20ſ   37₶
~~for bloodlettings and assorted remedies~~   ~~15₶2ſ~~
for remedies and ointments   12₶   49₶
                                                                  219₶10

[page break in original]
The preceding amount—   219₶10
No 6 Thomas pollard[13] Entered the hospital 12th of
February 1776, left the 26th of the same month
making 14 days of room and board at 20ſ   14₶
For bloodlettings and assorted remedies   15₶2   29 2
                                                                  248₶12

For the invalid from the garrison here, Entered the
hospital without certificate and was there 4 days,   4₶
making he took one medication   3   7
Sister La Nativité,[14] Bursar of the poor
                                                                  255₶12

To the Ursulines of 3 Rivers, 8 March 1776
farther down the following is written.
March 12th 1776. I acknowledge per the Evidence of
Mr Bado, that the above account is just, Gvn me

---

12. The BAnQ version identifies "McDonnall" as serving in "Captain Knights Company" (most likely Ten Eyck's company, as there is no documentation of a Captain Knight serving in Canada). Probably James or Peter McDonald, originally of Barent Ten Eyck's Company, Second New York Regiment, who may have been among the 120 men that Major Peter Gansevoort led from Montreal on January 17. They were to be the first reinforcements to the Quebec siege after Montgomery's defeat (see Goforth's January 19 letter and note). "Copies des comptes des Dames . . . ," BAnQ,; "Muster Roll of Captain Barrent J. Ten Eyck's Company . . . ," September 12, 1775, NARA, M246, rg93, r67, f19, p8.

13. Thomas Pollard, unidentified. The BAnQ version of the accounts notes that he was "in Richmons Regt," possibly making him a volunteer from the town of Richmond, western Berkshire County, Massachusetts; "Copies des comptes des Dames . . . ," BAnQ. However, Pollard's name does not appear on any extant muster rolls from Cady's Detachment, nor in the archival compilation *Massachusetts Soldiers and Sailors of the Revolutionary War*, vol. 12 (Boston: Wright and Potter, 1904), 506.

14. Sister Marie-Josephte Paquet *dite* de La Nativité. *Ursulines de Trois Rivières*, 317; Raymond Douville, "Guillimin, Marie-Françoise, de Saint-Antoine," in *DCB*, 4, http://www.biographi.ca/en/bio/guillimin_marie_francoise_4E.html (accessed October 16, 2014).

Appenedix 1 / 177

William Goforth 4. B.
Commander of three Rivers
A true copy of the original
Sent to Philadelphia
Attested before me   Wm Barr C.P.[15]

Second Ursuline Claim, March 8 to 30, 1776[16]

State of the invalids of the Continental army who were cared for and medicated at the Ursuline hospital in 3 Rivers and their expenses after 7 March 1776.

No 1 Jean Rains[17] from Captain Goforth's company.
Entered the hospital 10th of March, left the 26th,
making 16 days of room and board at 20ſ   16lt
for remedies   4lt   20lt

No 2 Jacques Kelly[18] from Captain Joons's company.
Entered the hospital 23rd of March to the 30th,
making 7 days   7lt
for remedies   4lt   11lt

---

15. William Barr, British Purveyor of Hospitals in Canada, March 16, 1776 to December 24, 1783. "An Account of such Money as has been paid by the several Public Accounts . . . ," June 23, 1798, *Reports from Committees of the House of Commons*, vol. 13 (London: 1803), 135.

16. NARA, M247, rg360, i35 r41, p125/125a. The text presented here is translated from the NARA copy, however, this account is also included in the 1792 copies discussed in the note to the *First Ursuline Account, 5 December 1775 to 7 March 1776* (above).

17. John Rains, of Goforth's Company. "Muster Roll of Captain Goforth's Company," NARA, M246, rg93 r65 p33.

18. Corporal James Kelly, Captain Jonathan Jones Company, First Pennsylvania Battalion. He was later murdered by one of his fellow soldiers near Pointe-aux-Trembles (Quebec District) on May 7. John Blair Linn and William H. Egle, eds., *Pennsylvania in the War of the Revolution, Battalions and Line, 1775–1783* (Harrisburg: Lane S. Hart, 1880), 1: 57.

19. William Ward, Captain Joseph Stout's Company, Second New Jersey. "Muster Roll of Captain Joseph Stout's Company," NARA, M246, rg 83 r57 f20 p17.

20. Note that Joseph Stout's company had an unusually large number of sick soldiers. Badeaux observed that the New Jersey troops claimed to be "dying of hunger" during the few days that the unit's main body spent in Three Rivers. See Badeaux's March 19 entry. None of these company's veterans' Revolutionary War pensions shed light on unusual health issues they faced, and their regimental orderly book does not include any entries from February 4 until March 26; Salsig, *Parole: Quebec*, 51–53.

No 3 William Ward[19] from Captain Stots's company.[20]
Entered the hospital 17th of March. Died the 27th
making 10 days   10₶
for remedies   7₶4ſ
for coffin and shroud   9₶   26₶4ſ
No 4 Bainjamain Larrabi[21] and thomas Crook[22] from
Major Cristi's company.[23] Entered 11th of March to the
30th, making 19 days each
In all 38   38₶
For remedies   10₶   48₶
No 5 Jean Molonie[24] from Captain Stouts's company.
Entered the hospital 19th of March, left the 29th
making 10 days   10₶
for remedies   6₶   16₶14
No 6 Jean Huntly and thomas sainds[25] from Captain
Stouts's company. Entered the hospital 20th of March
to the 30th making 10 days each.   20₶
For remedies   9₶   29
                                                                    150₶18

[page break in original]

---

21. Benjamin Larrabee, Captain Joseph Estabrook's Company, Bedel's New Hampshire Regiment. Isaac W. Hammond, ed., *Rolls of the Soldiers in the Revolutionary War, 1775 to May 1777* . . . (Concord, NH: Parsons B. Cogwell, 1885), 263.

22. Thomas Crook served in Abraham Palmer's Company, Bedel's (New Hampshire) Rangers, around St. John's in 1775. He continued serving in Canada through June 1776, probably in Major John Brown's composite "regiment" of New Englanders. The deposition supporting his service record noted that he returned with accounts of "suffering & sickness." "A Pay Roll of Colonel Timothy Bedel's Company . . . 1775," NARA, M246, rg93, r49, f49, p6; NARA, M804, rg15, pension S.12638 (Thomas Crook).

23. Major Cristi here is almost certainly a transcription error by Badeaux. The BAnQ version of the accounts identifies the company commander as "major Curtis." Israel Curtis was known to have remained in Quebec in Brown's composite regiment in 1776, and it would be logical for these New Hampshire men to have served under him; see note to Walter West entry above.

24. John Maloney, Captain Joseph Stout's Company, Second New Jersey. "Muster Roll of Captain Joseph Stout's Company," NARA, M246, rg 83 r57 f20 p17.

25. John Huntly and Thomas Sands, Captain Joseph Stout's Company, Second New Jersey. "Muster Roll of Captain Joseph Stout's Company," NARA, M246, rg 83 r57 f20 p17.

The preceding amount—   150₶18
No 7 Ebenezer William[26] from Captain Seavens's
company. Entered the hospital 7th of March to the 30th
making 23 days   23₶
for remedies   10₶   33

No 8 Joseph Grennoy[27] officer in Colonel deherse's
regiment. Entered the hospital 23rd of March, left
the 30th, 7 days at 45ſ per day[28]   15₶15
for remedies   7₶   22₶15

No 9 Gesse Heth[29] of Captain Israel Courtis's company,
Entered the hospital 12th of March, left the 26th,
making 14 days   14₶
for remedies   4₶   18₶

For remedies given to several invalids outside the
hospital   18₶16   18₶16
                                                                      243₶5

To the Ursulines of 3 Rivers
30 March 1776
Sister la Nativité, Bursar of the poor
And below is written the following
acknowledge good by me William Goforth

---

26. Ebenezer William, Captain Zebadiah Sabin's company of Massachusetts volunteers, attached to the Green Mountain Boys, see Appendix 2 and notes. Since Captain Sabin's detachments had passed Three Rivers heading toward Quebec City on January 31 and February 22, William may have been a straggler, or may have been released early from the Quebec City camp, perhaps due to his illness.

27. Ensign Joseph Greenway, as spelled in the BAnQ version of the accounts, from De Haas's First Pennsylvania Battalion. This name matches First Pennsylvania Regiment records, however, other documents show that Ensign Greenway resigned his army commission and was appointed a third lieutenant in the provincial naval service on March 21, 1776—this may have been done by proxy while Greenway was in Canada. "Copies des comptes des Dames . . . ," BAnQ; Linn and Egle, *Pennsylvania in the War of the Revolution*, 1: 56 and "Pay of Officers aboard the Provincial Ship," Pennsylvania Committee of Safety, March 21, 1776, in *AA4*, 5: 729.

28. Note that this officer was charged more than twice as much for room and board as a private soldier.

29. Jesse Heath, Israel Curtis's reenlisted New Hampshire company. There is not an extant muster roll for this unit, however Heath was recorded as having served in Canada with "Bedel's Regiment" in 1776. For details on Curtis's company, see note to Samuel Rocks, above. "A Return of Men in the Haverhill Company," May 1, 1777, Hammond, *Rolls of the Soldiers*, 546.

Commander at three Rivers april 2d 1776.
a true copy of the original
Send to Philadelphia
attested before me [signed Wm Barr C.P.]

Third Ursuline Account, March 31 to April 30, 1776[30]

State of the invalids of the Continental army who were lodged and medicated at the Ursuline hospital in three Rivers from the cessation of accountings on 30 March to 24 April 1776 and expenses.
Be it known
For those who stayed after the cessation of the accounts[31]
No 2 jacques Kelley from Captain Joons's company from 30th of March to 5th of April when he left, 6 days of room and board   6lt   6lt
No 4 Binjamain Larrabi and Thomas Crook of Major Cristi's company. Binjamain left 5th of April, 30th of March to 5th of April makes 6 days. Thomas Crook left 17th of April, from 30th March to 17th April makes 18 days, in all 24 days   24lt
No 5 jean huntlir and Thomas Sainds of Captain Stouts's company from 30th of March to 5th of April when they left makes 6 days each, twelve in all   12lt
No 7 Ebenzer William from Captain Savens's company from 30th of March to 2[0th] of April, when he left makes 21 days   21lt
for remedies for the pilot[32]   5lt
Sick having entered since 30th of March   68
An invalid received based on a promissory note from an officer. Entered the hospital 18th of March 1776, left 11th of April making 14 days   14lt

---

30. NARA, M247, rg360, i35 r41, p129/129a.

31. See previous accounts running through March 30 for these soldiers' identification information.

32. The "pilot" is unidentified. He may have been captaining one of the ships that the Continentals had resumed using in late April—for transporting reinforcements down the St. Lawrence to Quebec City, and for carrying discharged troops up the river.

for remedies	9₶18
An invalid received based on a promissory note from Captain William Goforth. Entered the hospital 11th of April, left the 18th making	
7 days	7
for remedies	6
	104₶18ƒ

[page break in original]

Preceding amount		104₶18
For remedies furnished upon promissory notes from the garrison commander		
No 1 for		4₶
No 2 for		2₶
No 3 for		3₶15
No 4 for		8ƒ
No 5 for	2₶10	12₶13
		117₶11

To the Ursulines of 3 Rivers
24 April 1776
Sister La Nativité, Bursar of the poor and those of the hospital order

A "Bostonian" received into our hospital by order of Captain Pierre Cassel 30th of April, died 13th of May, making 13 days	13
	130₶11

A true copy of the original
Sent to Philadelphia
attested before me
Wm. Barr C.P.

Jean-Baptiste Badeaux's Personal Claim[33]

I John Baptist Badeaux Publick Notary of three Rivers, in the Province of Quebec do hereby Certify that I have in my Possession ever since the year 1776 the following Philadelphia Bills, or paper money. Vizt.

---

33. NARA, M247, rg360, i35 r41, p117.

No. 73451.
38470
73508
47195
Hallifax curr[34]
Three Rivers 23rd of March 1784
[signed Badeaux P.N.]
Attested before me
Wm B. S. P

one four dollar bill	£ 1 "	0 "	0
one Dollar bill	0 "	5 "	0
one Six Dollar bill	1 "	10 "	0
one Dollar bill	0 "	5 "	0
	£ 3 "	0 "	0

Godefroy de Tonnancour Claim[35]

Account for two hogsheads[36] of rum that I turned over to Mr. Haron Hurte[37] and delivered by order of Misters Price and Hourde.[38] Which Mr. Hurte did [order] once in two parts for the former Continental Army. Which makes still owing
Canviv[?]
One hogshead 117 Gallons of rum }

---

34. Badeaux based his claim on the Continental bills' original stated value in Spanish milled dollars. In the eight years since Badeaux received these notes however, the Continental dollar had been devalued to roughly one-fortieth of its face value, before the Continental dollar was completely revalued in 1781. Wayne E. Lee, "The American Revolution," in *Daily Lives of Civilians in Wartime Early America: From the Colonial Era to the Civil War*, ed. David S. Heidler and Jeanne T. Heidler (Westport, CT: Greenwood Press, 2007), 51.

35. NARA, M247, rg360, i35 r41, p133. This simple accounting was extremely difficult to decipher. Tonnancour's handwriting on this claim epitomized a German staff officer's description of the French-Canadians from 1776: "But few people are able to write, and the orthography of the rich who can write may be compared with that of our common classes at home. I have read letters written by Captain of Militia, Tournencour [Tonnancour] a prominent banker and one of the wealthiest men in Canada which would require a key in order to understand them. They write as they speak, and contract several words into one." "Letter from Canada, by a German Staff-Officer, Batiscamp, a Parish in Canada," November 2, 1776, Stone, *Letters of Brunswick and Hessian Officers*, 37.

36. *tonnes* in the original French. A hogshead was a large cask, twice as large as a standard barrel.

37. Aaron Hart, see December 4 entry in Badeaux's journal, and note.

38. Montreal merchant James Price, staunch advocate of the Continental cause, and his business partner William Haywood. Price accompanied General Montgomery when he traveled from Montreal in November 1775, to join Benedict Arnold and besiege Quebec City. See Badeaux journal entry for beginning of December and note.

One hogshead 116 Gallons of rum } making
together 233 gallons of rum
constituting a property of the province   67:19ƒ
the present affirmed to be a true accounting
Amounting to the sum of sixty-seven pounds and 19 dulafaxe[39]
In Three Rivers, March 22, 1784
God. Tonnancour[40]
Three Rivers 22nd March 1784
Affirmed before me Wm. Barr, C.P.

Disposition of the Claims

Congress received all of these claims on July 8, presented by Isaac Melchior. As indicated on the cover letter, Congress referred the claims to the Committee of the Week for consideration, and on the fourteenth of that month, the committee then presented the documents for considerations of the assembly.[41] Congress, however, did not make any resolution of the claims. Presumably, debt payment was caught up in the broad, complex issues related to both sides' compliance with the terms of the 1783 Treaty of Paris. In the end, Badeaux and Tonnancour never received anything in return for their claims. The Ursuline Sisters did not receive any compensation for the services and materials they provided to the Continental Army in these accounts either, until 2009, when the United States Consul General provided symbolic compensation, more than two centuries after the fact.[42]

---

39. Halifax currency.
40. Louis-Joseph Godefroy de Tonnancour.
41. July 8, 1784, *JCC*, 27: 578; NARA, M247, rg360, i35 r41, p109.
42. In 2009, as part of the Trois Rivières 375th Anniversary celebration, United States Consul General David Fetter symbolically repaid the debt with C$130 delivered personally to the Ursulines. A 1957 article by Canadian Raymond Douville had examined the claims and calculated the interest that the United States theoretically owed to the nuns was more than $4 million by that time. Marie-Ève Bourgoing-Alarie, «Mieux vaut tard que jamais!,» *L'Hebdo Journal* (Three Rivers, QC), 4 July 2009; Raymond Douville, "La dette des Etats-Unis envers les Ursulines de Trois Rivières," *Les Cahiers des Dix* 22 (1957): 137–62.

Appendix 2

Officers and Unit Identification for Goforth's March 24, 1776, Letter to Reverend John Gano

Ja^n 31	Captn Seaban from the Bay Government, the first Hero that Came to our assistance	25
	Captain Zebadiah Sabin's Company of Massachusetts Volunteers attached to Seth Warner's Green Mountain Boys.[1]	
31	Captn Smith with	19
	Captain Simeon Smith, Cady's Detachment (Massachusetts).[2]	
Feb 9	Leiutenants Munson and Pettibone with part of two Company's	25
	Probably Sergeant Abel Munson, Captain Jacob Person's Company, Cady's Detachment (Massachusetts).[3]	
	First Lieutenant Eli Pettibone, Captain Nathan Peirce's Company, Green Mountain Boys.[4]	

---

1. These men answered General Wooster's call for immediate reinforcements, after receiving news of Montgomery's defeat at Quebec City. The appeal was originally addressed to Seth Warner and the Green Mountain Boys, but sparked responses by western New Englanders, too. *A History of the County of Berkshire, Massachusetts, in Two Parts* . . . (Pittsfield, MA: Samuel W. Bush, 1829), 409; NARA, M804, rg15, p5, pension W.22467 (Hezekiah Tuttle); Philip Schuyler to John Hancock, January 22, 1776, *AA4*, 4: 804.

2. "A Pay Roll of Captn Simeon Smith's Company . . . ," January 14 to June 6, 1776, NARA, M246, rg93, r40, f49, p23.

3. Captain Jacob Person's Company, Cady's Detachment (Massachusetts); "Pay roll of Captn Jason Person's Company . . . ," January 14 to June 6, 1776, NARA, M246, rg 93, r40, f49, p17; NARA M804, rg 15, p11, pensions S.45407 (Clark Hyde).

4. NARA, M804, rg15, p13–14, pension S.14878 (Richmond Worden); Muster Roll and Subscription, January 15, 1776, *The New England Historical and Genealogical Register* (April 1922): 155–57.

21[5]	Leuit Walker with *Lieutenant Jonathan Walker, Captain Simeon Smith's Company, Cady's Detachment (Massachusetts).*[6]	17
21	Capt[n] Wetherby with *Captain Samuel Wetherbee with Charlestown, New Hampshire, volunteers, incorporated into Seth Warner's Green Mountain Boys.*[7]	33
22	Leuit Meacham with *Lieutenant Jonathan Meacham of Sabin's Company of volunteers.*[8]	12
24	Capt[n] Hinman with *Captain Reuben Hinman, Cady's Detachment (Massachusetts).*[9]	23
24	Capt[n] Peirce with *Captain Nathan Peirce, Cady's Detachment (Massachusetts).*[10]	25
24	Uzziah Wright, Gentleman Volunteer with *Azariah Wright of Westminster, in the New Hampshire Grants.*[11]	8
26	Leuit Sunderland with *Ensign Peleg Sunderland, Oliver Potter's Company, Green Mountain Boys.*[12]	32
26	Serjeant Clark with *Most likely Sergeant Elisha Clark, Captain Wait Hopkins's Company, Green Mountain Boys.*[13]	20

---

5. Goforth was away from Three Rivers on February 20, and may have missed some troops passing through; see Badeaux's journal.

6. "A Pay Roll of Captn Simeon Smith's Company . . . ," January 14 to June 6, 1776, NARA, M246, rg93, r40, f49, p23.

7. Charleston, New Hampshire, sits on the Connecticut River adjacent to Vermont. NARA, M804, rg 15, pension S.14565 (John Spafford), p68. A number of parties were gathered in western New England and the New Hampshire Grants (Vermont), to provide immediate reinforcements to Canada; George Washington to Philip Schuyler, Chase, *PGWRWS*, 3: 142.

8. NARA, M804, rg 15, Pension S.23030 (Isaac Train), p4; this was a seventeen-man detachment when it departed Berkshire County.

9. NARA, M804, rg 15, p10, pension W.19003 (Josiah Sabin).

10. NARA, M804, rg 15, p4, pension S.13867 (Mathew Mason); Muster Roll and Subscription, January 15, 1776, *The New England Historical and Genealogical Register* (April 1922): 155–57.

11. Benjamin H. Hall, *History of Eastern Vermont*, vol. 2 (Albany: J. Munsell, 1865), 730.

12. NARA, M804, rg 15, pension S.41267 (John Train), p4.

13. Ibid., pension S.14324 (Joseph Rowe), p9.

1 March[14]	Leuitenant Loomis with *First Lieutenant Michael Loomis of Captain Isaac Vosbrough's Company, with Cady's Detachment (Massachusetts).*[15]	58
1	Leuitenant Talbert with the first Pennsylvania Company *Second Lieutenant Samuel Tolbert, unidentified company, First Pennsylvania Battalion, Colonel John Philip De Haas.*[16]	60
1	Leuitenant [Dean] from the Bay Government with *Lieutenant John Dean, Captain Jacob Person's Company, Cady's Detachment (Massachusetts).*[18]	4[8]
4	Serjeant Saint John with *Sergeant Jacob St. John, Captain Simeon Smith's Company, Cady's Detachment (Massachusetts).*[19]	15
4	Serjeant Gidion Brenson with *Captain Gideon Brownson, Green Mountain Boys.*[20]	07
5	Captn Goodridge with *Captain Daniel Goodrich, Cady's Detachment (Massachusetts).*[21]	35

---

14. Goforth was away from Three Rivers on February 29, and may have missed any troops passing through that day.

15. NARA, M804, rg15, pension R.3206 (Peter Eastman), p3.

16. Montgomery, *Pennsylvania Archives*, 2: 68.

17. Second digit illegible in original. The version printed in the *Constitutional Gazette* (above) lists "40," however 48 results in Goforth's total sum of 1362.

18. Illegible name in original is listed as Lieutenant Deane in a reprint of the letter in "New York, May 1, Extract of a Letter from an Officer in the Continental Army, dated Trois Riviers [*sic*], March 24, 1776," *Constitutional Gazette* (New York City), 4 May 1776. "Pay roll of Captn Jason Person's Company . . . ," January 14 to June 6, 1776; NARA, M246, rg93, r40, f49, p17.

19. "A Pay Roll of Captn Leicester Grosvenor's Company . . . ," January 14 to June 6, 1776; NARA, M246, rg 93, r40, f49, p13.

20. Curiously, Gideon Brownson was a Green Mountain Boys captain, not a sergeant. He was known to be leading his company from Montreal to Quebec City at this time. "A List of Capt Brownsons Company Montreal Febr 26 1776," and "A muster Rool [*sic*] of Capt Gideon Brownsons Company," May 9, 1776; in *The State of Vermont, Rolls of the Soldiers in the Revolutionary War, 1775 to 1783*, ed. John E. Goodrich (Rutland, VT: Tuttle, 1904), 635–39.

21. "A payroll of Captn Daniel Goodrich's Company . . . ," January 14 to June 6, 1776; NARA, M246, rg93, r40, f49, p8.

5	Leuit Frisby with *Probably Captain Isaac Vosbrough, Cady's Detachment (Massachusetts).*[22]	31
5	Leuit Walbridge with *Adjutant Enock Woodbridge, Cady's Detachment (Massachusetts).*[23]	49
6	Captain Gidion Dowd *Possibly Militia Captain Charles Dowd of Berkshire County (Massachusetts).*[24]	48
6	Captain Wright *Possibly Captain Robert Wright, First Canadian Regiment.*[25]	63
10	Leuit Hughs from Philadelphia with *First Lieutenant Peter Hughes, unidentified company, First Pennsylvania.*[26]	60
10	Leuit Grant from New England *Lieutenant Benjamin Grant, Captain Ebenezer Green's Company, Bedel's Regiment (New Hampshire).*[27]	30
10	Leuit Jenkins from Philadelphia with *Captain William Jenkins, First Pennsylvania.*[28]	45
10	Major Safford of Col Warner['s] Regiment with *Major Samuel Safford, Green Mountain Boys Regiment.*[29]	60

---

22. NARA, M804, rg15, pension R.3206 (Peter Eastman), p3.

23. "A payroll for Majr Jeremiah Cady and the Staff Officers," January 14 to June 6, 1776; NARA, M246, rg93, r40, f49, p2.

24. Only a single account can be found mentioning any Captain Dowd heading to Canada at this time. It is Charles Dowd of Berkshire County, rather than "Gideon"; NARA, M804, rg15, pension S.44645 (William Beatman), p4.

25. There is no extant record of a Captain Wright in any of the reinforcing units passing through Three Rivers at this time. Given that Goforth did not provide any additional identifying information, Captain Robert Wright of Livingston's Canadian Regiment is a possibility. Some of his company seems to have passed through the city in early December 1775 (see notes to Samuel Rocks entry in Appendix 1—The Accounts of the Three Rivers Ursuline Nuns). However, it is possible that Wright may not have been with that earlier detachment, or may have been sent back to the Richelieu Valley to return with men left behind, new recruits, or maybe even deserters.

26. Montgomery, *Pennsylvania Archives*, 2: 67.

27. "Officers' Receipt—Bedel's Regiment," March 8, 1776; NARA, M246, rg 93, r49, f49, p13.

28. Montgomery, *Pennsylvania Archives*, 2: 66.

29. New York Congress, 1 September 1775, *AA4*, 3: 571.

10	Captain Grosvenor with *Captain Leicester Grosvenor, Cady's Detachment (Massachusetts).*[30]	42
12	Captⁿ Jenkins with [*sic*] from Philadelphia, with his company chiefly passed before *Captain William Jenkins, Sixth Company, First Pennsylvania.*[31]	08
12	Captⁿ Colay from New England with *Unidentified.*[33]	46[32]
16	Leuit Yard, the first of the Jersey forces with an escort with provisions *Lieutenant Thomas Yard, Captain Joseph Braley's Company, Second New Jersey Regiment (Colonel William Maxwell).*[34]	34
17	Major Ray of the Jersey Batalion *Major David Rhea, Second New Jersey.*[35]	179
20	Captⁿ Carlisle with *Captain Daniel Carlisle, Bedel's Regiment (New Hampshire).*[36]	29

---

30. "A Pay Roll of Captn Leicester Grosvenor's Company . . . ," January 14 to June 6, 1776, NARA M246, rg93, r40, f49, p13.

31. NARA, M246, rg 93, r80, f2, p7.

32. "40" in 4 May 1776 *Constitutional Gazette* version.

33. The version of this list published in the *Constitutional Gazette* (New York), 4 May 1776, lists this officer as "Capt. Cooley from New-England. . . ." None of the rolls of known units passing to Quebec City around this time show anyone with a name similar to this, presumably a western New England volunteer, perhaps from the Connecticut Valley, where a number of prominent Cooleys lived.

34. "A Muster Roll of Captain Joseph Braley's Company . . . ," January 15, 1776, NARA, M246, rg93, r57, f20, p3. Colonel William Maxwell's Second New Jersey Regiment was hastily rushed north with marginal time to organize and equip. It is notable that the vanguard moved in these two large detachments, which would have helped maintain discipline. The regiment had experienced many challenges in controlling its soldiers on its march through New York; Harry M. Ward, *General William Maxwell and the New Jersey Continentals* (Westport, CT: Greenwood, 1997), 27–29.

35. "A Muster Roll of Captain William Falkner's Company . . . ," January 17, 1776, NARA, M246, rg93, r57, f20, p5.

36. NARA, M804, rg15, pension S.42403 (Ephraim Stone), p11. *Note:* Bedel's Regiment was deployed piecemeal; some detachments like these went northeast to join the Quebec City blockade under the overall command of Lieutenant Colonel Joseph Wait, others remained in the Montreal area under Colonel Timothy Bedel and Major Isaac Butterfield. Most of the latter were surrendered at the Battle of the Cedars, on May 20.

20	Leuitenant Grant with *Lieutenant Benjamin Grant, Captain Ebenezer Green's Company, Bedel's Regiment (New Hampshire).*[37]	14
22	Leuit Stone with *First Lieutenant Ephraim Stone, Captain Daniel Carlisle's Company, Bedel's Regiment (New Hampshire).*[38]	34
22	Captn Wait with *Captain Jason Wait, Bedel's Regiment (New Hampshire).*[39]	47
22	Leuitenant Stainer with *First Lieutenant Roger Stayner, Captain Thomas Dorsey's Company, First Pennsylvania.*[40]	81

Of new forces Total amount	1362
about three hundred of Montreal Garrison moved down	300
about six hundred I suppose left after the defeat according to accounts th[at] hear I can obtain Recruited by, or among Canadians	600
First Canadian Regiment, Colonel James Livingston, and Second Canadian Regiment, Lieutenant Colonel Jeremiah Duggan, later Colonel Moses Hazen.[41]	500
You must make allowance for the sick and wounded at the Camp	2762

---

37. "Officer's Receipt—Bedel's Regiment," March 8, 1776, NARA, M246, rg 93, r49, f49, p13.
38. NARA, M804, rg15, pension S.42403 (Ephraim Stone), p11.
39. Ibid., 15, pension W.2044 (William York), p25, and pension W.17893 (Eben Farnam), p4.
40. Montgomery, *Pennsylvania Archives*, 67; NARA, M804, rg15, pension S.41,197 (Roger Stayner), p4.
41. General Montgomery, with Congressional authority, formed the First Canadian Continental Regiment on November 19, 1775, under Colonel James Livingston, and Benedict Arnold, without authorization, directed Lieutenant Colonel Jeremiah Duggan to form a second Canadian Continental regiment in January 1776. Unaware of Arnold's action, Congress authorized a second regiment later that month, appointing Colonel Moses Hazen to command, who subsequently replaced Duggan; see note to Badeaux's March 24 entry. Richard Montgomery to Philip Schuyler, November 19, 1775, PSP, microfilm reel 12, NYPL; Benedict Arnold to Continental Congress, January 12, 1776, in Roberts, *March to Quebec*, 113; January 22, 1776, *JCC*, 4: 78.

Select Bibliography

Archives

American Philosophical Society

Benjamin Franklin Papers (Mss B F85) Part 1—Letters to Franklin

Bibliothèque et Archives National de Québec

CN 401, S60, Fonds Cour Supérieure. District judiciaire de Trois-Rivières. Greffes de notaires—Benoit Leroy.
CN 401, S5, Fonds Cour Supérieure. District judiciaire de Trois-Rivières. Greffes de notaires—Jean-Baptiste Badeaux (microfilm M146/36).
P98, Fonds Famille Gugy.
S2 Fief Grand-Pré.
S8 Rivière-du-Loup
P1000, Collection Centre d'archives de Québec.
S3, D254, Mémoire sur les actions du capitaine Bouchette lors de l'invasion de Québec en 1775.

Public Library of Cincinnati and Hamilton County

Goforth Family Bible

Columbia University

The Papers of John Jay, Columbia University, Butler Library, Rare Book & Manuscript Division. Available at http://www.columbia.edu/cu/lweb/digital/jay/search.html.

Indiana Historical Society

John Armstrong Papers, 1772–1950 (microfilm).

Library and Archives of Canada

MG-21. Haldimand Papers. Microfilm A-616.
MG23-B4. Moses Hazen Collection.
MG23-B7. Journal of the most remarkable events which happened in Canada between the months of July 1775 and June 1776.
MG23-B25. Certificate of Lt. Col. Allan Maclean.
MG23-B35. Collection Amable Berthelot.
MG23-B40. Robert R. Livingston Collection.
MG23-GV7. Fonds Hospice-Anthelme-Jean-Baptiste Verreau.

New-York Historical Society Archives

Horatio Gates Papers (microfilm).
Alexander MacDougall Papers, 1756–1795 (microfilm).

New York Public Library Archives

Philip Schuyler Papers (microfilm).

United States National Archives and Records Administration

M246, Revolutionary War Rolls, 1775–1783.
M247, Papers of the Continental Congress, The Correspondence, Journals, Committee Reports, and Records of the Continental Congress (1774–1789).
M804, Revolutionary War Pension and Bounty-Land Warrant Application Files.
M853, Numbered record books include indexes, records of military operations and service, records of accounts, and supply records.
M881, Compiled service records of soldiers who served in the American Army during the Revolutionary War, 1775–1783.

Université de Montréal

Programme de recherche en démographie historique/Research Program in Historical Demography. Parish records database. Accessed September 29, 2014. http://www.genealogie.umontreal.ca.

Published Primary Sources and Collections

Ainslie, Thomas. *Canada Preserved: The Journal of Captain Thomas Ainslie*. Edited by Sheldon S. Cohen. New York: New York University Press, 1968.
Archives de la Province de Québec. *Recensement des Gouvernements de Montréal et des Trois-Rivières pour 1765*. Québec: Imprimerie du Roi, 1937.
Boyd, Julian P., ed. *The Papers of Thomas Jefferson*. Volume 1. Princeton: Princeton University Press, 1950.
Carter, Clarence E., ed. *The Correspondence of General Thomas Gage with the Secretaries of State*. New Haven: Yale University Press, 1931.
Chase, Philander, ed. *The Papers of George Washington: Revolutionary War Series*. Charlottesville: University of Virginia Press, 1985–1991.
Cist, Charles, ed. *The Cincinnati Miscellany, or Antiquities of the West . . .* Cincinnati: 1845.
Clark, William Bell, ed. *Naval Documents of the American Revolution*. Washington, DC: Government Printing Office, 1964–1970.
Davies, K. G., ed. *Documents of the American Revolution, 1770–1783*. Dublin: Irish University Press, 1975.
"Diary of the Weather kept at Quebec in the year of the siege by the Americans in 1776." *Transactions of the Literary and Historical Society of Quebec* 9, no. 22 (1898): 1–5.
Doughty, Arthur, ed. "Appendix B: Papers Relating to the Surrender of St. Johns and Chambly." In *Report on the Works of the Public Archives for the Years 1914 and 1915*. Ottawa: L. Taché, 1916.
Fassett, John Jr. "Diary of Lt John Fassett Jr. during a trip to Canada and return in Captain Weight Hopkins' company of Colonel Warner's regiment, under General Montgomery, from September 1st to December 7th, 1775." In *The Follet-Dewey Fassett-Safford Ancestry of Captain Martin Dewey Follett*, edited by Harry P. Ward. Columbus, OH: Champlin, 1896.
Force, Peter, ed. *American Archives: Fourth and Fifth Series*. Washington, DC: M. St. Clair Clarke and Peter Force, 1837–1853.
Ford, Worthington C., ed. *Journals of the Continental Congress, 1774–1789*. Volumes 1–5. Washington, DC: Government Printing Office: 1904–06.
Foucher, Feu. "Journal Tenu Pendant Le Siege du Fort Saint-Jean, en 1775, Par Feu M. Foucher, Ancien Notaire de Montréal." *Le Bulletin des Recherches Historiques* 40 (1934): 135–59, 197–222.
Freeman, James. "Record of the Services of Constant Freeman, Captain of the Artillery in the Continental Army." *Magazine of American History* 2 (1878): 349–51.
Gabriel, Michael P., ed. *Quebec during the American Invasion: The Journal of François Baby, Gabriel Taschereau, and Jenkin Williams*. Translated by S. Pascale

Vergereau-Dewey. East Lansing: Michigan State University, 2005.

"Journal of the Most Remarkable Occurrences since Arnold Appear'd Before the Town on the 14th November 1775." In *Historical Documents Relating to the Blockade of Quebec by the American Revolutionists in 1775–1776*. Quebec: Literary and Historical Society of Quebec, 1905.

"Journal of the Siege and Blockade of Quebec by the American Rebels in Autumn 1775 and Winter 1776." In *Historical Documents of the Literary and Historical Society of Quebec*. 4th Ser. Quebec: Literary and Historical Society of Quebec, 1876.

Laterrière, Pierre de Sales. *Mémoires de Pierre de Sales Laterrière et de sus traverses*. Quebec: L'Evenement, 1873.

Leake, Isaac. *Memoir of the Life and Times of General John Lamb*. Albany: Joel Munsell, 1850.

Lorimier, Claude. *At War with the Americans: Translation of 'Mes services pendant la guerre américaine.'* Translated and edited by Peter Aichinger. Victoria, BC: Porcépic, 1987.

Maseres, Francis. *Additional papers concerning the province of Quebeck: being an appendix to the book entitled, "An account of the proceedings of the British, and other Protestant inhabitants, of the province of Quebeck, in North America, In order to obtain an House of Assembly in that Province."* London: W. White, 1776.

Minutes of the Supreme Executive Council of Pennsylvania. Harrisburg: Theo. Fenn, 1853.

Parke, Andrew. *An Authentic Narrative of Facts Relating to the Exchange of Prisoners Taken at the Cedars*. London: T. Cadell, 1777.

Prince, Christopher. *The Autobiography of a Yankee Mariner: Christopher Prince and the American Revolution*. Edited by Michael J. Crawford. Washington, DC: Brassey's, 2002.

"Recensement des Habitants de La Ville et Gouvernement des Trois-Rivieres, 1760–1762." *Rapport de L'Archiviste de la Province de Quebec pour 1946–1947*. Quebec: Redempti Paradis, 1947.

Ritzema, Rudolphus. "Journal of Col. Rudolphus Ritzema, of the First New York Regiment, August 8, 1775 to March 30, 1776." *Magazine of American History* 1 (1877): 98–107.

Roberts, Kenneth, ed. *March to Quebec: Journals of the Members of Arnold's Expedition*. Garden City, NY: Doubleday, 1938.

Salsig, Doyen. *Parole: Quebec; Countersign: Ticonderoga, Second New Jersey Regimental Orderly Book, 1776*. London: Farleigh Dickinson, 1980.

Smith, Paul H., ed. *Letters of Delegates to Congress, 1774–1789*. Washington, DC: Library of Congress, 1976–2000.

Stone, William, transl. *Letters of Brunswick and Hessian Officers during the American Revolution*. Albany: Munsell's, 1891.

Verreau, Abbé, ed. *Invasion du Canada, Collection de Memoires Recueillis et Annotes.* Montreal: Eusebe Senecal, 1873.

Willcox, William, ed. *The Papers of Benjamin Franklin.* Volume 22. New Haven: Yale University Press, 1982.

Wurtele, Fred, ed. *Blockade of Quebec in 1775–1776 by the American Revolutionists (Les Bastonnais).* Quebec: Literary and Historical Society of Quebec, 1906.

Secondary Sources

Aldrich, Edgar. "The Affair of the Cedars and the Service of Colonel Timothy Bedel in the War of the Revolution." In *The Proceedings of the New Hampshire Historical Society.* Volume 3, *June, 1895 to June, 1899.* Concord: New Hampshire Historical Society, 1902.

Anderson, Mark R. *The Battle for the Fourteenth Colony: America's War of Liberation in Canada, 1774–1776.* Lebanon, NH: University Press of New England, 2013.

Audet, Francis-J. *Les Députés des Trois-Rivières (1808–1838).* Trois-Rivières, QC: Bien Public, 1934.

Barck, Oscar. *New York City during the War for Independence, with Special Reference to the Period of British Occupation.* New York: Columbia University Press, 1931.

Becker, Carl L. *The History of Political Parties in the Province of New York, 1760–1776.* Madison: University of Wisconsin Press, 1909.

Bellemere, J. E. *Histoire de Nicolet, 1669–1924.* Quebec: Athabaska, 1924.

Bennett, David. *A Few Lawless Vagabonds: Ethan Allen, The Republic of Vermont, and the American Revolution.* Havertown, PA: Casemate, 2014.

The Catholic Encyclopedia. New York: Encyclopedia Press, 1911.

Cécil, Pierre. "La bataille de Trois-Rivières, 8 juin 1776." *Traces* 38, no. 2 (mars-avril 2000): 25–27.

Chambers, Ernest. *The Canadian Militia: A History of the Origin and Development of the Force.* Montreal: L. M. Fresco, 1907.

Champagne, Roger J. "New York's Radicals and the Coming of Independence." *The Journal of American History* 51, No. 1 (June 1964): 21–40.

———. *Alexander McDougall and the American Revolution in New York.* Schenectady, NY: Union College Press, 1975.

Chatfield, William H. *Two Revolutionary War Patriots: Major William Goforth and Captain John Armstrong: Epic Struggles Against British Suppression and Indian Warfare.* Cincinnati: Pendleton House, 2011.

Commission des biens culturels du Québec. *Étude de caractérisation de l'arrondissement historique de Trois-Rivières.* Quebec: Commission des biens culturels du Québec, 2005.

Cubbison, Douglas R. *The American Northern Theater Army in 1776: The Ruin and Reconstruction of the Continental Force.* Jefferson, NC: MacFarland, 2010.

Desjardin, Thomas. *Through a Howling Wilderness: Benedict Arnold's March to Quebec, 1775.* New York: St. Martin's Press, 2006.

Dictionary of Canadian Biography Online/Dictionnaire biographique du Canada en ligne. Library and Archives Canada. Accessed September 30, 2014. www.biographi.ca.

Everest, Allan S. *Moses Hazen and the Canadian Refugees in the American Revolution.* Syracuse: Syracuse University Press, 1976.

Fryer, Mary Beacock. *Allan Maclean, Jacobite General: The Life of an Eighteenth Century Career Soldier.* Toronto: Dundurn Press, 1987.

Fyson, Donald. "Judicial Auxiliaries Across Legal Regimes: From New France to Lower Canada." A paper presented to the colloquium *Les auxiliaires de la justice: intermédiaires entre la justice et les populations, de la fin du Moyen Âge à l'époque contemporaine,* Québec, September 2004. Accessed January 17, 2010. http://www.hst.ulaval.ca/profs/Dfyson/Auxiliaries.pdf.

Gabriel, Michael. *Major General Richard Montgomery.* Madison, NJ: Fairleigh Dickinson University Press, 2002.

Greer, Allan. *Peasant, Lord, and Merchant: Rural Society in Three Quebec Parishes, 1740–1840.* Toronto: University of Toronto Press, 1985.

Harris, Richard C. *The Seigneurial System in Early Canada: A Geographical Study, with a New Preface.* Montreal: McGill-Queen's University Press, 1984.

Ketchum, Richard M. *Divided Loyalties: How the American Revolution Came to New York.* New York: Holt, 2002.

Lanctot, Gustave. *Canada and the American Revolution, 1774–1783.* Translated by Margaret Cameron. Cambridge: Harvard University Press, 1967.

Lefkowitz, Arthur S. *Benedict Arnold's Army: The 1775 American Invasion of Canada during the Revolutionary War.* New York: Savas Beatie, 2008.

Legge, Arthur E. E. *The Anglican Church in Three Rivers, Quebec, 1768–1956.* Trois-Rivières: 1956.

Lynd, Staughton. "The Mechanics in New York City Politics, 1774–1788." *Labor History* (Fall 1964): 225–46.

Mason, Bernard. *The Road to Independence: The Revolutionary Movement in New York, 1773–1777.* Lexington: University of Kentucky Press, 1966.

Monette, Pierre, ed. *Le Rendez-vous manqué avec la révolution américaine.* Montreal: Chez Triptyque, 2007.

Montgomery, Thomas Lynch, ed. *Pennsylvania Archives, Fifth Series.* Volume 2. Harrisburg: State Printer, 1906.

Neatby, Hilda. *The Administration of Justice under the Quebec Act.* Minneapolis: University of Minnesota Press, 1937.

Ouellet, Fernand. "The British Army of Occupation in the St. Lawrence Valley, 1760–1774: The Conflict between Civil and Military Society." In *Armies of Occupation*, edited by Roy A. Prete and A. Hamish Ion. Waterloo, ON: Wilfrid Laurier, 1984.

Porter, John R., and Léopold Désy. "L'ancienne chapelle des Récollets de Trois-Rivières." *Le Bulletin et le Bulletin annuel du Musée des beaux-arts du Canada* 18 (1971): 5.

Robert, Daniel, and Norman Séguin, "Trois-Rivières, 1634–2009, Chronologie essentielle du patrimoine bâti." *Patrimoine Trifluvien* 19 (2009).

Roy, Joseph-Edmond. *Histoire du Notariat au Canada, Depuis la Fondation de la Colonie Jusqu'à Nos Jours*. Volumes 1 and 2. Levis: La Revue du Notariat, 1899–1900.

Roy, Pierre-Georges. *La Famille Godefroy de Tonnancour.* Quebec: Laflamme, 1904.

Samson, Roch. *The Forges du Saint-Maurice: Beginnings of the Iron and Steel Industry in Canada, 1730–1885*. Quebec: University of Laval Presses, 1998.

Shelton, Hal. *General Richard Montgomery and the American Revolution*. New York: New York University Press, 1994.

Smith, Justin H. *Our Struggle for the Fourteenth Colony: Canada and the American Revolution*. 2 volumes. New York: Knickerbocker Press, 1907.

Stanley, George F. G. *Canada Invaded, 1775–1776*. Toronto: A. M. Hakkert, 1977.

Stevens, Paul L. "His Majesty's 'Savage' Allies: British Policy and the Northern Indians during the Revolutionary War, The Carleton Years, 1774–1778." Doctoral dissertation, State University of New York-Buffalo, 1984.

Sulte, Benjamin. *Histoire de la Milice Canadienne-Française, 1760–1897*. Montreal: Desbarats, 1897.

Tanguay, Cyprien. *Répertoire Général du Clergé Canadien*. Montreal: Eusèbe Senecal et fils, 1893.

Trudel, Marcel. *Mélanges historiques; Trois-Rivières d'Autrefois*. Volumes 18–21. Montreal: 1931–34.

———. *Le régime militaire dans le gouvernement de Trois-Rivières 1760–1764*. Trois-Rivières, QC: Bien public, 1952.

Les Ursulines de Trois Rivières Depuis Leur Établissement Jusqu'à nos Jours. Tome Premier. Trois-Rivières, QC: Pierre Ayotte, 1892.

Vachon, André. *Histoire du Notariat canadien, 1621–1960*. Quebec: Les Presses de L'Université Laval, 1962.

Watt, Gavin. *Poisoned by Lies and Hypocrisy: America's First Attempt to Bring Liberty to Canada, 1775–1776*. Toronto: Dundurn, 2014.

Wertenbaker, Thomas. *Father Knickerbocker Rebels: New York City during the Revolution*. New York: Charles Scribner's Sons, 1948.

Index

Allen, Ethan: captures Ticonderoga, xvii, xxi, 4n8; defeat at Longue-Pointe, xxvi, 12, 16–17, 24; Fort St. John's raid, xxi, xxvi, 4n9
Angelus, 74, 130
Anglo-Canadians, xviii, xix, 2n4, 39; anti-administration, xx, xxi, xxii
Aorson, Aaron, 74, 130
armies. *See* regiments
Arnold, Benedict: captures Ticonderoga, xvii, 4n8; Fort St. John's raid, xxi, xxvi, 4n9; Kennebec expedition, xxiii, xxvi, 39, 61; outside Quebec City, 45, 57n10; Three Rivers transit, 116, 119–20
artillery: Fort St. John's siege, 16–18, 31–32; Quebec City defense, 112, 118, 130, 144; Quebec City siege, 45–46, 62, 63, 84, 85, 88, 123–24; Richelieu Rapids defense, 127, 135; Sorel defense, 154

Baby, Pierre, 37–38, 40, 68, 118
Badeaux, Jean-Baptiste: claims on United States, 181–82; loyalist views, 1–2, 124; Ursuline nuns' attorney, xxxii, 37, 109, 169, 171–81. *See also* journals

Bailly, Charles de Messein, 92n45, 93, 111
barracks: Montreal, 58; Three Rivers, xliii, xliv, 36, 66, 72, 128, 147, 150
Baucin, Michel, 6, 49, 159
Beaujeu, Louis-Liénard de, 92n45, 110–11
Bécancour, 9, 69, 154
Belette, François, 112, 125, 147
Bellefeuille, Antoine Lefebvre, 9, 68, 70, 124, 157
Berthelot, Amable, 1n1, 2n3, 168, 170
Berthier, 25, 40, 159
Bostonians, 4n7. *See also* Continental soldiers; regiments, Continental
Brogden, Jonathan, 104, 129n66, 133n76
Brown, John: envoy to Canada, xx–xxi, xxvi; liaison with rebel Canadians, 11n17, 12n21, 16–17, 31n46, 32; siege of Quebec, 90n36, 144; stops British ships at Sorel, 39, 41

Campbell, Donald, 57, 149
Canadians, 2n4; Continental views of, 41, 76–77, 91–92, 97, 137, 141. *See also* Anglo-Canadians;

Canadians *(continued)*
  Congress supporters; French Canadians; Loyalists; rebels, Canadian; regiments, Continental
Cap-de-la-Madeleine, 26, 128, 135
Carillon. *See* Ticonderoga
Carleton, Guy: escape from Sorel, 38n12, 45; governor, xix, xxi, xxv; lieutenant governor, xxxi; martial law, xxvi; military leader, 4, 7–8, 30, 53, 84; Three Rivers visits, 7, 38–39, 165; treatment of rebel prisoners, 156, 158
Castle, Peter (commander), 124, 144n107, 150n29, 151, 153
Catholicism, xviii, xix, xx, xxx
Caughnawaga, 18n44, 89, 150
Cedars, Battle of The, xxvii, 155, 156–58
Chabot (ship captain), 29, 165
Chambly (parish), 18, 29
Chambly, Fort, xxvi, 31–33
Chambly River. *See* Richelieu River
Champlain, 26, 70, 158, 163
Charlesbourg, 93, 114
Chaudière River, xviii, xxiii, 94
Cheesman, Jacob, 52, 130–31
chevalier (title), 5n18
church: Recollet (Three Rivers), xxx, xliii, xliv, xlv, 5, 21, 36; Three Rivers parish, xliii, xlv. *See also* Catholicism; convent
Clinton, James, 19n47, 58
clothing, winter, 44, 45, 71
Congress, Continental: xvii, xix, xx, xxv, 47; letter to Canadians, xvii, xxv, 2
Congress supporters: advise Goforth, 128, 134; response to loyalist prisoners, 147; Three Rivers, 22, 55, 83, 86, 90, 118, 120–21, 152, 163; treatment by Americans, 119–20; Whig Canadians, xxi, 156
Continental soldiers: demand services from habitants, 86–87, 88; harass loyalists, 153, 155, 158–59, 163–64; Montreal unrest, 57, 82; pillage and threaten Canadians, 100–102, 107, 139, 150–51, 158–59; poor discipline in Three Rivers, 84, 86; poor appearance, 140, 147; Quebec siege unrest, 145; sickness, 111, 129, 130, 133, 137, 139, 147; treatment of loyalists, 48, 53; views of Canadians, 41, 119–20. *See also* regiments, Continental
convent: Ursuline, xliv, xlv, 21; Recollet, *see* church: Recollet (Three Rivers)
Courval, Joseph Claude Cressé, 116, 119
Crévier, Jean-Baptiste *dit* Descheneau, 79–81
Crown Point: capture of, xvii, 4; Continental use, xxii, xxvi, xxvii, 89, 150
currency: British/colonial: 7, 72n21, 80, 174n4; Canadian: 29, 175n8; Continental, 181–82. *See also* money

Delzene, Ignace, 86, 116
Deschambault, xxvii, 150, 153
Descheneau, Jean-Baptiste Crévier *dit*, 79–81
Duggan, Jeremiah: 31n46, 49, 99n71, 190

Easton, James, 39n16, 41, 43
economic relationships, intercolonial, xvii, xviii, 135

elections, militia: Continental, 67–71, 73, 97, 103, 126, 128; provincial British, 6
enlistments: expiration of, 57, 94, 100, 115, 118, 138; reenlisted troops, 46n40, 60
Evans, Israel, 17, 33

Forges St. Maurice, 116, 145
Franklin, Benjamin, letter to, 74–78
Fraser, Malcolm, 39, 124
Freeman, Constant, Jr., 121–22, 129n65
French Canadians, xxiii, xviii, xix, xxi, 2n4. *See also* Congress supporters; habitants; militia; rebels, Canadian; regiments, Continental; seigneurs

Gano, John (Reverend), xxxv; letter to 95–102
Garneau, François-Xavier, 1, 167n1, 170
Goddard, Stanley, 84, 105
Godefroy de Tonnancour. *See* Tonnancour
Goforth, William: hospital accounts, 174n5, 177, 179, 181; privateer captain, 144, 160–61
Government House. *See* barracks: Three Rivers
Green Mountain Boys, xxi, 4n8, 4n9, 12n22, 100, 134. *See also* regiments, Continental: Warner's
Gugy, Conrad: relationship with Badeaux, xxx, xxxi, xxxiii; legislative councilor, 6n22; abused by rebels, 49–51, 90, 151–52, 153, 155, 159
Guillot, François. *See* La Rose

habitants: defy government, xxi, xxvi, 8, 28–29; description, xviii; support for Americans, 91. *See also* Loyalists; rebels, Canadians
Hart, Aaron, xxxiii, 49, 122, 182
Hazen, Moses: alleged loyalism, 88–89, 113; commander at Montreal, 105, 113n15, 137, 140, 141; Continental regimental commander, 88, 99n71, 126n60, 190; Richelieu valley seigneur, 4, 11. *See also* regiments, Continental: Second Canadian
hospital. *See* Ursuline nuns: hospital
Hurons, 154, 157

Ile-aux-Noix, xxii, xxvi, 6n23, 15n29
Indians: Continental army soldiers, 147; join British in up country, 113, 120, 122, 152; participants in Battle of The Cedars, 155, 159; supporting British, 6n23, 30n40; supporting rebels, 79; terminology, xlvii; threat from up country, 84, 89, 93, 106, 107; trade, 135. *See also* Caughnawaga; Hurons; St-François
Isidore, Father, 21, 124
Isle of Orleans, 141, 146

Jay, John, xl, 13; letter to, 132–38
journals: Badeaux (description), xiii–xvii, xxi, xxiv, xxxiii; Berthelot and Sanguinet, xiii, xiv

Kennebec expedition, xxiii, xxvi, 39, 40n17, 45, 61, 152n33

Lachine, 93, 157, 158
La Corne, St Luc, 18, 45, 64n42
Laforce, Henri, 115, 165

Laframboise, Jean-Baptiste: advises Goforth, 128n63; militia captain, 67, 80, 142n99, 158; unofficial interaction with Americans, 68, 85, 91–92, 116
La Galette. *See* Oswegatchie
Lamb, John, 15, 16, 46n40, 53–54, 73
Lamothe, Joseph-Marie, 81n11, 83, 84
Lanaudière, Charles-Louis de, 24, 25–26, 28, 38, 165
La Pointe. *See* Crown Point
La Rose, François Guillot, 49–51, 90, 152n36, 164
Launière, Joseph, 84, 90
Leproust, Antoine-Claude, 48, 68, 124, 152, 154, 155
Leproust, Louis-Joseph, 14, 25, 157
Livingston, James, xxii, 42n29, 49–51, 99n71, 190
livre, 7n3. *See also* currency: Canadian
Loiseau, Augustin, 47–48
Longue-Pointe, Battle of, xxvi, 11–12, 24
Longueuil, Battle of, xxvi, 30
Lorette, 154, 157
Lorimier, Claude, 84, 105, 120n39, 146n6
Loyalists: American treatment of, 48, 53, 55–56, 58, 63–64, 76; in Montreal, 57–58, 64; in Three Rivers, 68, 124, 125; Quebec District uprising, 104–105, 110–11; rallying in up country, 113, 152, 155; views, 1–2. *See also* Continental soldiers: treatment of loyalists

Machiche (Yamachiche), 9, 39, 40, 151, 152, 159, 165
Maclean, Allan: advances through Three Rivers, 26–27; key loyalist leader, 53; rumors about, 81, 112, 125; Sorel operation, 29; threatens Nicolet, 27–29; withdraws through Three Rivers, 30, 35–36
Maillet, Louis, 39, 124
Marsolet, Charles-Antoine (Father Isidore), 21, 124
McCord, Jonathan, 129–30
McDougall, Alexander, xxxvi, 15, 16n30, 19n47, 102; letters to 16–19, 31–33, 44–46, 52–53, 56–63, 72–74, 104–107, 126–30, 138–44
McDougall, John, 17, 32
McDougall, Ranald Stephen: at Fort St. John's siege, 17n41, 32–33; at Montreal, 46, 53, 58, 59–60, 62; at Three Rivers, 65–67, 72, 84; expected to leave Goforth, 63, 143; joins Goforth for privateering, 144, 161
Measam, George, 105–107, 140n95
Melchior, Isaac, 54, 56, 60–61, 172, 183
Merlet, Ardouin, 25–26, 40, 152n36
messengers, secret, 81n11, 83, 84, 93–94, 113, 118, 122–23
militia, Canadian: disbanded, xxv; mobilization, xxi, xxii, 5, 6, 23–24, 27; resistance, xxi, xxii, xxvi, 7n2, 9, 23, 26–27, 28–29; under government orders, 7, 9, 12–13, 27, 30n40, 35. *See also* elections, militia
money, American shortage of, 42, 61, 105, 109, 139–40
Montgomery, Richard: care for troops, 44, 45; death at Quebec

City, 51; leads invasion, xxii, 6n23; takes Montreal, xxvi; Three Rivers surrender to, 36, 39, 42–43, 48n7; travel to besiege Quebec City, 47; treatment of loyalists, 18, 58n14
Montreal: Badeaux visits, 42; suggested measures for defense, 128, 134–35; under American occupation, 57–58, 64, 94, 114; Whig activity, xxi
Morriss, William, 37, 39–43, 124
Mott, Gershom, 33, 52, 56, 62, 64, 130; reports from Quebec City siege, 129n66, 133n76

Nicolet, 9, 23–24, 27, 29, 81, 163
Niverville, Joseph Boucher de, 38, 48, 124
Normanville, Joseph Godefroy de, 124, 151
novena, 22, 121

Oswegatchie, 120n38, 152, 159

Papineau, Joseph, 81n11, 83–84
pay, military, 7, 44, 45
Payne, James, 59, 72n19
Pélissier, Christophe: advises moderation, 156; goes to Sorel, 153, 155; meets with generals, 116, 123; militia colonel; 118, 143; supports Americans, 83, 91, 145
Platt, Richard, 32, 74, 130
Pointe-aux-Trembles (Montréal District), 42, 43, 159
Pointe-aux-Trembles (Québec District), xxvi, 39, 114–15, 161
Pointe-du-Lac, 9, 164, 165
Pratte, Charles Dupras, 27, 48n6

Prescott, Richard, xxvi, 30, 41, 45
Price, James, xxi, 47, 55, 77, 115, 182

Quackenbos, John, 17, 33n56, 52
Quebec (city): American plans if captured, 127; battle, xxvii, 51, 53, 64; blockade, 58, 64, 81, 119; siege conduct, xxvi, 85, 88, 94, 111–14, 115; siege needs, 61–62, 63, 78, 83, 123; British relief, xxvii, 148; refusal to surrender, 45, 51. *See also* artillery; messengers, secret
Quebec Act, xix, xx, xxi, xxv, xxvi, 136

Rainville, François-Marie, 113, 165
rebels, Canadian: assist Goforth, 128, 134; betray and oppose Maclean, 29, 30, 80n5; Chicot rebels, 25–26, 40; Longue-Pointe participants, 17, 24; pillage and threaten loyalists, 151–53, 155, 159, 164–65; Richelieu Valley support for invasion, xxii, 8, 9, 11–12, 17n38, 41n20, 47n3; support Quebec City blockade, 91; Three Rivers loyalist fear of, 42–43
Recollets, xxx, 5n17, 21; alleged spies, 55–56
regiments, British: Eighth (King's), 58, 84n18, 105, 120, 122, 152, 155; Royal Highland; Emigrants, 26, 27, 28, 30, 81; Seventh, 5n13; Twenty-Sixth, 4, 5n12
regiments, Continental Burrall's (Connecticut), 147 Cady's Detachment (Massachusetts), 185, 186, 187, 188, 189

regiments, Continental *(continued)*
  First Canadian:
    in Continental strength assessments, 99, 126n60
    in Three Rivers, 47–51, 119, 188, 190
    soldiers in hospital, 175n7, 175n9
  First New York, xxxvi, 32–33, 96
  First Pennsylvania:
    as reinforcements, 98, 100, 126n60, 134, 187, 188, 189, 190
    soldiers in hospital, 177n18, 178n27
  Fourth New York, 62n35, 62n37
  New Hampshire Rangers (Bedel's):
    reinforcements in 1776, 136n86, 140n94, 148n15, 188, 189, 190
    Richelieu Valley campaign, 16n37
    soldiers in hospital, 178n21, 178n22
  New York (composite, 1776), 46n40, 126n60, 143, 144
  Second Canadian, 80, 88, 99, 126n60, 190
  Second New Jersey:
    as reinforcements, 99, 100, 126n60, 134, 189
    misbehavior of, 85n23, 107
    soldiers in hospital, 177n19, 177n20, 178n24, 178n25
    uniforms, 101
  Second New York, 62n34, 176n12
  Third New York, xxxvii, 18n45, 19n47
  Warner's (Green Mountain Boys):
    as reinforcements, 98, 100, 130, 185, 186, 187, 188
    diminishing strength, 130, 134; reenlist at Quebec City siege, 144
  Wooster's (composite), 59, 144n107, 148n16, 150n29, 175n10, 178n23
  See also volunteers, American
Richelieu Rapids, 127–28, 135, 149n22
Richelieu River, 9n6, 27n31, 100
Ritzema, Rudolphus, 19n47, 32, 52, 53, 56, 64n42
Rivière-du-Loup, 6n21, 9, 37, 49, 90, 158

Sabin, Zebadiah, 64, 98, 179n26, 185, 186
Saint-Ongé, Pierre Garreau, xliv, 21–22, 83, 86, 114, 121, 124
Sault-St-Louis. *See* Caughnawaga
Schuyler, Philip, xxii, xxxvii, xxxviii, 6n23, 161
seigneurs, xviii, xx, xxii, xliv
seniority, principle for rank, xxxviii, 60–61
ships: activity on St. Lawrence, 83, 89, 93, 105, 114–15; American use of captured, 47, 144, 145, 147, 160–61; British surrender, xxvi, 38n12, 40, 41, 43, 45, 112n10; Royal Navy, 158, 161, 163
Sills, Samuel, 68, 91–92, 158
Society of Dissenters, xxxv, 76n34
Sorel (parish): American batteries at, 38n12; American retreat to, 149, 150, 151, 154, 155, 156; British operations at, 27, 29, 30
Sorel River. *See* Richelieu River
Stansfield, Joseph, 124, 153, 154
St-Cuthbert, 25–26
St-Denis, 30, 155
Ste-Anne-de-Beaupré, 113
Ste-Anne-de-la-Pérade, 27, 69
St-François: Indians (Abenakis), xxxiv, 23, 160; parish, 23, 79, 160

St. John's, Fort: prisoners, 91; raids, xxi, xxvi, 4; siege, xxvi, 11, 16–18, 31–32, 35, 60; target of invasion, xxii, 6, 8, 9
St-Maurice Forges, 116, 145
St-Ours, 137, 140
St. Pierre, Lake, 116, 118
St-Pierre-du-Sud, xxvii, 92n45, 93, 104–105, 110–11, 136
St-Pierre-les-Becquets, 9, 70–71, 86

Te Deum, 9, 149
Thomas, John, xxvii, 149n20, 150, 153, 156n49
Thompson, William, 163n1, 165
Three Rivers: battle of, xxviii, 164–65; city descriptions, xviii, xliii, xliv, xlv, 36n4; city surrender, 36–38, 39–43, 48n7
Ticonderoga: capture of, xvii, xxi, xxvi, 4; Continental post, xxii, 32, 121
Tonnancour, Charles-Antoine (Chevalier), 5, 23–24, 28–29, 39, 66, 124
Tonnancour, Louis-Joseph Godefroy de: claims against United States, 174, 182–83; hosts Carleton, 7; militia colonel, 23, 39, 158; militia commission, 66–67, 73–74; prominent loyalist, 48, 85–86, 87–88, 111, 124; supports Badeaux, xxxiii; threatened by Continentals, 150, 151
Tonnancour, Joseph-Marie, 9
Tonnancour, Pierre-André, 24, 25–26, 27, 85, 124, 147, 151

Traversy, Joseph, 79–81
Trifluvien (meaning), 36

Ursuline nuns: hospital, xxiii, xliv, 109, 156, 157, 171–81, 183; religious practice, 21–22, 121, 149; represented by Badeaux, xxxii, 37, 168. *See also* convent: Ursuline

Van Wagenen, Gerrit, 33n56, 130
Verreau, Hospice-Anthelme, xiii, 167–68, 169
Viger, Jacques, 168–69
volunteers, American, 175n10, 176n13, 178n23, 178n29, 185, 186, 188, 190

Walker, Richard, 84, 105
Walker, Thomas, xxi, 43, 77, 115
Warner, Seth, 100, 104, 130, 134
Weisenfels, Friedrich, 32, 52, 63
Whigs. *See* Congress supporters
Whitcomb, Benjamin, 136, 140
Willett, Marinus, 52, 61
Wooster, David: issues new militia commissions, 97, 103, 126–27; loyalist policies of, xxvii, 55, 66–67; Montreal commander, 57, 60, 72, 93, 115, 132, 135; Quebec City siege, 91, 112, 125n57, 144, 146; retreat from Quebec City, 149; Three Rivers visit, 90, 99, 104, 105, 129, 136, 142

Yamachiche. *See* Machiche

www.ingramcontent.com/pod-product-compliance
Lightning Source LLC
Chambersburg PA
CBHW070759230426
43665CB00017B/2423